CIRCLES, GROVES
&
SANCTUARIES

About the Authors

Pauline and Dan Campanelli are author and illustrator of *Wheel of the Year* and *Ancient Ways*, and have contributed to Llewellyn's *1991 Magickal Almanac*. Pauline has also written for *Witchcraft Today: The Modern Craft Movement* and *The Witches Almanac 1991*.

Pauline and Dan have been practicing Wiccans since 1968. Because of their deep religious beliefs they have evolved a lifestyle based on Natural Magick. In their 18th century home in western New Jersey, Magick is a part of their everyday life.

Pauline and Dan have written and illustrated articles on Witchcraft as well as their personal experiences with the Spirit World for *Circle Network News* and *Fate* magazine. Other paranormal experiences shared by Pauline and Dan have been included in *Haunted Houses: U.S.A.* and *More Haunted Houses*, and in Alan Vaughan's *Incredible Coincidence*.

Both Dan and Pauline are professional fine artists. Dan works in watercolor, Pauline in oils. They are each listed in thirteen reference books including *Who's Who in American Art* and *The International Dictionary of Biographies*. Their home and artwork were featured in *Colonial Homes*, March/April 1981 and *Country Living Magazine*, April 1985 and October 1992. New Jersey Network produced a program on their artwork and lifestyle for PBS in 1985. Their paintings have been published as fine art prints and are available throughout the United States and Europe.

To Write to the Authors

If you wish to contact the author or would like more information about this book, please write to the author in care of Llewellyn Worldwide and we will forward your request. Both the author and publisher appreciate hearing from you and learning of your enjoyment of this book and how it has helped you. Llewellyn Worldwide cannot guarantee that every letter written to the author can be answered, but all will be forwarded. Please write to:

Dan & Pauline Campanelli
c/o Llewellyn Worldwide
P.O. Box 64383-108, St. Paul, MN 55164-0383, U.S.A.

Please enclose a self-addressed, stamped envelope for reply, or $1.00 to cover costs.
If outside the U.S.A., enclose international postal reply coupon.

Free Catalog from Llewellyn

For more than 90 years Llewellyn has brought its readers knowledge in the fields of metaphysics and human potential. Learn about the newest books in spiritual guidance, natural healing, astrology, occult philosophy and more. Enjoy book reviews, new age articles, a calendar of events, plus current advertised products and services. To get your free copy of *New Worlds of Mind and Spirit*, send your name and address to:

Llewellyn's New Worlds of Mind and Spirit
P.O. Box 64383-108, St. Paul, MN 55164-0383, U.S.A.

Llewellyn's Practical Magick Series

Circles, Groves & Sanctuaries
Sacred Spaces of Today's Pagans

Compiled by
Dan & Pauline Campanelli

1993
Llewellyn Publications
St. Paul, Minnesota 55164-0383, U.S.A.

FIRST EDITION
Second Printing, 1993

Cover art by Dan Campanelli

Library of Congress Cataloging-in-Publication Data

Campanelli, Dan, 1949-
    Circles, groves & sanctuaries : sacred spaces of today's pagans /
compiled by Dan & Pauline Campanelli.
        p.   cm. — (Llewellyn's practical magick series)
    ISBN 0-87542-108-3
    1. Sacred space. 2. Paganism. 3. Goddess religion. I. Campanelli, Pauline, 1943- .
    II. Title. III. Title: Circles, groves, and sanctuaries. IV. Series.
    BL580.C36   1992
    291.3'5—dc20   92-19357
                                                                                  CIP

Llewellyn Publications
A Division of Llewellyn Worldwide, Ltd.
P.O. Box 64383, St. Paul, MN 55164-0383

About Llewellyn's Practical Magick Series

To some people, the idea that "Magick" is practical comes as a surprise. It shouldn't. The entire basis for Magick is to exercise influence over one's environment. While Magick is also, and properly so, concerned with spiritual growth and psychological transformation, even spiritual life must rest firmly on material foundations.

Magick can, and should, be used in one's daily life for better living! Each of us has been given Mind and Body, and surely we are under spiritual obligation to make full usage of these wonderful gifts. Mind and Body work together, and Magick is simply the extension of this interaction into dimensions beyond the limits normally conceived. That's why we commonly talk of the "super-normal" in connection with the domain of Magick.

The Body is alive, and all Life is an expression of the Divine. There is god-power in the Body and in the Earth, just as there is in Mind and Spirit. With Love and Will, we use Mind to link these aspects of Divinity together to bring about change.

With Magick we increase the flow of Divinity in our lives and in the world around us. We add to the beauty of it all—for to work Magick we must work in harmony with the Laws of Nature and of the Psyche. *Magick is the flowering of the Human Potential.*

Practical Magick is concerned with the Craft of living well and in harmony with Nature, and with the Magick of the Earth, in the things of the Earth, in the seasons and cycles, and in the things we make with hand and Mind.

Other Books by Dan & Pauline Campanelli:

Wheel of the Year: Living the Magickal Life
Ancient Ways: Reclaiming Pagan Traditions

Forthcoming:

Rites of Passage: The Pagan Cycle of Life

Dedicated
to
The Old Gods

Contents

dha • Dragon Magick • ShadowCat's Sunrise Ritual • The Studio Sanctuary at Flying Witch Farm • Ancient Sacred Pre-Columbian Artifacts • Magickal Books • Sacred Artifacts of the Ancient World • The Witches Almanac • An Indoor Witches Garden • Bay Laurel • Rosemary • Myrtle • The Sanctuary of Silver RavenWolf • Decorating Ideas for Indoor Sanctuaries

Section II
OUTDOOR MAGICKAL SPACE

the Saudi-Iraq Border • Ritual in the Desert • An Imbolg Circle • An Altar of Snow • Luminaries for the Four Quarters • Colored Icicles • Blessing the Area • An Imblog Song • Ending the Rite • A Circle of Flowers • Creating a Magick Garden • Flowers for the North Quarter • Flowers for the East Quarter • Flowers for the South Quarter • Flowers for the West Quarter • Flowers for the Center • Coven of the Spiral Castle • A Degree System • The Celtic Faith • A Gaelic Dance Chant • A Native American Ceremony • The Sweat Lodge • Making the Prayer Bundles • The Four Directions • Another Sweat Lodge Experience • Letting Go • A Sense of Unity • A Wood Henge • Using the Circle for the First Time • Setting up the Samhain Ritual • Casting the Circle • The Samhain Ritual • Group Scrying • The Geis • The Stone Circle at Circle Sanctuary • Constructing the Circle • Contributing Stones to the Circle

Magickal Rituals, Charms & Spells

Chapter Nine

Sabbat Rituals

Introduction

On a farm in western New Jersey, a figure of the Venus of Laussel seems to breathe in the flickering light of a votive candle, while in Finland, between two modern highways, a coven of Witches gathers at a secret shrine to honor the Old Gods. In an enchanted garden in New York City's Greenwich Village, pomegranates are offered to Demeter, while in California, a best-selling author makes an offering at a table-top altar in her bedroom. In England, Pagans gather in a circle of sacred trees, and in a house in France, a coven of Witches invokes the ancient gods in a circle defined by copper wire, while an American commuter carries his circle in his suitcase. A coven of contemporary Witches casts its circle network across the country to do sabbat rituals by computer, and on a forested hillside in Germany, an ancient stone altar is once again the site of Pagan rituals performed by contemporary military personnel.

This book is not another listing of ancient sites, but a cross section of contemporary Pagans and Witches performing Magick and rituals in sacred spaces they have created. Here, well-known writers and leaders of the Pagan community, as well as solitary Witches and private individuals share with us the magick and mystery of their sacred spaces.

Circles, Groves and Sanctuaries fills a need for a book descriptive of contemporary, rather than ancient magickal places, and in the more than three years we spent compiling the material, we solicited hundreds of Witches and Pagans, and hundreds more solicited us. Ultimately, we were in contact with nearly a thousand Pagans around the globe, many representing large groups or covens. Most met the idea with enthusiasm, while some shunned it, feeling that their religious practices were far too private to share with others or, for one reason or another, were afraid to come out of the "broom closet."

Those who did agree to share their magickal places with us range from a very young child who, encouraged by Pagan parents, created his own sacred space, to an octogenarian who, in his advanced years, found his way back to the Old Religion and is proud to share his sanctuary with us. Among those who contributed material, many shared with us how their sacred space evolved and what rituals were used to create them or performed in them. Some are still in the process of evolving. Many of the people who submitted material for *Circles, Groves and Sanctuaries* included charms and rituals for the major sabbats from various Wiccan-Pagan traditions, which can easily be adapted to group or solitary practice.

The kinds of sacred spaces included in *Circles, Groves and Sanctuaries* are, by our definition:

ALTAR—The object upon which ritual tools are placed during a ritual.

SHRINE—A small permanent or portable space created for a specific deity (usually represented by a statue or object) at which daily, monthly, seasonal or annual devotions are made.

CIRCLE—The working space in which rituals are performed.

GROVE—A natural outdoor space where some seasonal or annual rite is held.

SANCTUARY—An indoor or outdoor space that contains more than one shrine or altar or where a specific deity or spirit is believed to dwell from time to time.

Some of these definitions overlap. The book, however, is simply divided into indoor spaces and outdoor spaces and then subdivided into the above categories. Some of the places in this book are open to the public, and addresses are given wherever appropriate (as indicated with an *, and listed in the back of the book).

Among the people who contributed material to this book are those who live in city apartments and can only spare a small corner for the God and/or Goddess. There are many who live in suburbia and have both indoor and outdoor spaces, and some who live and worship on large tracts of land where many acres have been dedicated to the old Pagan Gods by building Old World megaliths. Regardless of the amount of space involved, these people are all doing the same thing, devoting a part of their world to the love of Nature, the Old Gods and ultimately the whole Earth!

It is hoped that *Circles, Groves and Sanctuaries* will be a book of inspiration for all contemporary Pagans to create their own sacred spaces, no matter how large or small, and that by doing so they will become a part of a greater network that will one day en *circle* the Earth.

SECTION ONE

Indoor Magickal Space

CHAPTER ONE

Indoor Altars

Nestled among the rolling hills of the Delaware Valley are a few acres of land called Flying Witch Farm. All that is within the boundary of this tract of land is a sanctuary for the creatures of Nature and the old Pagan gods. High on a hill within this sanctuary is a wood lot that Dan and I have named the "Grove of Faunus," dedicated to this ancient god of fertility and the hunted animals over which he presides. Below this grove, among shrines to the Lord and Lady, is the old stone farmhouse in which we live, and where, on nights when the Moon is full, or on days when the Sun has reached its zenith, or the harvest has begun, we cast our circle. The circle, within which all of our rituals take place, becomes a magickal place between the world of everyday life, and the realms of spirits and of the mighty gods themselves, and in the center of the circle, at its heart, stands the altar.

The altar that Dan and I use for our sabbat and esbat rituals, like so many of our magickal objects, found us. Everything about it has symbolic meaning. It is of oak—sacred to and symbolic of the God. It is round and has three legs, symbolic of the Goddess. It dates to about 1690, the time when the Salem witch trials were taking place in this country, and it still carries with it the Puritan fear of and pre-occupation with the occult, which when tapped by a true Witch, comes through as the excitement and mystery of real Magick.

Fifteen years ago friends of ours who were antique dealers invited us to their home to see the latest acquisition for their own collection—a Pilgrim century tuck-away table. Since we were antique collectors they thought we would appreciate it. We not only appreciated it, we loved it! Several months later our friends lost interest in the piece and decided to sell it. Unfortunately, we were unable to afford to buy it, so we bid it farewell. Seventeenth century furniture is very rare and many collectors simply don't recognize it when they see it. Our friends took it to several shows, but the only response it got was raised eyebrows. No one would buy it! There came a point when something had to happen—and it did. A woman offered to buy a set of ice cream parlor chairs that we had acquired but didn't want. We were not in the business of selling antiques so we didn't know what to charge. Instead we asked her to make an offer. She named exactly the price marked on the Pilgrim century table. It was in our home that very night.

On the night of the next Full Moon we asperged the table with salted water, passed incense and a lit candle around it and consecrated it in the names of the

Old Gods. We then anointed it with altar oil (oil in which ground frankincense and myrrh have been dissolved), forming a pentacle with an oiled fingertip and left the altar to bathe in the moonlight.

When it is not being used for ritual this table has a place of honor in our living room where it is usually adorned with a bowl of fruit in season. We serve wine to guests on it and often eat special meals on it ourselves because, in the words of the Goddess, "All acts of pleasure are my rituals."

When the table is prepared for ritual it is covered with an altar cloth that has a pentagram which I embroidered in the center. Behind the pentagram stands a large wooden box that Dan made and carved in the tradition of 17th century "Bible boxes." This box, made of wood that was once used to seal off one of the fireplaces in our house, holds all of our ritual tools. During most rituals, a pair of beeswax candles, representing the Lord and Lady, stand on this box casting their light over the whole altar. The symbols of the elements stand on this box as well. They are: an earthenware dish containing salt for Earth (salt is a soil contaminant, so if you are in the habit—like we are—of returning the elements from your altar back into the natural cycle after a ritual, take it easy on the salt), incense for Air, a cup of water for Water, and a lit red candle for Fire.

On the altar itself are two wine cups (as we are a solitary couple), our athames, and our wands of hazel wood inscribed with runes. My wand is tipped with a quartz crystal, the other end with a spiral of copper wire. Dan's wand, which is only used to invoke the God, is tipped with a small pair of stone horns and a tiny bronze bell which makes it much like a shaman's rattle. Our athames are very similar with blackened horn handles and inscribed with runes. Dan's is larger than mine. Only we can tell our bronze wine cups apart, and this is important because only Dan's is used for blessing the wine. A friend gave us a blank book hand bound in silk and leather—the third copy of our own Book of Shadows I've made. With the exception of our cups, athames, wands and amulets, all of our other tools are used by both of us.

For Dan and me the altar is the focal point of our rituals and as such it has, like our magickal tools, acquired a great deal of magickal energy. In order to enhance this energy between sabbats, because this is a part of the energy we tap into when doing ritual, after each lunar esbat it is sprinkled with an infusion of mugwort and salted water and left in moonlight overnight. Beltane, however, is traditionally the time to purify sacred spaces. This is easily done by sprinkling the altar, circle, grove or sanctuary, and all of the magickal tools with a branch of pine or fir, symbolizing birth and renewal, dipped in a bath of vervain and spring water. In the case of our Pilgrim century altar, it is then scrubbed with this mixture which removes the old wax, and then it is given a new coat of wax to protect the ancient oak wood from the salt water and wine spills of future rituals. Finally, it is draped with the altar cloth, bedecked with the flowers of May and arranged with the tools for the celebration of the Beltane sabbat.

A Pilgrim century table, here arranged for Beltane, used as an altar at Flying Witch Farm (photo by Dan Campanelli).

Far from Flying Witch Farm, in fact, across the country in Berkeley, California, author Marion Zimmer Bradley, best known for her novel The Mists of Avalon, *has this to say about the personal altar.*

Almost everyone in what many Pagans and neo-Pagans call the Craft—which I and mine prefer to call the Path—knows that his/her transition from dilettante and apprentice to serious student comes when they are willing to commit themselves to having and maintaining, in their domicile, a permanent altar to that facet of the Mysteries which he/she has chosen as his/her own. (This double pronoun nonsense is getting too much for me. As a woman, I am one half of mankind, and therefore I feel that male pronouns can include me, too. When I think what we lady writers went through to get rid of such designations as poetess and authoress and be referred to simply as poets and authors. I am appalled when I see a lady chairman demanding to be called a chairwoman, or, even more barbarous, a chairperson.)

To return to our muttons—or, rather, our altars. There have been times when I have brought this up, and the budding priest or priestess will say to me, "Keep a temple in my house? I don't have the room."

This, of course, is nonsense and deserves no answer other than the old cliche, "Where there's a will, there's a way." I can imagine no one except the Army private, in boot camp, whose living space consists of a cot or bunk, and whose personal possessions are all kept in a footlocker, open to inspection by his sergeant, who would be completely incapable of keeping the tiniest of altars. (And I knew one of those who kept his personal altar in a folding stationary case, with his paraphernalia symbolically suggested by careful drawing of his gods and all tucked up inside, which he could open for a private moment or two of his devotions.)

It is only those affluent householders who have inherited, or acquired, an enormous ancestral mansion, who can be reasonably expected to devote an entire room to a temple. For every-one else, a table, folding desk or bureau makes an excellent altar. It can be kept in a small corner of the bedroom, a niche in a sewing room, a convenient closet, or what have you. My partner and I keep our altar in a niche behind the chimney in our bedroom. We impose a severe discipline upon ourselves, that no secular item, however innocuous, must ever be laid on the altar. Since our altar is between a bookcase and a laundry hamper, and neither of us are by nature tidy or orderly people, this isn't as easy as it sounds, but since the accidental tossing of a pair of socks or the novel I was reading on the altar involves us, by agreement, in various purifications, we're learning. (Let me hasten to add that I am not superstitious enough to think that a pair of socks, however grubby, or a novel, however trivial, could "contaminate" the altar. The prohibition, and the lustrations, are for our benefit, not the altar's. It is to emphasize the whole point of an altar—its psychological and suggestive effect on us; that in this mundane room devoted to mundane life and the daily round, a tiny corner protrudes, like the tip of an iceberg above the ocean, a doorway into the unseen; that by approaching the altar, kept carefully apart from our all-too-trivial daily lives, we step emotionally and psychologically into a whole other dimension, as if we were stepping through a gateway leaving the bedroom behind and entering an astral temple which we have built here, with the doorway kept uncluttered.)

Morning Glory Zell's altar to Ganesha—Lord of Prosperity, Wisdom and Time (photo by Otter G'Zell).

Morning Glory Zell's altar to Istar and Tiamat—Keeper of the Dragons of Water (photo by Otter G'Zell).

Size does not matter. I have a dear woman friend who lives in a house trailer with three daughters and four large dogs. Her altar is a folding shelf which she has fastened to the wall of her bedroom. When the trailer is moved, or mundane types are about, she folds up the altar and there is nothing but a shelf folded against the wall. When there is privacy and time the shelf comes down; the god-forms behind it are revealed and she sets up her chosen decorations—usually flowers which she has grown herself. A tiny altar but a beautiful one.

It need not be large, or expensive, but it should be as lovely as you can manage to make it. Its beauty or lack of it reveals the part which your Work plays in your life. If you are only trifling, playing games with occultism, and you choose for your altar only a few cheap and shabby things, by them you will be judged. On the other hand, expensive and fancy things bought in "occult gift shops" are often mass-produced trash.

Altar furniture will vary according to the Path you have chosen. Some people who are on one of the Eastern Paths find it sufficient to place a portrait of their guru there and wreath it about with flowers.

My own order suggests that the four elements—Earth, Water, Fire, and Air—be present on the altar. Once you have chosen your altar (and if you buy it at a secondhand shop be certain that you wash, clean, polish, and garnish it first, following this with whatever exorcism you see fit—there is no need to take someone else's personal magnetism into your sphere of intimate contact) you may do as you like about an altar cloth, although if you choose to have one, it is well to make it yourself and preferably to embroider it with such symbols as you choose. One thing I do consider absolutely necessary, if you ever work with the element of Fire, is an asbestos pad, or one of those metallic table protectors. Incense burners, especially those which burn charcoal, get very hot. So do candles when they are in metal or ceramic holders and are allowed to burn down to their cups or sockets. The leather top of our altar (which began life as a beautiful library table probably, from its size, intended to hold *Webster's Unabridged*) has an ugly charred ring from the time when my espoused priest/husband and I fell asleep after working an extended and weary ritual, leaving our ten colored Qabalistic lights burning in their candle cups. Any device sold in a kitchenwares department intended to protect your tabletop from hot pans and dishes will serve your purpose. Ours is an attractive copper-colored one (the metal of Venus).

The element of Water can be represented by your chalice which can be anything large enough to hold water and/or drink from. Stained glass ones are sold by local craft shops and are beautiful. Mine is a silver communion cup from some church, and I am sure it wonders sometimes what it is doing on a Pagan altar. Despite its recognizable origins it was too beautiful to resist. Your chalice should obviously be the most beautiful vessel you can afford, or one with a deep meaning to you. I know a married couple on the Path who use their first child's christening mug as a chalice, and why not? You could even go into a bridal silver shop, buy a silver goblet or wineglass and have it engraved (silver engraving is often included in the price) with your initials or those of your order or coven. This would indeed personalize it to its intended use.

The element of Fire is, of course, found in your candle. Some lodges always have two candles present on their altar: a black and a white one for the Twin Pillars of the Great Temple (see the High Priestess card in the Waite Tarot). Others prefer a single candle in the chosen color associated with their ritual. If you choose to use colorless beeswax candles (we do, not for ritual purposes but because I detest the smell of paraffin which comes from non-wax candles, even when covered with cheap perfumes) you can put them into colored vigil light cups of the proper colors. Candleholders can be cheap, dime store ones, or handmade pottery ones fashioned in symbolic shapes. I was lucky enough to find a set of six brass pentagram candle holders in an import shop.

The simplest way to represent the element Earth is a pottery dish with coarse rock salt in it. Another way is a geode, or a beautiful crystal from a rock shop. Other ways will doubtlessly occur to those who work in other traditions.

Diane Darling's altar to the Goddesses of Love—Venus and Tara (photo by Otter G'Zell).

The element of Air is often controversial. Some feel that incense represents the element Air. Others dislike incense and burn it only when necessary to cover up unwanted smells. I own three incense burners. One is brass for burning resin or gum incenses on charcoal. (Note what I said about asbestos protectors if you use this kind.) The second is also a small brass one, shaped like a symbolic female organ, for burning powder incense or cones or pastilles. The third is a glass ball with a hole in the top to serve as a holder for the kind of stick incense which the Hari Krishna people give away on the street. This simplifies the daily tending of the altar, since no matter how busy or fussed I am I can light a stick of incense.

Another Air symbol is the magical weapon known as the air dagger. Some covens refer to it as an athame and if you work that tradition you probably have one and know how to display it. Obviously keeping a dagger on display is impractical if you have small, meddlesome children, cats (if someone could work out a ritual to keep cats off altars, I would welcome it), or many mundane types passing in and out of your temple. My own air dagger is a small knife which a friend wrapped for me in Samurai sword fashion with a tiny green dragon (another Air symbol) resin, cast from a Samurai *minuke*, on the hilt. It is truly a thing of beauty but I keep it in our cabinet unless I am alone in the house. Another friend had a beautiful and valuable Malay *kris* stolen from his household altar. Knives attract thieves more than anything else except cash, typewriters, drugs or guns. An obviously valuable antique is an open invitation to a sneak thief.

In addition to the symbolic four elements your altar should have items of deep emotional meaning to you which you wish to consecrate to your work. Some groups feel that symbols of the Great Polarities—the male and female principles—should be present. The black and white pillar candles will serve for this, if desired. Our own symbols include a cowrie shell for the female principle. I've seen everything from a sword to a package of Trojans laid on altars to symbolize the male principle. I know a man of Indian ancestry who has a group of Indian totem items on his altar and it is one of the most powerful I know; it feels like a great electric force field when your palms are held flat, two feet above the surface. I know a woman who kept her first husband's wedding ring on her altar as a magical object; since he had been her initiator this was obviously reasonable. (And I heard of, although I do not know her personally, a Witch versed in sex magick who kept on her altar a lock of hair from every lover. I don't know whether she asked her lovers for them, in a spasm of passion, or clipped them surreptitiously while their attention was elsewhere.)

Unless you are working in a completely Christian tradition you will want god-forms on your altar. Reproductions of the Greek gods can be had from many museums. The same, I understand, is true of the Egyptian gods. If you have the slightest artistic ability it is well to draw or paint your own. Even without artistic ability most people can make a drawing of the Tree of Life or the signs of the zodiac, which can be used as a reminder of the multiplicity of the created Universe and Nature. Our Triple Goddess consists of a detail from the Botticelli *Venus*, a painting of a young girl by an artist friend, and an imitation ivory-on-black-velvet Kwan Yin from Chinatown hung up three-in-a-row. One woman from my own order chose as her sign of the Great Goddess three snapshots matted side-by-side in a large frame—her mother, her sister, her twelve-year-old daughter. Since a portion of our consecrational vow runs "that in the name of the Mother, every woman shall be to me as my own mother, my sister, or my child ... " this is obviously a valid representation. Another woman I know uses only a mirror as a symbol of the god-within. Certain saints used in the Catholic Church—the Virgin of Guadalupe, Saint Brigid—are obviously more Pagan than Christian. I am not exactly recommending the use of these images, but they are easy to come by and no one is going to ask you, when you buy them, what use you will make of them. (Examine the symbols on conventional pictures of the Virgin of Guadalupe and then ask yourself if you can still consider her Christian, or if the Catholics have simply stolen the Great Mother for their own rituals!)

My own altar contains a simple head of Christ, without halo; not because I am a Christian, which I am not, but because our order regards Christ as one of the Initiated Masters. No virtuous Pagan could quarrel with the simple teachings of the Sermon on the Mount, and if Christianity had gone no further, repeating the simple ethic of love of God and one's fellow man, the various sects, schisms and stupidities of the Church would never have happened.

I do not personally care for Buddhist symbols in my temple, and when a few have found their way in, they have found their way out again, almost as quickly. (Some workers prefer them. I have seen a temple elaborately furnished with Nepalese temple gongs, etc.)

My own feeling on this matter is that I was born in the Western world for the purposes appointed by the Lords of Karma and if it had been intended that I should follow the Lord Buddha, I would have been born somewhere east of Suez.

More than half the human race lives in the Orient and I could easily have incarnated there. But this is, of course, a matter for everyone on the Path (or, if you prefer, in the Craft) to choose for himself.*

In stark contrast to the subtle symbolism employed by author Marion Zimmer Bradley, here we are told of the direct and simple symbols on the altar of a four-year-old boy, Erin, by his proud Pagan parents, Taerie and Jim of central Pennsylvania.

Our son has his own altar in his bedroom that he set up himself. A feather and plastic knife are tools that he chose for the east. He has used the feather in rituals that draw the power of the wind into him. This power can have a very calming effect that seems very reassuring to him.

His yarn decorated wand takes the south spot on Erin's altar. This is the tool he is most proud of. He took special care, wrapping part in purple and black string. His wand also has a clear crystal on the projecting end. "I needed help to make it fit in because I'm not allowed to use a sharp knife by myself yet," noted the four year old.

A blue cup filled with water and a Batman canteen honor the west. Being a water sign, this is an important element to Erin. He makes sure there is fresh water every night and takes the plastic canteen for any outdoor magic he works.

The north direction on his altar has a piece of agate and a large metal ball bearing from his great-grandfather. Erin used to have salt, "but the cats kept knocking it over when they used my altar to get to the window."

He also put an old bottle with magick dried plants in it in the center of his altar. He uses them for healing the unexplainable hurts a young child has such as hurt feelings, disappointments, and general "yucky feelings." Center on his altar embraces the unknown. This helps Erin deal with many thoughts and fears that come to him in the middle of the night or when he feels alone.

Erin has a lot of pride in his altar and shares it with many of his friends—children and adults. Most of his friends are not familiar with Wicca or any Pagan religion but Erin's enthusiasm makes it easy for them to openly ask any questions that they might have about why he has his own personal altar.

*Article courtesy of Green Egg Magazine.

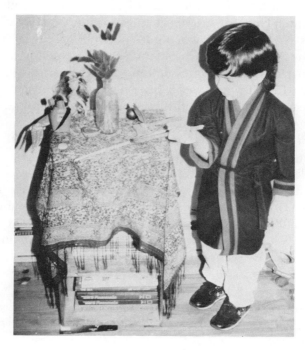

Erin, aged 4, and his personal altar.

Taerie and Jim tell us of another altar.

Our living room also has a permanent altar honoring our ancestors. This is decorated with pictures and treasures that once belonged to them. On Samhain, it is the perfect spot for offering and remembering those that have returned to our Mother. Our son, Erin, honored his recently dead fish with an offering of fish food on this altar. It is a corner of our home that allows reflecting and memories of our loved ones.

Limited space seems to be a factor for many Pagans and Wiccans, especially those living and practicing the Old Ways within the confines of a city apartment. Here Patricia Menzel Tinkey of Woodstock, Illinois tells us how she does her Witchin' in the kitchen.

Because my husband, Jerry, and I live in an apartment, we have limited space and also survive on a limited budget. What you see in this photograph is a picture of my permanent altar. It stands in a corner of our kitchen, on the top of a stack of six steel shelves. The top shelf is the altar itself, dedicated to the ancient Egyptian deities to which I feel most attuned—Anubis and Bastet and Isis. On it are six candles, these particular ones shown are green, still there from the rites of spring recently celebrated; a cauldron, bowls for salt and water, my athame, a crystal ball in a dragon stand, a wand with a crystal tip, recently made at a meeting of my coven, two scarabs my father brought me back from a trip to Egypt, a mortar and pestle, still containing the herbs ground for incense, and a figure of Anubis, Bastet and Isis. The shelf is covered with a permanent altar cloth—it is sheer purple with multi-colored sparkles. Because the shelf is six feet high, six inches taller than me, it is difficult to continually change the cloth so I chose the one color I like best and because the colors used in the sparkling effect are multi-colored.

A kitchen altar dedicated to Egyptian deities (photo by Patricia Menzel Tinkey).

The shelf below the altar houses all of my miscellaneous objects that I may need during a ritual: oils, wine glasses, my Book of Shadows, incense and charcoal and my incense burner. There are four shelves below these, which house my kitchen "stuff"—cookbooks, iron, Fry Daddy and other things I use in my daily kitchen duties.

I obviously didn't find this altar and it certainly isn't arranged in any particular fashion. It is my own design and it works quite well for me. I was afraid I would never be able to have an altar in a small apartment, but this works perfectly. It is a space-saver as well as a functional decoration. People who come by to visit and who don't know of my religious beliefs don't even question it. It looks a little mystical, but that is all.

I use this altar for all of my personal rituals, ones that I don't do in the presence of my coven, the Web of Isis. My personal rituals are all done off the top of my head. I cast the circle either very formally, providing I have the time, or very casually if I am rushed. The rituals are rarely spoken, but rather are communicated to whatever deity I am speaking to by meditation. The most recent ritual I performed at this altar was a spell of protection/healing placed around my father who underwent surgery for kidney stones. I simply cast my circle by calling to the Egyptian elements of the four quarters and then prayed to Isis to help my father through his pain and suffering that he was going through, and then to Anubis to guide my father back to the path of good health. This was done through meditation before the altar.

This altar is a larger version of the first. The objects are laid out from my personal altar onto the kitchen table. The table is covered with a cloth of the appropriate color first and then I take down the items I will need and lay them out. This arrangement is used for my coven rituals. The table usually sits against the wall but we pull it out if we are going to be dancing around it. The arrangement you see in the picture was used for the New Moon Ceremony we recently had. There are the candles, bowls for salt and water, the cauldron for the burning of the fire, the wand, the athame, my head of Anubis, crystal ball, glass for wine and incense burner. This particular burner was made specifically for me by my husband, Jerry. I originally didn't have a censer and was continually burning my hands on the hot burner, trying to infuse the air of the circle. Jerry saw my dilemma and made me this one, complete with handle for ease.

An altar arranged for coven use, on a kitchen table in a city apartment (photo by Patricia Menzel Tinkey).

When I set up this altar, I simply call to the elements of the four quarters for them to bless and consecrate our small space. This is nothing formal, just in my mind.

For being in a severe lack of space, I think we do quite well!

The creation of a personal altar to the Old Gods seems to be instinctive to those of us who have found our way back to the Pagan faith of our ancestors. Brigid Hagan of western

New York State is a free-lance writer and designer of original needlepoint. Her life turned in a new and positive direction when she discovered the Old Ways of Wicca and the feminine side of spirituality. Here she tells us of the creation of her personal altar.

A detail of Brigid Hagan's altar.

I have always had "mini-altars," little scenes on table tops or window sills which have included a picture of my grandmother, a seashell, something dear to my heart . . . together. Intuitively, I've hung corn on the door, sung and chanted during sweeping and cleaning, and imbued hand-made articles with spirit of one kind or another during the creation. It wasn't until I began studies with Shekninan Mountainwater (a goddess woman/Witch in Santa Cruz, California) that I put together my first indoor altar.

Being a perfectionist, I was afraid that I was going to "do it wrong" and was anxious about what to put on the altar and what if I made a mistake? I've since come to understand that altars are very personal and each article and object are there for a reason (my own reason).

For anyone just starting out, aside from the traditional directions of north, east, south and west, usually signified by Earth, Air, Fire and Water respectively, the rest is really up to your imagination! I thought about what I do to "dress" the house at the Yule holiday season: the tree, the windows, mantelpiece, floors, etc. What do I want to convey? What am I saying?

My altar said who I was. I love quartz crystals and I put some of them at the north point of my altar. (The altar is the length of the top of a bookcase, it is on a north wall of the room.) For the east direction, I put a stick of my favorite incense, and to the south, a candle. To the west, I have a small brass bowl in which I put fresh water when I do my rituals. The objects on the altar change from season/holy day to season/holy day.

A friend gave me a small art nouveau mirror which I put on the wall above the altar and directly at eye/face level. My altar area continues on the wall above the shelf with an impressionistic print of a Native American woman, a framed needlepoint of my own design which represents a Tarot card (9 of discs of the Motherpeace deck), an astrological chart done by an old friend, and a framed photo of a very old woman from Sicily (a Crone offering bread). My oils and incense are on a shelf to the right. I also keep various colored candles there, matches, red yarn, colored note paper and two pens.

To the left of the main section of my altar is a smaller area, circular in shape, on which I have arranged my anniversary coins from my 12-Step Program, special objects which represent my recovery, and usually something which stands for the season it happens to be (a leaf for autumn, holly for winter, a small bouquet of violets for spring, berries for summer).

Once a year, just prior to Hallowmas, I take all my crystals, gemstones, magickal objects etc. and put everything on the altar . . . this is to charge and purify them for the coming year. I'm great dressing my altar from Lammas through Winter Solstice . . . actually even into and past Candlemas and Brigit's Day (which is also my sobriety day). I am a dark time person and enjoy the months when the days grow short and the nights are cold. (Incidentally, in past years, I never liked Halloween very much, it was always an imposition. When I started studying and getting into the holy days and the *whys* and *wherefores* . . . I decorate and look forward to playing music and handing out the goodies to the costumed children who come to the door! A change of focus changes everything, doesn't it!)

From Candlemas through Lammas, I have a white satin piece of material that is draped over the altar and everything is arranged on it. Last summer I framed a postcard of Temperance (from the Rider-Waite deck) and that angel stood as guardian of my altar.

I've picked up some wonderful altar objects in my travels. We were in a little country shop outside of Niagara Falls, New York and I found a little 3-inch high cornhusk doll—a woman holding what looks like a spade or shovel—if her arm is raised just a bit, she points the spade directly at me from the middle of my altar circle! Very effective! I have a small pewter Witch who is always near the crystals, and an amulet which I made with a tiny crystal, homemade potpourri and a very old dime which was my maternal grandmother's. They are all tucked into a pendant-like holder on a silver chain ... I have that in the center of the circle often, for charging and purification. I also charge any jewelry on the altar. The more of my energy I put into the altar and its surrounding space, the more magickal and part of me it is.

I've decorated for Autumn Equinox and Hallowmas by draping a dark red cloth over the altar. (This goes great with the browns and blacks of the dark time, and stays on through Yule because it lends itself to the greens and golds and silvers of the season.) This year, while on a walk around the neighborhood, I picked up a maple leaf, an oak leaf and linden leaves and placed them around the corn lady ... I made a circle around them with my crystals and other stones (all touching). I found a fall decoration of acorns and leaves and put it around my mirror. Very autumnal! For Hallowmas, I added a tiny Witch and pumpkin to the circle and pinned a cat riding a broom to a black piece of cloth ... for a bit of humor. Oh yes, there are a couple of framed postcards (I'm great for frames and pictures!) that I add to the altar in the fall: one is a 1930s photo which shows a parade and on a banner is written, "World Leaders Are Meat Eaters!" The other is a sepia-colored shot of a very down and out street gentleman and we are looking over his shoulder to a sign which says, "Eat The Rich!" (Two obviously pointed ideas ... brings my '60s days back to me!) These are good dark-time, black humor bits and pieces. (For springtime, Beltane, I have a picture of a pretty maiden, bunnies, birdies, you know, I really *am* more of a dark-time person!)

A personal altar created by Brigid Hagan.

Last April I was into making dream pillows and made up a wonderful blend of rose buds, petals, lavender and mugwort. I left the directions and the bag of wonderful smelling stuff on the altar to "cook!" Also, throughout the room (and house, for that matter) were my books and articles, written and half-written, and ideas, and pictures, all very Witchy and Goddessy and feminist and Pagan!

My eldest daughter, Laura, and her (new) boyfriend, Mike, came over to take care of our dog and cats while we went away for a weekend. Apparently Mike started looking around the house and found my altar upstairs. He stared at it for a short time and said to Laura, "What's your mother like?" then he looked at the dream pillow instructions and said to her, "Laura, what does a dream pillow *do* to you? Does it make you *do* things or what?"

Well, no one said anything to me about it until the family was all together for some reason and Debbie (middle daughter) was laughing with Barbara (young-est) about how Mike was "afraid to meet Mom" and what I might "do" to him! We all got laughing so hard . . . it was *really* hysterical! So, my altar has different effects on different people. Most of the women (and my husband, Dave) think it's pretty neat and look forward to what I put on it from season to season. Right now I have a pentacle pendant getting purified and charged for Yuletide . . . very powerful stuff! Good, positive, interesting, funny, focused and thoughtful.

When I consecrated the altar initially, I made the space sacred with incense (clearing and purifying), and sprinkled sea salt from the door into the room, all around the area and in a circle (more purification). I tossed droplets of water over the same area (more purification) and lighted white candles and red candles on the altar itself. I asked that whatever deities were watching over me and mine would bless and protect this holy space of mine . . . that I would be consistent about taking care of the spot (which sometimes gets overloaded with all the stuff I want to include) . . . that I was sincere about learning and sharing what I'm about . . . that I was dedicating my life to good, to recovery, to living and let live! That I would do what I could for others, and carry whatever message it was that I was supposed to carry . . . which I'm trying to do. Ethics are important to me . . . Law of Three-fold Return has *always* been a part of my inner knowledge (even if I didn't know about it consciously). It's one of those Universal Laws . . . it is true whether one *knows* about it or not . . . if one practices what is commonly known as The Golden Rule, this is a form of the Return Law. I remember being very affected by "She changes everything she touches; everything she touches changes." And somewhere in the Charge of the Goddess where it says that if we don't find the answers inside ourselves, we will *never* find them outside ourselves. I know this to be true to my very marrow.

In 1962, a year before The Beatles' "British Invasion," another young man from Eng-land began a quieter revolution. At his home in Brentwood, Long Island, New York, Raymond Buckland began what is believed to be the first coven of Witches in the United States. Ten years later Ray Buckland left the Gardnerian Tradition, into which he had been initiated, to found the Seax-Wica.

This tradition was founded by myself in 1973. It has a Saxon basis but is, in fact, a new denomination of the Craft. It does not pretend to be either a continuation or a recreation of the original Saxon religion. Main features of the tradition are the fact that it has open rituals (all of them are published and available), it has a democratic organization that precludes ego trips and power plays by coven leaders, there can be coven or solitary practice and there is the reality of self-initiation in lieu of coven initiation, if desired. Covens are led by Priest and/or Priestess and decide for themselves whether to work skyclad or robed. The Seax-Wica is found throughout the United States and in many countries around the world.

A rumor published in one popular book on the Craft, that Seax-Wica was begun as a joke and made up of bits and pieces from various sources, is untrue on both counts.

Since I left the Gardnerian Tradition after more than a decade of great activity in it, in order to found and promote the Saxon tradition, and since the Seax-Wica has been my life for well over another decade, it should be obvious to anyone of any intelligence that it was not a joke! Far from it; it was very carefully constructed as an answer to the corruption (a harsh word but, I feel, the appropriate one) that seemed prevalent in some sectors of the Craft, and in much of Gardnerian specifically, at that time. (I have no reason to believe that this is still the case.) Far from drawing on other sources, with the exception of using Saxon deity names, all of the tradition as I presented it was new and of my own authorship. I was particularly careful to still honor my original Gardnerian oath and not to include any of that tradition's secrets.

Happily, many people felt the same way that I did at the time of the Seax-Wica's inception and many have welcomed it since. Today the Saxon tradition flourishes and grows at a steady rate.

The worship of a God and a Goddess ties in Saxon Witchcraft with other traditions of the Craft as being essentially a Nature religion. Everywhere in Nature is found a system of male and female; because that is the way of the Gods—a God and a Goddess—believe the Witches. No all-male or all-female deity. It is, then, a duotheistic religion. It stems, as has been well pointed out in such works as Murray's *God of the Witches*, Lethbridge's *Witches*, and this author's *Witchcraft from the Inside*, from early man's animistic beliefs. With man's original belief in many deities the two most important to his existence were a (horned) God of Hunting—later, generally, to become a (foliate) God of Nature—and a Goddess of Fertility. To the Seax-Wica these are now Woden and Freya.

In common with all Craft traditions the Seax-Wica meet in a circle. This is nine feet in diameter. A traditional size used solely to limit the physical size of the working area and, therefore, the maximum number of coven members. This maximum would be about a dozen. This is felt to be a "comfortable" size for compatibility—there should be complete harmony within the coven. (In Gardnerian Witchcraft the circle is also nine feet in diameter, but for a definite magickal reason.)

In the center of the circle is the altar, which should be circular. When meeting out-of-doors a rock or a tree stump would be ideal for the purpose. There are certain "tools" kept on the altar top, and others are held by the Witches themselves. At the center back of the altar stands a single tall white candle. Figures to represent the God and Goddess (Woden and Freya) may be placed on either side of it. Before the candle stands the censer. On one side of the censer stands a dish of water together with a dish of salt, and on the other side stand drinking horns or goblets for the Priest and Priestess. Across the center of the altar lies the sword and before it, facing the Priest(ess), is the green-covered book known as The Tree. Spaced around the circle itself are lighted candles. Their number and relative position being unimportant. Most traditions have four such candles placed to mark the north, east, south and west points. The Saxons, however, use them purely for illumination. Some Saxon covens use seven candles (seven is a "magical" number) but any number may be used.

What sets the Seax-Wica aside from other traditions is that in addition to the tools on the altar, the individual Witches will each have a Seax, or short dagger (the equivalent to the athame of some other traditions). It should have a straight, double-edged blade, but other than that may be of any type. The handle may be of wood or bone (a natural substance is preferred) and may be of any color. There are no signs or symbols of any sort carved or written anywhere on the Seax.

Ray Buckland's altar arranged in the Seax-Wica Tradition.

The altar pictured here was made and presented to Ray as a gift by members of his coven in New Hampshire. It is made from a slice of an oak tree which has been set on carved wooden legs (not visible in the photo), and is approximately 3 feet in diameter. It is arranged with the tools of the Seax-Wica Tradition, and was at the center of the indoor circles which were held in the upper half of the ell-barn that was attached to the Buckland home. When Ray and his wife and high priestess left New Hampshire, he left the altar with his coven and today it is, no doubt, a treasured coven heirloom.

Among Ray Buckland's numerous books are: Witchcraft from the Inside *(Llewellyn, 1971),* The Tree: The Complete Book of Saxon Witchcraft *(Weiser, 1974), and probably his greatest contribution to the literature of the Craft,* Buckland's Complete Book of Witchcraft *(Llewellyn, 1986).*

Like the Craft that he has done so much to foster, Raymond Buckland has gone a long way from those early days on Long Island. He now resides in Ohio, and has truly earned his place among the elders of the Craft.

Gloria Rivera of New York State has made a pilgrimage to a sacred site that is the goal of most on the Wiccan/Pagan path—Glastonbury Tor. Here she tells us how the magick of that place has become a part of her altar and the rituals she performs at it.

My altar consists of two parts. I have a set of shelves that holds my tools, books, jewelry and incenses, and a long table where I lay everything out for rituals. On one shelf I have an altar set up with feathers and my athame for the east, a candle for the south, shells and my chalice for the west, and a quartz formation with a small angel and tree for the north. In the middle of all this rests my wand. Although all my tools mean very much to me, I must admit that my wand is extra special.

Two years ago I went to England with special friends of mine. One day, and it just happened to be my birthday, we went to Glastonbury Tor. At the bottom of the Tor were hawthorn trees with fallen branches below them. It wasn't until some months later that I made one of the branches into a wand. It was a few weeks before the Summer Solstice. I was with Suzan, who had been with me at Glastonbury, and her husband David. We lit candles and incense and had Pagan music playing while I dug into the branch so that it would become home to stones I favored. Opal, amethyst, moonstone, tiger-eye and azurite all brought their special energies to the wand. A large quartz crystal was put on the tip to direct energy. With a soldering tip I engraved astrological symbols from my birth chart and a large ankh which I covered with my blood which was spilt while making the wand. Every few months I go over the ankh with some of my menstrual blood. I feel that this strengthens the bond between myself and the wand.

I consecrated my wand at the beach on the Summer Solstice with the help of the wind, sun, ocean and sand. I plan bringing my wand to the ocean whenever possible to give it an extra dose of power!

When I'm ready for ritual I place my tools and other appropriate objects on a table in my bedroom. On one corner of the table is a statue of Botticelli's *Venus* that my friend Debbie sent from Italy. Venus always has shells, flowers, plants and other magickal objects near her. She is a very powerful goddess figure for me. Often she stands in rays of moonlight that stream in from the windows and bless her.

An altar on a shelf in Gloria Rivera's bookcase.

Although the rituals I perform are not always the same I tend to burn one particular incense. I take a charcoal block, cover it with frankincense, myrrh, sandalwood powder and dragon's blood powder and hold it with ice tongs over a candle. As the charcoal heats and the sparks fly I chant incantations for the incense to smolder and for their purifying powers to be released.

To symbolically "sweep away" any remaining negativity I take my besom and sweep around the ritual area. Sometimes I really get going and ride around on it for a while, singing and chanting, letting it take me away!

Tools, including a wand made of wood from Glastonbury Tor, arranged on Gloria Rivera's altar.

To call the quarters I take my athame and draw an invoking pentagram in the east, south, west and north respectively. At each point I request the energies of that element to be with me for the ritual. Once the circle is cast I do whatever feels right for that particular ritual. I will often have thought out certain things I want to do, but I never write things first then read from a paper because to me that makes things a little too sterile and takes a lot of the spontaneity away.

When I feel the ritual I've set out to do is complete, I close the circle by going to each quarter once again, thanking the elements for being with me.

Kyle and Penny Peterson of the Kansa Holt Circle* have been outreach coordinators for the group holding the Heartland Pagan Festival in Kansas City, Kansas. Here they describe for us their altar and some of the rituals performed at it.

For rituals that we hold indoors, we use a dining table as our altar. It is a large medieval looking table that is octagonal in shape. Along the sides and on the base are ornate, handmade carvings. There are four matching chairs which we bring back into the circle for "cakes and ale" feasting.

Upon the altar is a sword, a censer, a dish of salt and a dish of water. There is also a goddess figure, one altar candle and goblets. The remaining items are a Book of Shadows, the altar cloth and a libation dish with earth in it for inside rituals.

The set up is as follows: In the center of the altar is the censer. To the immediate left are the goblets and just below them is the libation dish. On the right, closest to the censer, is the water dish, with the salt dish next to it. Above the censer is the Goddess figure with the altar candle above her. Below the censer is the sword and the Book of Shadows.

An altar arranged for coven use by the Kansa Holt Circle. High Priest Kangra stands in the background (photo by Penny M. Peterson).

The area that we use for our circle is our dining room, which with our small numbers, fits us just right for any rituals that have to be held indoors. When we cast our circle, the size roughly measures out to 8 feet in diameter. Randomly placed about the circle are four candles, mainly for illumination. At the beginning of each ritual, an altar candle is lit along with the incense. The altar candle is then used to light the outer candles. It is then replaced upon the altar. Consecrated water is then sprinkled about the circle, followed by the censer of incense.

The following ritual, from Raymond Buckland's *The Tree: The Complete Book of Saxon Witchcraft*, is used to formally consecrate a circle.

Thegn: *The temple is about to be erected.*
Let all within this temple be here
of their own free will and accord,
in peace and in love.

Priestess: *Salt is life. Let this salt be*
pure and let it purify our lives,
as we use it in these rites, dedicated
to Woden and to Freya.

Using her seax (athame) she lifts three portions of salt and puts them into the dish of water. As she stirs, she says the charge.

Priestess: *Let the sacred salt drive out any*
impurities in this water so that
together they may be used in the
service of Woden and of Freya;
throughout these rites and at any
time and in any way we may use them.

The salt water is sprinkled around the circle as described earlier. Incense is passed around next to finish consecrating the circle. For the present, our dining room will remain our indoor circle and when weather permits, we hold ceremonies outside in our grove.

Here is an initiation ritual that one of our members put together for his own initiation. With his permission, we give it here (as he put it) for posterity.

Consecrating the temple/circle is performed first then players are positioned for their roles.

Priest: *Let there be none who suffer loneliness;*
none who are friendless and without
brother or sister. For all may find love
and peace within the circle.

Priestess: *With open arms the Lord and Lady*
welcome all those present for this
occasion.

Squire: *We celebrate the affirmation of faith*
of one seeking that which we enjoy.

Priestess: *Of whom do you speak?*

Maiden: *Of he, who even now, awaits outside*
our temple, seeking entry.

Priestess: *Who has caused him to come here?*

Squire: *He came himself, of his own free will.*

Maiden: *He seeks to become one with the Lord*
and Lady, and to join with us in our

worship of Them.

Priestess: *So, he would like to join with us in*
our worship of the Lord and Lady.
How do you all feel about his petition?

All: *So be it!*

Priest: *The seeker now stands outside the*
circle, waiting to enter this, our
temple.

Priestess: *Then prepare him to be brought before us!*

The Squire takes up a cord while the Maiden takes up a blindfold. The Priest opens the circle for them to exit where they then proceed to bind and blindfold the Initiate. They re-enter the circle with the Initiate remaining outside. The Priest closes the circle before the Initiate who now awaits the summoning.

Priestess: *I am she who speaks for the Lady.*
What is thy name?

Initiate: *I am known as Tanis Silversea.**

Priest: *I am he who speaks for the Lord.*
Why do you come here?

Initiate: *To worship the Gods in whom I believe*
and to become one with them and with
my Brothers and Sisters of the Craft.

Priestess: *What do you bring with you?*

Initiate: *I bring nothing but my True Self,*
naked and unadorned.

Priestess: *Then I bid you enter among us so that*
I may duly consecrate you, in the
eyes of the Lord and Lady.

The Priestess anoints the Initiate with the sacred water, marking a pentagram on his forehead, breasts and genitals.

Priestess: *In the name of the Lord and Lady, may*
this sacred water cleanse you. Let
it drive out all impurities, all of
your sadness and all of your hate.

The Priestess kisses the Initiate, then replaces water on the altar.

Priestess: *May you be filled with the love that*
should be borne by and for all beings.

---

*At the Initiate's request, we are using a pseudonym to protect his identity.

Maiden: *You have been bound as to be brought*
before Death, as many have done though
every one was unique. Now it is time
to face those whom you seek.

The Priest and Priestess hold up athames while the Maiden removes the blindfold. The Initiate then kneels.

Maiden: *Behold, in these two priests do we see*
the Lord and the Lady. With that knowledge,
know that we and they are the same.

Priestess: *I am she who speaks for the Lady, yet*
are you and I equal.

The Priest and Priestess lower athames and present the blades to the Initiate who kisses the blades.

Priestess: *What are the names of the Gods?*

Initiate: *We know them as the Lord and the Lady.*

Priestess: *Are these the Gods you wish to worship*
above all others?

Initiate: *Yes, they are.*

Priestess: *Do you promise faithfully to attend the*
rites held in their honor, so far as you
are able?

Initiate: *I do.*

Priestess: *Do you promise to love and honor*
thy brothers and sisters of the
Craft; to aid them when in distress;
to care for them when sick; to protect
and defend them from their
enemies, so far as you are able?

Initiate: *I do.*

Priestess: *Know then, that in these things are*
we equal. In all things do we seek
for the good of us all. Love is the
law and love is the bond.

Initiate: *Love is the law and love is the bond.*
The Initiate rises and they kiss.

Priestess: *Let your bonds be loosed so that you*
may be reborn.

The Squire unties the cord and gives it to the Priestess, who then ties it about the waist of the Initiate.

Priestess: *Now do I give you a new name to further emphasize your rebirth. To your brothers and sisters of the Craft you shall be known henceforth as Arion. You shall meet with us here in this circle, or some other like spot, to worship the Lord and Lady, and to learn and love in their sight.*

All: *So be it!*

Priest: *Now are you truly one of us. As such will you share our knowledge of the Gods and of the mystic arts, learning as you progress.*

Priestess: *But we caution you, ever remember the Wiccan rede: An' it harm none, do what thou wilt.*

Initiate: *An' it harm none, do what thou wilt.*

Priest: *Now is the time for us to celebrate the rebirth of Arion upon us. PARTY ON!*

All: *So be it!*

Next would follow cakes and ale with much celebrating, until it is time to clear the temple. We are serious in our beliefs but we also believe in having a fun time and a good sense of humor to help liven things up.

We are still a minority religion, far outnumbered by members of mainstream religions in most areas. This is as true of people in prisons as elsewhere. But for a Pagan in prison things are not as simple as they are for the practitioners of other religions. Ron E. of Henderson, Kentucky, who has written articles for Harvest *and for* Magi, *and who plans to produce a newsletter along with a friend in the near future, here describes how he has overcome many obstacles that a Pagan in prison might face.*

This is a typical altar set-up for someone who is incarcerated. First you must understand that someone in prison is extremely limited to the availability of the proper tools needed to practice the Craft. Upon first arriving at an institution, normally a person has nothing to work with at all. Here I've created an altar and I've had to make due with the few items that are available to me to use. I also have to do a lot of visualizing for the tools that I cannot find or cannot make a substitute item for, such as an athame or a sword. Listed in the diagram of my altar are items that I have found that work well as substitutes for me. Use your imagination when coming up with makeshift tools you can use while one is incarcerated.

First of all to find an altar. I have found that the desk in my cell, or the top of my locker works rather well. The fold-up desk measures 23″ wide by 26″ deep. The locker top measures 18″ wide by 21″ deep. Cover the top of either one with a towel, which I use for an altar cloth. You may even use a towel on the floor as an altar if need be. Now place your tools on the altar, using the diagram I've made, or be creative and place your tools so they may be comfortable for you to use. If there are items you cannot find a substitute for, just visualize the tool being there.

After deciding on an object to use for an altar you need to get some warm water and salt if possible and ritually cleanse the altar to purify it. After cleaning your new altar, you're ready to consecrate the altar. Here is the ritual I have made for consecrating my altar and tools. Remember, while being incarcerated, this may need to be done every time you move to another cell because of all the negativity inside a prison. I personally cleanse and consecrate my altar at least once a month to rid it of the negativity that's around in this type of environment. This is totally up to the individual on how often this is done.

Assuming that you have already cleansed the altar here are the steps for consecrating your altar and tools:

1. Get the tools necessary to consecrate the altar. They are:
    a. Cup or bowl for water
    b. Cup or bowl for salt
    c. Candles
    d. Incense
    e. Book of Shadows or written ritual

    These are the tools you will need. You may have others if you wish.

2. Cast a circle around yourself and the altar. I know that space is limited in prison so keep this in mind when you cast a circle. Only use the space that is needed. You will need to cast a circle using visualization, because I know you are not allowed to cast a magick circle physically on the floor.

3. Now you need to light your candles and incense. If you are not using real tools, but instead, you are using substitute items to represent these tools, *do not* light them. This too can be visualized.

4. Now consecrate the salt and water. Mix them together and charge them with your own personal power and energies.

5. Now meditate for a moment on what you are about to do. Place all your concentration on the ritual you are about to perform. Then, after meditating, stand in front of your altar.

6. Hold up your right hand in salute to the Lords and Ladies. Say, "Lord and Lady, God and Goddess. In your presence I (your name), present my personal altar for your approval, that henceforth it may serve me as a tool in service unto you."

Now dip your fingers into the salt water and sprinkle it over the altar. You may walk around it if possible sprinkling each side, starting in the east. Place the saltwater back on the altar. Take up the incense and walk around the altar holding the incense as close to the altar as possible. Again starting in the east, place the incense back on the altar when finished. Remember, if you do not have these items, visualize the procedure described. Now say, "May the sprinkling of the salted water representing the elements of Earth and Water, and the smoke of the ritual incense, representing the element of Air, drive out any and all impurities or negative vibrations within. May this altar be pure and cleansed, ready to serve me and the God and Goddess. So mote it be!" You may add to this by walking around your altar with a candle to represent the element of Fire.

Now concentrate all of your energies (your spiritual power) into the altar to charge it, then say, "I, (your name) charge this altar with my energy from the God and Goddess and their wisdom and might. May it serve well in protecting me and in serving the God and Goddess in all that I do. So mote it be!"

7. Your altar is now consecrated and you may use this ritual to consecrate all your tools by simply replacing the word "altar" with the name of the tool you are cleansing and consecrating. Remember to thank the God and Goddess for their attendance and to watch over you in all that you do.

The following are some suggestions on items you may use as substitutes for the tools that you need to place on an altar. Remember that if you're in prison you have to use some imagination. You are also restricted by rules and regulations that govern the institution you may be in. Don't do anything that may get you into trouble.

1. Either drawn or traced from a book, a picture to represent the God and Goddess. Add some color to add beauty to your activities.

2. Use a plain piece of typing paper rolled up into a tube to represent white candles. *Do not* burn these. You could even use menthol cigarettes if need be.

3. Use any type of cup you may have to represent your chalice. You can also use the same type of cup for your salt and water. It is best if these cups are only used for ritual purposes.

4. Use an ashtray with some after-shave in it to represent incense.

5. Use a piece of cardboard or even paper to draw your pentacle on.

6. Take a regular wooden pencil, strip off all the paint and also take off the eraser. You can use this for your wand.

7. Use a towel for an altar cloth.

Remember to use some imagination when coming up with some items to use as your tools for the Craft. It is best if these items are all used only for ritual and Craft activities. A diagram of my altar appears on the following page. I hope the suggestions that I have given you will help.

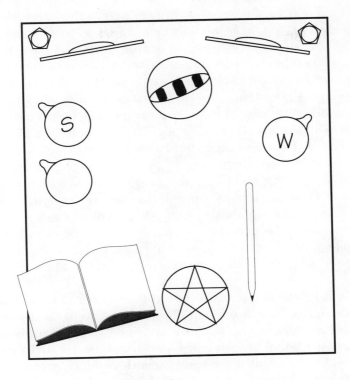

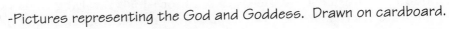 -Pictures representing the God and Goddess. Drawn on cardboard.

 -White candles. Paper rolled into tubes.

 -Chalice. Plastic cup.

 -Salt and water. Plastic cup used for both.

 -Pentacle. Drawn on heavy cardboard.

 -Incense. Aftershave in ashtray.

 -Wand. Pencil, stripped of paint and metal to be all natural material.

 -Book of Shadows.

-Altar cloth. Towel used for this purpose.

Nothing in Nature ever remains the same. Change is inevitable. Everything is born to die and dies to be reborn. We of the Pagan faith, as followers of a Nature-centered religion know this well. Still it is good to be reminded from time to time. Here Roslyn Reid of Bridgewater, New Jersey tells us of her altar which like Nature Herself is ever-changing.

This is the altar on my bookcase, consisting of items I have accumulated from different parts of the country over several years. Its dimensions are about 1 x 2 feet. It is not based on another altar but was created totally spontaneously and continues to change. For instance, the Buddha is now under a Japanese maple in the garden, which I considered a more appropriate place, and a carving of the Egyptian goddess Selket has taken his place. To consecrate the altar I set out a bowl of water, a bowl of salt, and then I light a white candle and cast a circle while calling the spirits of the four directions.

Objects in the picture include a plaster Buddha, given to me by my best friend, which I was using as a platform to hold some other items. On the Buddha's lap is a Nazi war games medal depicting Demeter—a reminder that familiar and honored figures can be perverted for personal gain. Beware! (This was captured by my uncle in WWII.) On the knee of the Buddha is a pewter sorceress with a crystal ball in her upraised hand—a representation of me, also a gift from a perceptive friend.

Behind the Buddha, barely visible, is our family crest. This also appears on the glasses to the right of the Buddha in the picture. Also to his right is a cypress knee from a Florida swamp (Earth Spirit), topped with a nautilus shell (Sea Spirit, as well as a symbol of growth and something I like to work on).

In the front of the picture are several candleholders, given to me by my mother and sister. I use the silver ones for rituals involving the Moon. Behind them are 2 beer steins my grandfather brought over from Germany at the turn-of-the-century. His spirit will help me out if I need it.

The round object seemingly floating in the background is a carving my niece, an artist in Oregon, did out of horn, shell, wood, and various other natural materials. She carved this for our wedding cake, and it represents the astrological glyphs for Aquarius (me) and Taurus (my husband). Festive memories are attached to this piece.

I use this altar for all my rituals. One of the rituals is for dispelling bad luck and should be done during the waning Moon. The procedure (borrowed mostly from Starhawk as well as various other places) is as follows: anoint a black candle with exorcism oil, protection oil, or any oil of this nature. Inscribe a rune on the back of the candle. Call the four directions and put salt and water on the altar if you wish—I don't always do this. Light the candle and sit or lie in front of it, envisioning roots going down into the Earth Mother from your body. Draw the power of the Goddess up into yourself, picture a cord running from your body to the candle, and imagine your bad luck melting as the flame burns. Burn the candle long enough to melt the entire rune. Chant or play music if you wish. To finish up, tie off the spell by envisioning a string tightly wrapped and knotted around the cord. Use your athame or sword to sever the cord between the knot and your body. Then let the power of the Goddess run back into the earth, and blow out the candle. I have had success with this spell.

The ever-changing altar of Roslyn Reid.

Not pictured is my altar at work because the photograph didn't turn out too well, but I'm going to describe it. It consists of a clock that revolves to reveal the stages of the Moon. On the base of this clock I keep the following gems:

Clear quartz—charged to be protective
Moonstone—for calmness
Bloodstone—for strength and courage
A crystal pyramid which is mostly decorative
Blue quartz—charged to be a career enhancer
Watermelon tourmaline (pink and green)—enhances the effect
of the other stones

I use these stones every now and then as the need arises, but I always keep them handy.

Thomas of the suburban Philadelphia area shares with us his thoughts about sacred space.
Let me begin by first saying that sacred space is not created by gold plated shrines, acres of pristine wilderness, or ancient relics. Sacred space is created more by intention than by external trappings, no matter how beautiful or moving we may find these to be. The inherent value of the physical is its ability to move us to that magickal state of consciousness. Ritual objects, especially those that are

aesthetically pleasing, help to remove us from the mundane sphere of our every-day lives.

Please don't think for a moment that I am denying that some objects, particularly natural objects, possess their own unique characteristics and energies. What I am saying is that by deliberately charging these items with our will and purpose, we imbue them further. For example, herbs and stones possess their own qualities, but by charging these to our purpose we increase their immediate usefulness. I believe the same applies to the creation of sacred space. Some spaces seem to possess a certain natural energy of their own, while some spaces are created by determination and will. Ideally, we should search out those spaces which we find naturally to possess the qualities we wish to take advantage of, and work to strengthen them magickally and ritually.

For those of us who for one reason or another are forced to take advantage of limited space, this provides ample opportunities for the creation of sacred space, while at the same time not intruding on the rights and the "space" of others (especially those who may or may not share our beliefs or even tolerate them!). Space may vary from the inside of a box or drawer to an outdoor grove. The main consideration in creating sacred space is not to focus on the space but to focus on the sacred.

Many Witches and other practitioners of magick routinely create sacred space without giving the matter much thought. I am firmly convinced that ritual objects and magickal items should be stored in specially chosen places when not in use. For most of us these specially chosen places are boxes, especially wooden or stone, which are used for no other purpose. These also serve to keep undesirable energies and/or prying eyes away from them. Even a spare drawer or shelf can acquire an aura of its own when it is used over time for no other purpose. Personally I store herbs, oils, stones, ritual objects, and most especially power objects in space which is used for no other purpose. Even if you have only the right side of a dresser or a desk draw with which to work, this serves the same function as a custom-made, silk lined chest, although many would argue not as well.

I say not as well, only because by using items designed specifically for the purpose, they strengthen the adoption of ritual and magickal consciousness. Part of my rituals has always been the preparation before and afterward, such as the unwrapping of the tools, setting up the altar, preparation of the simple feast . . . all of these signal both the conscious and the unconscious mind that a break from the mundane is about to occur.

The first guideline for the creation of ritual space should be that ideally it should be used for no other purpose, especially one that is mundane and unconnected with the task at hand. Yes, magickal tools can be stored in your sock drawer, but please, not with the dirty socks! If a space cannot be permanently utilized for your purposes, simply cleanse the area both physically and psychically before it is used for any ritual or magickal purpose.

Another point which can be made here is that if at all possible, use the same space each time for whatever your purpose may be. Using the same physical space over and over again seems to charge the space psychically and makes the task of raising and directing power much easier each successive time. This can be especially apparent when casting the circle. Try casting the circle in a location other than the one you usually use, and you will notice the difference.

The second guideline for the creation of sacred space is that it should be in an area in which you or your tools, altar, etc. can be assured privacy and that you will be able to work undisturbed. Ideally altars should include an area in which spell materials and other items can remain undisturbed. If this is not possible, reassemble the altar each time as identically as possible. Better to have to extinguish candles after a meditation than for some well-meaning individual to come along behind you and clean up that mess on top of your dresser (by the way, what was all that crap anyhow?).

This leads to the third and final guideline for our topic: discretion. I am very proud to be a Witch and a Pagan, but I also realize the value in not alienating any other faiths. I know not everyone will agree with me, but getting along with the neighbors will be much easier without a thirty foot pentagram laid out in stone with a fire pit in the middle of your backyard. How about a border of herbs, a round patio or small gazebo? These would work just as well, without risking having the fundamentalists videotaping your next sabbat gathering.

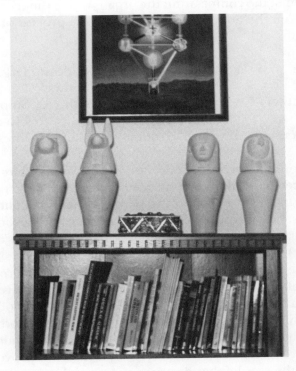

Photo I. Canopic jars, representing the Four Sons of Horus, mark the four cardinal points of the circle in the Theban Wicca Tradition.

While most Pagans or Wiccans, practice a tradition based on the mythologies and beliefs of the pre-Christian Celts, Norse or Anglo-Saxons, Thomas practices something a bit different, and in doing so he shows us the universality of basic Pagan beliefs.

The tradition I practice is called Theban Wicca. It is a very ancient and little known branch of the Craft which dates back at least several years ago when I made the whole thing up. On a more serious note, I call my solitary practice Theban as it recognizes the Isis and Osiris aspects of the Goddess and the God. Few would argue Egypt was entirely without influence in Western occultism, and the mystery religion of Isis had one of the greatest followings in the ancient world. As a representation of the Great Mother and the Sacrificial God, I can think of no more appropriate aspects with which to attune.

I am first and foremost a Witch, and in our society this makes me somewhat unusual. For the ancient Egyptians, the practice of magick was the accepted norm. Certainly priests, healers, magicians, etc. were more advanced in their use of the powers of nature than the local farmers, but all people in all walks of life believed in the efficiency of magick. By adapting an Egyptian veneer to my Wiccan practice, I have found a very personally satisfying and effective tradition which I would stack up against the best of "established" traditions.

Photo I shows the Four Sons of Horus which are used to mark the four cardinal points of the circle. Each of the Canopic jars was associated with a goddess as well as a direction of the compass and the organs which they contained after they were removed from the body in preparation for the process of mummification. From left to right:

Direction	Name	Representation	Goddess	Organ	Element
North	Hapy	Ape-Headed	Nepthys	Lungs	Earth
East	Duamutef	Jackal-Headed	Neith	Stomach	Air
South	Imset	Man-Headed	Isis	Liver	Fire
West	Quebensenenuf	Hawk-Headed	Selket	Intestines	Water

The Four Sons of Horus are addressed as one would address the Guardians of the Watchtowers, and the same associations are used for each. (Above the Guardians is a print of the Kabalah, and between Duamutef and Imset is a silver box inlaid with semi-precious stones in which I keep stones for magickal purposes. The bookcase below exclusively houses many of my texts on Wicca, Paganism, and magick.)

Photo II is an example of an altar which could be erected regardless of available space. This altar, which I think of as my nature altar, was created in a corner of my living room on top of a stereo receiver. The dimensions of the receiver top are approximately 16 1/2" x 16 1/2", while the Goddess and God image is about 6 1/2" x 3 1/2". The altar is dedicated to the aspects of the Goddess and God in nature and features a variety of shells, crystals, stones, and a pyrite "Sun." Fresh flowers decorate the rear left-hand corner and a small incense burner sits to the right of the altar. Large reproductions of scarabs sit before the altar in the front, and a geode of amethyst crystals creates a dramatic backdrop. When creating sacred space, I generally like to keep the importance of symbolism in mind by utilizing colors (such as the purple of the amethyst, sacred to Isis and objects (such as the scarabs) which are appropriate to the task at hand.

Photo II. A geode is the centerpiece of the Nature altar created by Thomas of suburban Philadelphia.

Photo III. The ritual altar arranged for an esbat ritual in the Theban Wicca Tradition.

Photo III shows a photo of my ritual altar set up for an esbat ritual. The altar is situated in my bedroom to ensure privacy and limit possible interruptions. The location also guarantees that I can leave materials on the altar and they will not be disturbed. This is my "sanctum sanctorum," the psychic center of my home. Here is where I perform my magick and rituals indoors. The area is kept clear of psychic and physical disturbances by its location, and the presence of many magickal and power items lends efficiency to my rituals. In the background directly behind the altar are my boxes. Magicians in Egypt customarily utilized boxes to contain magickal items in sacred space, and several accounts of ancient papyri speak of the magician calling for his box before magick can be wrought. The larger white wooden box on the bottom is decorated on four sides. The panel which is visible depicts my natal horoscope and the position of the planets at my place and time of birth. I feel this personalizes the box and its contents, and aids me in attuning with its energies. The opposite panel in the rear shows a pentacle with the appropriate corresponding alchemical signs for the elements. The two smaller panels on the sides are decorated with the Kabalistic Tree on one side and the interlocking triangles of the "alchemical star" on the other.

The altar consists of a 15 1/2" Goddess and God image in the rear. Directly in front of this is an amethyst cluster, a large red altar candle, and the incense burner on a tripod, and finally the pentacle. The right side of the altar is dedicated to the Goddess and items such as the amethyst crystal sphere for divination, the silver chalice in an Egyptian lotus motif, the Full Moon anointing oil, and the plate of small loaves are arranged here. Note the "ears" on the small loaves on the pentacle plate. Although they are difficult to see, small indentations, ears, are given to the loaves before they are baked. The ears enable the Gods to hear our offerings and our prayers and other communications to them. The left side of the altar is dedicated to the Lord. Here we find the earthenware container of salt, the horned bell, the black-handled athame and white-handled bolline. Some items which occupy this side such as the fresh flowers in the rear, the incense in the middle of the altar, or the wand on the far left could arguably be placed on the side of the Lady and are here more for convenience sake than anything else. The Book of Shadows occupies the foreground. In Theban tradition, this book is known as Pert Em Hru or Coming Forth by Day. This is the title of the ancient Egyptian Book of the Dead and contains a variety of spells, magickal formulas, and rituals.

The altar is approximately 30" in diameter, and is located in the middle of a circle which is approximately 5 1/2 feet in diameter. While the circle is a great deal smaller than the traditional nine foot circle, I find this to be a more ideal size to work in. Thus, the altar serves as a focal point of energy in the midst of the circle. As Joseph Campbell said, "The world is a circle," and the design of the altar helps to remind me of the microcosm and the macrocosm.

In closing, I would just like to offer some additional insights which have occurred to me while composing the above. A properly constructed altar, or indeed any sacred space, should "live." By this I mean that an altar should become, over time, a living psychic organism. It, like an organism, is composed of organs which cooperate for the benefit of the whole. Your athame, your Goddess and God images, your chalice and choice of incenses and burner … these are the organs which make up the being of your altar. The altar should possess a life of its own, and the relationship should be symbiotic, not parasitic. More simply stated, I am repeating myself by stating that you should not be spending more than you can reasonably afford. It is much better, in my opinion, to personalize your altar and make it your own. Your altar is a unique living being, created by you, and given life by you and the energies of the Earth. Whatever can be done to help you to tap in and attune with its unique energies should be done. Making the altar uniquely you will certainly help. Use your own judgments when attributing correspondences, make or personalize as many of the items on your altar as possible, don't feel restricted by anyone's opinion, including my own. Search out those items which you feel attuned to or comfortable with. For myself, I've found museums to be an excellent source for historically accurate and beautiful altar items. Most museums have a gift shop with a wide variety of items from jewelry to statues. Keep in mind too that as a living being, an altar is never fixed or static. I am constantly looking for suitable altar items and "upgrading" wherever and whenever possible. For instance, rather than invoking the Four Sons of Horus as the Guardians of the Four Quarters, it would be just as appropriate to call upon the four Goddesses associated with each direction as detailed above. Artists Guild International has an impressive set of the four Goddesses and is on my "want list." Also on the list is a small offering dish from the Metropolitan Museum in New York. The dish is in the form of the hieroglyph, "to bring," which is a small bowl with feet. Finally, it is important to remember that we can create special, magickal space all around us. Especially for those of us who don't have a great deal of space to begin with, we can surround ourselves with symbolic and special objects which help to remind us of our special relationship with the Earth and all life. Personally, I have always had a strong attraction to Egyptian items and have furnished my home with a variety of reproductions, artwork, and objects which recall my special relationship with Isis and Osiris. Usually the only comment this raises with others is, "I guess you like Egyptian stuff." As Pagans, we should remember that wherever we are, we are creating magickal space around us, simply by virtue of our being Pagans.

Any ritual you are currently using would be more than adequate for the Theban tradition. One would simply alter (if you'll pardon the pun) the names of the Goddess and God and the four quarters to those of Isis and Osiris and the Four Sons of Horus or the four guardian Goddesses. If at all possible the traditions and customs of Egyptian worship should be followed, but I am also a firm believer in self-expression and individualism. If you're uncomfortable with something, change it! Almost all of the Theban rituals are based on or inspired by published rituals (such as Gardnerian) or those which are frequently published in Pagan periodicals such as *Circle, Harvest,* or *FireHeart.* Again, even published rituals should not be followed blindly just because they're published. Follow your own intuition, change what you don't like, and add what you feel is missing or should be there. Personalize the rituals with a poem, a song, or some other personal touch to make them uniquely yours. The only objection I have to some forms of Wiccan rituals is the veneration of the Goddess excluding the God. In my mind, this is just as wrong as the veneration of a God to the exclusion of the Mother. Please understand that this is simply my personal opinion. I don't begrudge Dianic Witches the right to express themselves in any way they feel particularly attuned to, I just feel that this is to an extent as one sided as some other religious practices we could mention.

Affectionately known as Kat to her close friends (which happily include Dan and me), Katharine Clark* is priestess of a teaching coven of a hereditary tradition of the Craft known as the Tuatha De Danann. Here she shares with us some basic observations on consecrating an indoor altar.

For many Wiccans and Pagans living in our overpopulated world, it has become necessary to establish our shrines and altars as part of our inner environment. Unfortunately, there is an attitude prevalent among some segments of the Craft that indoor worship is an inferior alternative to outdoor celebrations and sanctuaries. And yet—although it's true that our Path is one intimately linked to the spirit, breath and soil of a living Earth—artificial boundaries need not divorce or sever us from its embrace. As more and more of us are obliged to practice our Craft indoors, it is time to expand our concepts. Remember: everything has the potential to be one with Nature.

The wooden shelf set up as an altar, in an inconspicuous closet, was once a living tree, the pattern of its grain still echoing its history. The same holds true for wooden tables, cedar chests or even a sheet of lumber supported by bricks. In order to feel the energy of the indoor shrine or altar, one must re-discover—and honor—its organic roots. Indeed, it becomes our obligation to do so, for as an outdoor shrine reflects our affinity with the Earth and its Old Ones, so our indoor altars are our reminders of their subtle presence beneath our roofs.

As a teacher of the Craft for 19 years, I've found that there are basic, almost instinctive things that can be done to strengthen the bond between indoor altars and "outdoor" energy. In order to awaken their potential, it is crucial to enliven them with as many natural components as possible, experimenting with combinations until you feel a comfortable balance. For example: remove old paint and varnish from your altar shelf or table, and let the wood breathe. Anoint it with a natural oil of your choice (these are readily available at most health food stores). If you prefer stone altars, many suitable rocks can be found in local fields, especially around planting season. Even that eternal enemy of nature, "urban development," can have its small, redeeming quality if the contractors unearth a stone which you can rescue for an altar top. If fields or construction sites are inaccessible, local building supply houses and landscapers carry stocks of quarry stone and slate for cosmetic use on lawns. Many of these are suitable size for a small altar. Finally, if you are relegated to using manmade materials (glass., Formica, plastic, and the like), an altar cloth can be made from natural fiber cloth such as cotton or wool.

The elements you choose to represent on your altar can heighten its natural awareness. Many of us use commercial incense, and a number of these have been chemically processed. Yet a few brands are organic, using only flower essences for their aromatic base. Beeswax candles may be used in lieu of commercial paraffin, sea salt may be used in lieu of the processed variety, and clay chalices or wooden bowls can embody the elements of Earth, Water and Fire. Many of us have found an affinity with stones or crystals, and the inclusion of their Earth energy would be very appropriate. (In our Irish tradition, a stone with a natural hole worn through it is thought to hold the magick of the Gentry, or Old Gods, and would add their vibrancy to any altar. However, such a stone must be found, not bought.) The presence of wild flowers or living plants upon the altar completes its tie to the flow of life.

None of the above information is new. Most Wiccans would usually select organic substances with which to establish sacred space, no matter where they may be. The "newness" must lie in the conscious, deliberate awareness of our indoor altar's connectedness with the force of natural energy and light. As we envision, so we empower. If we actively feed the spark of life in our altars and their accouterments, we will always worship with the feel of moonlight on our faces and earth beneath our feet. To this end, the following dedication ritual for indoor altars (or shrines) is offered as a guideline for your own creativity and sense of celebration.

Unlike our dedication ritual for the outdoor grove or sanctuary, the indoor dedication starts with the bare essential—the naked altar. As the ritual progresses, the bond between nature and altar is forged and reinforced step-by-step. (This ritual is written as a solitary celebration, but can be adapted for groups by assigning ritual words/actions to various participants.)

Kneel or sit before your altar, and place before you a container of water, and a container or vial of oil. By dipping the index finger of your right hand into each, trace a pentagram upon the surface of your altar. (You may substitute any personal or group symbol that you wish. If you have an altar which will be marred or damaged by the elements used, you may wipe the surface dry immediately after anointing, or anoint the underside of the altar top.)

Celebrant: *I cleanse you with salt* (trace pentagram with salt)
        I bless you with water (trace pentagram with water)
        I anoint you with oil (trace pentagram with oil)
        I purge you of memories born in common use,
        and call forth the knowledge of your true design.
        May you be the table of spiritual feasts.
        May those that gather before you
        do so in peace and unity.
        May all that touches you
        fill you with pure and loving light,
        and may the Gods bless you as a mirror
        of their own sacred Earth.

If an altar cloth is to be used, it is draped over at this time.

Celebrant: *As grass covers soil, so this cloth covers our altar.*
        May their energies blend and become one.

Next, take incense and bless your altar. (You may draw a pentagram above it with the smoke, trace its perimeter with the smoke deosil or clockwise, or trace a personal/group symbol in the air before the altar. As an alternative to incense, some health food stores and New Age shops sell smudge sticks, or bundles of cedar and sage. Native Americans have used these for centuries in purification rites.)

Celebrant: *As the wind blows*
so may the breath of the Old Ones
find you here.
Summer to winter,
sunrise to moonset,
may the Sylphs and breezes
bless you with their song.

With your finger, take a bit of the incense ash and inscribe a pentagram in each of the four corners of your altar, or its under- side. Place the incense upon the altar and pick up the bell. This may be the bell you use in your circle rites, or one bought for the occasion. It can range from large and brassy to a string of tiny chapel bells, as long as the "voice" or tone of the bell(s) reminds you of the ringing of the wind.

The bell is next rung over each of the altar's four corners (or quarter points if circular). This represents the call of the four winds of the world, the archetypal elementals of Air. The bell is now placed upon the altar.

Next, place the candles of the altar, left hand for the Goddess and right hand for God.

Celebrant: (lighting left side)
I light the candle of the feminine, the Divine.
May the fire of bountiful life
grant its blessing to this place
and seed it with eternal light.
(lighting right side)
I light the candle of the masculine, the Divine.
May the spark of knowledge and inspiration
purge the darkness from this place
and bless it with sacred flame.

At this point you may wish to let a drop of wax from each candle fall upon your altar to seal its bond with the elemental of Fire, or press a drop of wax from each candle to the underside of the altar with your finger.

Lastly, elevate your chalice. (This may be filled with spring water, bottled water, rain water or whatever feels best to you, as long as it is technically drinkable.) Breathe across its surface three times and take a sip, then asperge the four corners (or quarter points) using your fingers, a fresh flower, a lotus pod, or whatever you choose.

Celebrant: (elevating the cup once again)

Water is the timeless wine of the Earth,
the elixir of the spirit
poured out from rock, and well
and temperate sea.
May you be one with the water,
a part of the river
of life, and departure and constant return.

The chalice is placed upon the altar. If there are live plants present, you may wish to pour a small libation into their soil.

Stand. Extend your hands over the altar. If you work with athame, wand or staff you may wish to pass it over the altar to add its energy to those you have already called forth.

Celebrant: *As above, so below.*
I bless you with the elements,
both seen and unseen;
I bless you with the spirit of life,
both hidden and revealed;
I bless you in the name of my people,
and the Gods my people swear by.
May you be a meeting place
of love, and peace and unity of mind.

You may allow the incense and candles to burn undisturbed, or extinguish them if necessary. The dedication of an altar should be a time of celebration; a feast of cake and ale, a special meal, or even a small party would be fitting!

Katharine now shares with us the setting up of the traditional altar of the Tuatha De Danann and a Yule and Lughnasad (Lammas) celebration ritual.

Over the course of my Eldership of the Tuatha De Danann (TDD) various surfaces have done duty as altar top: kitchen floors, piano benches, book shelves, desks, an assortment of stereo consoles, and even packing crates during one of our migrations. We are fortunate that a more permanent altar arrived in time to bless our new home.

As in the case of many Wiccans, the majority of our Craft tools were either gifted to us, found or purchased after being stumbled upon by "chance." This altar was no exception. It was a cedar chest belonging to my sister, a great lover of antiques, and was kept with similar pieces in her spare bedroom. I had admired it for years but had no hope that she would part with it. Then came a particularly lean year for all of us. Holidays were fast approaching, and my sister suggested that perhaps we'd accept the chest in lieu of a "new" Yule-tide present? It's been a welcome member of our circle ever since. All our rituals are presently performed at this altar, although this will change with the completion of the outdoor circle.

We've come to find that flexibility is the life-blood of the various Celtic traditions, and the TDD altar is reflective of this. Although it is natural cedar, we have a tendency to use a variety of altar cloths. One in particular is a beautiful red velvet runner, edged with brass lace and finished on either end by triangles of hand-worked tapestry. I discovered it years ago in a curio shop. The shopkeeper sold it to me for a pittance because she felt it was used for purposes "not Christian." As it's a perfect size for an altar, it has continued its history uninterrupted.

Beyond the elements arranged on the altar as part of its dedication, we also include the usual Craft tools. However, there is no hard and fast rule regarding their placement. We do strive to represent the elements in balance on either side of the altar. A typical example would be as follows:

Goddess candle		God candle
Chalice	Book of Shadows	Water bowl
Salt	Athame	Pentacle
Incense	Wand	Bell

The broom and sword usually rest on the floor before the altar, as does the cauldron, when ritual calls for its presence.

Most often, ritual actions are initiated at the altar, and then radiate outward. This could mean starting part of a ritual at altar-side (our altar is usually placed in the north) and continuing it at each quarter-point or starting at the altar and continuing in the center of the circle. The following two rituals each demonstrate one of the above actions. The photos provide an idea of how our altar set-ups can differ with each rite.

Yule

(Note: In our tradition, the ordering of the elements is quite different from the classical alignment. East is Earth, south is Fire, west is Air, and north is Water. However, the ritual is easily adapted to individual/group needs or traditions.)

The circle is cast. White candles are at the quarter points, and the altar abounds with holly, garland, and decorations of the season. The cauldron stands before the altar, inside is salted water and an unlit candle. A large bundle of evergreens and pine cones (and whatever else you choose) rests upon the altar. Surrounding the cauldron are four, smaller versions of this bundle. The celebrant stands before the altar:

As this night comes, let me sing with it.
Let my spirit dance in its circles.
Be with me, Old Ones; pour my sabbat mead.
Draw down stars to touch the bread.
Bless my altar of the Earth.

The fields are silent.
Under the snow, secrets lay hidden
and summers are born.
In the shadow of frost, there is rapture.
Old Ones, bless my altar of Earth.

Yule altar of the Tuatha De Danann (photo by Gary T. Niall).

Celebrant takes up the special bundle and elevates it, saying:

Lord and Lady, this time is yours,
a spiral of all being.
The seasons come and come again
from the completeness of your heart.
In your circle is life first born,
in this circle may life renew
with the glorious return of the Sun.

Celebrant stands with hands extended over the cauldron:

May the Yule take me,
gather me inward,
set my spirit to blaze.
I honor the waning Sun
as I do the waxing Moons.
You have found a new birthing,
oh glorious Lugh,
a phoenix song carried on the solar winds.
Now in your darkness, I await your light.
I call upon the elements of our world.

May they come and celebrate
the dancing of the dawn.

Celebrant takes a small bundle from the cauldron side and elevates it in the east:

Gentry, holders of the dream,
let my words echo in your halls.
Let their stones rejoice and join my spirit
in welcoming the Yule.

Celebrant places the bundle in the east and extinguishes the candle. A second candle is now taken from the cauldron side and elevated in the south:

Salamanders, holders of wisdom,
let my words be heard
on your plain of fire.
Kindle my heart, as the Sun grows
brilliant with life.

Celebrant places the bundle in the south, and extinguishes the candle. A third bundle is now elevated in the west:

Sylphs, weavers of magick,
temple bells of the soul,
teach me the songs of the morning
as the Sun starts its slow return.

Celebrant places the bundle in the west, and extinguishes the candle. The last bundle is now elevated in the north:

Undines, keepers of memories,
all life springs from your
cauldron of rebirth.
Bathe my being in wonder
and the touch of the Sun's new light.

The bundle is placed in the north. The celebrant extinguishes the candle and returns to the altar.

Celebrant washes his hands three times in the cauldron's salted water. He next takes the unlit candle out of the cauldron and lights it from both the altar candles. Finally he elevates the candle high overhead so that its light casts its reflection, flickering shadows across the entire circle:

This darkness, this circle, is my Sunless home.
On this night, it is also a living tomb.
But as of old, the Sun shall rise,
the light shall have its rebirth.
I set you free upon the land.
I banish darkness, in the Old Ones' names.
I light the Yule!

Celebrant re-lights the quarter points, starting in the east, then replaces the candle in the cauldron. This can be followed by any needful magickal work or meditation, or a small cake and ale ceremony.

Close circle.

(Note: Yule seems to mean the same to all Wiccans in all traditions. It is the shortest day of the year, and the rebirth of the "Sun," a time of renewal for the male principle of life. We of the TDD use live Yule trees in our rituals. When we "light the Yule" we light a series of small candles clipped on the tree's branches. They are quickly extinguished and the tree soon removed to our outside grove. Candles ablaze on a live tree are a wondrous sight, however respect for life is primary:

1. The tree must be *fresh* and *live*, not cut. Check to be sure the needles are soft and pliant, not dry.

2. Keep the root ball moist.

3. Air temperature in the room should be kept in the 50s or low 60s. Do not set the tree near a radiator or air vent.

4. It would be best to bring the tree indoors on the same day as the ritual, but no sooner than the day before.

5. Never risk human life by lighting candles on an artificial or cut tree.

6. Never endanger a live tree by treating it like an indoor ornament. Live trees should ideally remain indoors three days, but no more than seven.

Happy Yule!

Lughnasad

Lughnasad (August 1) celebrates the ripening of the grain crops as the fruit season comes to an end. It is a perilous time for the fields, as weather, vermin, and other caprices of nature pose a threat to the harvest. Our ritual invokes the blessings of the Old Ones upon the fields and those who labor within them, and invokes the spark of life in the fields themselves.

This was also the time of the great festival in Ireland, in honor of the God Lugh. It was a time of declared peace, a breathing space between fruit and grain harvests, when people can feast and retell the old tales of gods and heroes.

In the months to come, as summer fades to autumn and the harvest begins in earnest, the rind of the last fruits and the chaff of the grain will be buried in earth or thrown to the wind as a symbol of the people's intention to return life to the Earth, from which it was taken. But for now, the dust of labor is symbolically washed away by dipping a hem into sacred water. The Old Ones are remembered, and the celebration of life commences.

The circle is cast. There are green candles at the quarter points and on the altar. There must be an unlit candle, with a holder, before the altar—next to the cauldron. The cauldron is filled with spring water. Upon the altar are fresh flowers, and the breads, fruits and nuts of the season, along with a bundle of wheat, or fresh corn, to represent the ripening crops. Celebrant stands before the altar and elevates the bowl of fruit and grain:

> *Old Ones, I stand before you*
> *in the heart of your bounty,*
> *and the fire colors of growing fruit.*
> *My people once offered rind and chaff,*
> *casting it to your winds*
> *to still the face of hunger and cold.*
> *Still in my heart I seed the breezes,*
> *I sow the wind,*
> *I hold back the night*
> *and thunder with the bowing wheat.*

Celebrant lowers the fruit:

> *To you belongs the flavor of life.*
> *To you belongs the heat of the world,*
> *the embrace of my heart, my soul, my mind.*
> *May our spirits be one.*
> *May no sting of death or shadow*
> *befall the people, or fertile earth.*
> *May blessings find us, bind us, hold us,*
> *and flow through us once more.*

Celebrant removes the cauldron to the center of the circle, and takes the flowers from the altar:

> *I recall the ancient celebration,*
> *the festival of Goddess and God.*
> *At this time were both remembered,*
> *and peace was the law of the land.*

Celebrant walks around the cauldron deosil and drops the first flower into the water. (This is an old Irish tradition: the women would walk around the sacred wells three times sunwise, in order to obtain a wish—or bind a spell. The flowers symbolized the sacrifice they were willing to make to achieve their ends.)

> *I honor the Great One, the Mother of Life,*
> *companion of darkness and the Moon,*
> *spirit of moors and empty hills.*
> *Be bountiful to us and grace us with your blessing.*

Celebrant walks around the cauldron again, and drops the second flower upon the water:

> *I honor the Great One, the God of the Sun,*
> *the opener of the Way.*
> *Light of beauty and battle in one.*
> *Lugh of the Long-hand, be bountiful to us.*
> *Protect folk and field with your power.*

Loaves of bread, representing the start of the grain harvest, adorn the altar at Lammas in the Tuatha De Danann Tradition of Katharine Clark (photo by Gary T. Niall).

Celebrant walks around the cauldron for the last time, and drops the third flower upon its water:

*I call upon the spirit of Life,
the children of Earth, the children of Air,*

the web of all being,
the unquenchable fire.
From barren to ripe, from ripe to harvest
may the earth be blessed and grant us, again,
the bounty of its sacred feast.

Celebrant dips the hem of his robe (or clothing) into the cauldron water:

As of old, I dip my garment
into the waters of life.
Wash clean the dust of labors past.
Bless me as you find me; fill my heart.
Refresh me for the work yet to come.

Celebrant lights the spare candle before the altar and kneels before it:

Aliven my heart, Old Ones. Hear my voice.
In rivers and streams, hear me.
In the echoes of hills, answer.
In the voice of rye and barley, sing your song.
In the quiet of rowans catching the Moon,
or the leap of salmon in sacred pools,
show me your wonders.
Bless this time of growth into harvest.
Let me cherish your presence in the heart of the fields.
Fill me.

Celebrant passes his hands through the candle smoke three times, then touches his palms to the cauldron water. He presses his wet palms to his eyes momentarily, and meditates.

A cake and ale ceremony usually follows, then the circle is closed.

CHAPTER TWO

Indoor Shrines

Deep within an ancient Egyptian temple, beyond the great doors sheathed with bronze and the towering columns covered with hieroglyphs and brightly painted scenes there once stood an alcove. On the interior of this dimly lit space was painted a papyrus swamp in blue and gold. In the center of this alcove once stood a figure of Horus, the falcon-headed Sun God. This tiny alcove was the shrine of Horus and the spiritual focal point of the ancient temple.

Several millennia later and thousands of miles away, in a small alcove above a doorway in an old stone farmhouse, stands a replica of the Venus of Laussel. With her horn of thirteen segments poised, she almost seems to breathe in the flickering light of a votive candle, and casts her blessings of fertility and abundance on all in the room.

In ancient times such environments were created to contain representational figures of a particular deity. Such figures were sometimes ritually dressed or adorned, and at such shrines devotional offerings to the deity were usually made. In some cultures the representational figure of the deity was carried in procession to the shrines of other deities or to particular sacred sites, on days sacred to that deity, as a way of symbolizing his or her particular myth. Many of these practices were adopted by the Roman Catholic Church, and some are being reclaimed by contemporary Pagans and Wiccans.

Bob Place* of Saugerties, New York, a crafts person as well as a Craft person, tells us how he has applied his skills as a fine jeweler to the creation of such a shrine.

I started this shrine about sixteen years ago. I began with the temple structure, which is made of hand-me-down blocks, that I had when I was a child. They are made of hard maple. After modifying the blocks for the roof, I pegged and glued all of them together. When it was finished its dimensions were 16 1/2″ x 8″ x 3″. In spite of its small size the bare structure had a monumental classical, or archaic esthetic, that I find comforting. I would enjoy sitting and contemplating it. I knew it was a temple of the Goddess (this is the name I usually use for her although I occasionally use names like Gaia, or Aphrodite), and it was important to me to put a statue of her in it, but at this time I didn't have one that would fit.

I believe that the Goddess is everywhere. She is the space that is between everything, and in everything; the space that nurtures and brings into existence all matter. When we feel her presence it is because our attention is being drawn to something, or someone that was always there. So it is essential, when summoning the Goddess, to direct our attention toward her. The most powerful tool for doing this is symbolism. Symbols come to us from deep in the unconscious, where

A shrine to the Goddess by jeweler Bob Place (photo by Walt Lankenan).

The Goddess within the shrine created by Bob Place (photo by Walt Lankenan).

the individual mind merges with the collective mind. The Goddess lives here, as the archetypal feminine power. Essentially symbols come from the Goddess herself. By creating symbols she is summoning our consciousness to her.

For both conscious and unconscious reasons I decided to make a sculpture for the shrine. My first was made of wax sculpted in the round. The Goddess had her arms raised in the same position as the present one (I realized, years later, that this is a pose common to many ancient sculptures, and that the curve of the arms echoes the crescent shape of the moon). I brought it to a friend, who is a dental technician, to help me cast it. He had not cast pieces this large before, so this was an experiment for both of us. We made a lost wax mold and poured bronze into it with a centrifugal caster. The bronze cooled too fast, the sculpture was only half there.

For my next attempt I used ceramic clay to sculpt a Goddess in relief. Like the present one she had upraised arms, wavy hair, a Minoan inspired skirt, and the upper torso was nude. I glazed it in realistic colors and fired it. This sculpture was in the shrine for seven or eight years, but I was not entirely satisfied with it. It had some problems with the anatomical proportions.

During this time I had become a jeweler and had developed my skill at working with silver. So for my third sculpture the material that I chose was sterling silver, the metal of the Moon. Once again I started with a wax sculpture, but this time only for the upper part of the figure. This time I hired an experienced caster, but he still had trouble, and the surface of the casting came out pitted. It took a whole day of filing and buffing to give it a smooth finish. I made the skirt out of silver sheet and wire. In the center I set a carnelian, that was a gift from a friend. It has an intaglio carving of a dove, and the motto, "I love liberty" written on it in French. Around it I set nine turquoise stones, forming a triangle. Before attaching the sculpture I painted the background red-brown, and applied gold leaf over it, to bathe the Goddess in sunlight. I painted the background in the pediment deep blue to represent the sky.

Over the years I have attached small objects to the shrine to add to its power. Some of these things are simply purchased from mineral shops, or antique stores; such as the fossilized sea urchin with a natural five-pointed star on it, or the white shell cameo. Others are jewelry that I have made like the pentagram, and the labrys pendants, or the enameled figures. There are many small pieces that are repoussed, or carved models, that I made for castings. Some of the jewelry is made by friends of mine, like the pewter knight standing guard in the foreground, the bronze figure in fetal position, or the two scarf pins on top. The faience ankh and the scarabs were bought in Egypt. The red coral horn, and the kneeling figure from a creche scene, I bought in Spain; and the primitive jade carving in Mexico. Some are given to me by friends after they return from traveling. The amber pendants were brought from Poland by my wife's relatives. The cylindrical brass box contains miraculous ash that materialized in the hand of a guru in India. The porcelain, frozen Charlotte doll with the broken limbs is an antique that I found in the dirt in a field while I was hiking. The silver plated hand of power, and the gold plated scissors, I bought in a botanica in Paterson, New Jersey. Other pieces are from China, Tibet, Greece and Italy. Some I have had since childhood others are new. All of the pieces relate to the myths of the Goddess. I keep the shrine on top of a bookcase at chest level. It is currently in the corner of my office where I am writing this. I always keep it against the north wall, so that it is facing south. I think this is because the Moon travels through the southern half of the sky, and with the statue in this position it will catch moonlight throughout the night. Around the shrine are six candles, and tools representing the four elements. I use these for drawing a protective circle, and calling of the four directions before an invocation.

When calling the Goddess I use three words which she has given me, and which I must keep concealed. Along with these, I make up a new invocation every time I call. I let the words come to me as I speak. I call on her to ask advice, to ask for favors, and to dedicate things such as works of art. I always thank her afterwards.

Roslyn Reid of Bridgewater, New Jersey, who told us of her ever-changing altar in the previous chapter, tells us now of a most unusual shrine in her apartment.

Yule shrine of Roslyn Reid.

What's in this picture should be obvious—the Yule shrine of Puff the Magic Dragon! The large black object in the center is our portable fireplace, which is 3 feet tall by 3 feet wide by 2 feet deep. It arrived from the catalog store complete with artificial logs and a screen, making it an adequate facsimile of a genuine fireplace. It is ventless, burns canned heat, needs only a few inches of clearance, and can therefore be moved to almost anywhere in the house. (As you can see, right now we have fitted it into a convenient spot under the window, right next to that other American shrine, the TV set.) Such flexibility of location is wonderful for sorcerers with small apartments; and besides its "cozy" value, it has a practical application in that it warms our room quite well.

The dragon on top of it is the cover of a wood stove humidifier. The boughs of holly were cut from our yard to celebrate the Yule season, and the stockings were purchased for the same reason. (Of course, we remove the stockings when we start a fire, but we leave the boughs of holly on top. They don't seem to mind a bit. Also, a ceramic light ring anointed with oil can be placed on top of the fireplace to give the room an appropriate scent while the fire burns.)

Aside from decorating it in this manner for Yule, we usually don't hold rituals at this fireplace. One of the reasons is that because there is no vent, nothing can be burned in it except the canned heat, so it's useless for such rituals as burning the need-fire. However, one exception is when I use it for the Dumb Supper on Halloween night, when I set out a can of beer and a plate of cookies for my deceased cousin.

In Oregon, Sheila Castellanos, describes for us the construction of her shrine to the Goddess as well as the nature of the offerings and prayers that are made there.

This shrine is dedicated to the Goddess, it consists of an altar, an altar cloth, and a statue representing the Goddess. For the altar I chose a round table which was made by a member of my family several years ago. The altar is made totally of wood and its dimensions are 24 inches in diameter and 32 inches in height. The altar cloth is made from an old skirt which I found while cleaning out a closet. The design on the altar cloth is of flowers and birds. The statue took a little more time and effort to find. I searched garage sales, flea markets, and secondhand stores to find a statue which fit my image of the Goddess. I was unsuccessful. Finally, I found the perfect statue in a catalog which I received in the mail. The statue is made of permastone and its measurements are 13 inches by 11 inches. It is a figure of a nude woman stretching out on a cliff and holding a crescent Moon high above her head. It seemed so perfect, so I bought it!

The figure is adorned periodically—on greater sabbats and Full Moon esbats. Prayers of thanks are said and offerings are made. Some examples of offerings are bread, wine, vegetables, fruit, and flowers. Following are three prayers which I have written to the Goddess:

Samhain Prayer of Thanks
Goddess we give thanks for the beautiful summer.
We are grateful for the abundant crops

and the beauties of the flowers.

Thank you Goddess,
and farewell until you are with us again!

Prayer for the Goddess
Oh Goddess! We thank thee
for all you have sent
and blessed us with.
Please accept this small offering
as a token of our
appreciation and love!
Blessed Be.

Full Moon Prayer
On the night of the Full Moon,
we give thanks to
the Lady above.
Who brightens up the night
with the light of her love.

The photo shows on the altar the statue representing the Goddess and offerings made to Her. The offerings include a goblet of wine, a basket of vegetables (potatoes, onions, carrots, and squash), and a white rose.

A special place where offerings are made to the Goddess by Sheila Castellanos.

CHAPTER THREE

Indoor Circles

"Ring the bell, open the book, light the candles." So begin the instructions for casting the magick circle in more than one Book of Shadows.

Probably no one will ever know when or where the first magick circle was cast. Perhaps it cast itself as the circle of light and warmth that surrounded the first fire ever kindled in a cave. Of all of the magickal spaces ever created the circle is the most important, the most symbolic, and probably the oldest. The circle is in space what the Wheel of the Year is in time. In most traditions, the eastern point of the circle corresponds to spring and the element of Air; the southern point to summer and the element of Fire; the western point to autumn and the element of Water; and the northern point to winter and the element of Earth. The northern half of the circle represents the dark half of the Wheel of the Year, death and the Horned God, while the southern half represents the light half of the year, life and the Goddess of Fertility and rebirth. The whole circle symbolizes the place where all things meet their opposite, union of the Goddess and the God and the eternal cycle of birth, death and rebirth. Unlike the magician's circle of protection, the magick circles cast by Pagans and Wiccans are created to contain the power generated within this sacred space between the mundane world and the world of Spirits.

Adorned with the flowers of spring at Beltane, baskets of grain and the first fruits of the harvest at Lammas, with glowing jack-o'-lanterns at Samhain or with boughs of fir and sprays of holly at Yule, from the warm flickering firelight of the Stone Age down to the cool pulsing light of the computer age, the magick circle is ever-changing, ever-turning, ever renewing itself.

In the following pages Pagans from across the country and from Europe reveal to us their unique secrets for casting the magick circle.

We will begin with Lady Epona, High Priestess of the Coven of the Silver Mist as well as Treasurer of Philanor (Philadelphia Network of Old Religions).

When I first began my training many years ago, the altar set-up was the most important part of the ritual, the next group I trained with put emphasis on the quarters. Now, about eighteen years later, I have both altar and quarter set-up that I feel necessary to perform an effective ritual.

The nice thing about being a Wiccan is that I have learned to go with the flow. Some things you don't learn out of a book, you have to go the Her in your deep inner self and just do what you feel. I find using the things I have learned, the things I have taught, and just using what I feel is usually the best.

Sacred space can be anywhere you need it. If it is an appropriate area you will know, being Wiccan means listening to that inner voice that tells you what is right.

I usually put my altar table in the middle of my circle first. Then the quarters can be set up. I begin in the east, each element is placed with a quarter candle.

In the east to represent Air is the thurible. The incense can be any substance that relates to that ritual. I have gotten in the habit of making my own incense. This is easily done by using a wood base and oils and herbs that identify with what you are doing. Incense should be kept light enough to scent the air without being overwhelming.

In the south to represent Fire, I have a candle with the quarter candle. If the ritual is outside a small fire is great. Sometimes in winter when using my basement I use a kerosene heater, but even an electric heater would be all right. Don't fight modern times, use them to help you.

In the north to represent the Earth I use a large earthen bowl (my child made it when she was in kindergarten) and I fill it with sea salt. Sea salt can be purchased in the supermarket by the box, it's called kosher salt. I usually keep crystals and other Earth items that I would like charged in it.

In the west to represent the element of Water I just put water in my ritual chalice. One time I used a large glass bowl filled with water and put floating candles in it.

When I set up my altar I start with two altar candles to represent the God and Goddess, a chalice of wine, the athame, a candle snuffer, sometimes a wand, and whatever you may need to do the ritual. The last thing to go on the altar is the representation of the God and Goddess. Sometimes I use statues and other times just symbols of them. Horns can represent the God form. Sometimes the ritual centers around only the Goddess. I use flowers or a crystal or whatever fits for that ritual. I've always felt that sacred space could be created anywhere you need it. All it takes is a pure heart and good intentions.

This year for the Samhain or Hallowmas ritual, we started in the afternoon by carving pumpkins for each quarter. Osin was given the opportunity to express his feelings by carving each pumpkin as he felt it would relate to the particular quarter (element) that it would represent.

I set up my altar and quarters shortly before the ritual. The area is cleansed and blessed first by walking clockwise with a broom and sweeping the circle. Any area that is comfortable can be used for ritual work. Since I live in a town house, I use the area off the kitchen that allows me the most room.

This ritual was to the Goddess Hecate and I used three ears of corn to represent Her. They represented the aspect Maid, Mother, and Crone—the fullness of the harvest, the seeds of the future, and the end of the season with the promise of rebirth.

First everyone assembles in a circle around the altar. A brief moment of meditation and getting in tune with each other is spent by holding hands and be-

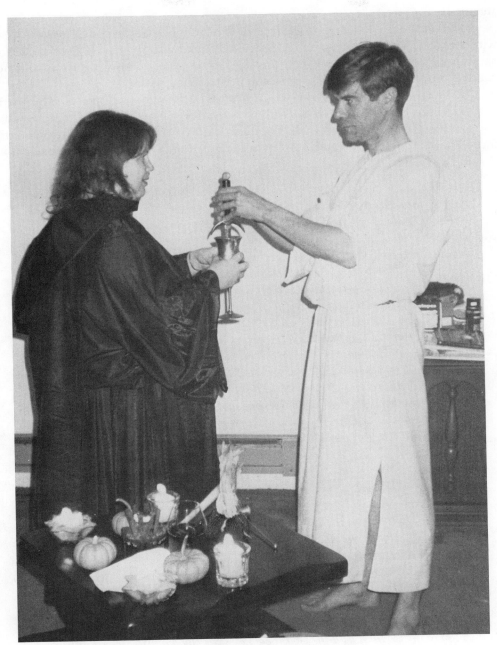

Lady Epona and Osin charging the wine in the symbolic Great Rite.

ing silent. Then we drop hands, I begin my rituals by clapping my hands three times above my head and saying, "Hekas, Hekas, Es ta Biblious, Be far O ye profane, for we are about to invoke the powers of the Old Gods. Enter into this place with clean hands and a pure heart, less you defile the source of life." This cleans up the area so that when you invoke all positive energy is around you and all negativity is gone.

The circle is then cast by starting in the east. The circle is drawn clockwise with a sword. Then the quarters are invoked starting in the east. I always use the same invocation for the quarters, this is a training coven and it is important to build a rapport with the spirits that you are working with.

Each ritual begins the same. The contents of the mid-section is done according to the seasonal holiday or the Full or New Moon. I borrow, invent, copy, and use anything that is ancient or has been written or that seems appropriate and mold it to our capabilities at this point in the training. This is the Halloween ritual I used this year:

This is the sacred night of Halloween, the Festival of the Dead, and the Mother that was the Maiden is now become the Crone. She is Dame Hecate, the Scribe of Souls, in whose dread Book of Shadows all names must be written with the ebbing blood of life . . . She is Dame Hecate, the Broomstick Hag, whose icy breath shakes us shivering from the naked Tree of Life, which She upends to sweep us as dead leaves from Her relentless path . . . She is Dame Hecate, the Destroyer, whose other face is the Lord of Shadows . . . She is Dame Hecate, the Old and the Wise, whose bittersweet gift is Death. In token and remembrance of this gift by which Life renews itself, do we bring to Her altar on this night the gift of ourselves, that we may thus renew ourselves. For we are the symbol in the eye and the reflection in the mirror; for we are the Goddess beholding Herself.

O Goddess, Queen of all Wiccans, on this sacred night of Halloween do I invoke thee as Hecate, Mistress of Death and Sorcery, Dark Lady of Spells and Shadows, Sovereign Queen of all Spectre and Spirits, and Queen of Light, so am I also Priestess unto Thee, O Queen of Darkness, for to deny Thee is to be blind in one eye, and but half alive. Therefore do I summon thee both from within and from without, for I am of Thee as Thou art of me; such is the mystery of the Goddess.

Let us reflect that the mysteries She shares with the Lord of Shadows, who is her Son and other Self, are part of the very fabric of the cosmos, and are not in themselves evil. For the waning Moon and all it symbolizes are as compelling to the mind and eye as the waxing Moon, and we as Wiccans are therefore wise to have an understanding of both.

Rose red, blood red, Wine of Life. O flowered cup, O thorned knife, drink deep the draught of peace from strife! Drink deep and see things yet unseen on this most sacred Halloween.

As the athame is to the male, so the cup is to the female and from this fruitful union of the Goddess and the God there flows the blood of life, rich and red and intoxicating as wine. Let us drink to Halloween, to Magick and to each other!

Pass chalice clockwise and everyone drinks:

Ye spirits of Wiccans who remain disincarnate, and who on this night of nights love best to return to this dimension we call the Earth plane, we Wiccans who are reincarnate welcome you to this our Feast of the Dead. In recognition of your presence do I pour forth this chalice of wine from which no mortal here may drink . . . likewise do I set forth this sabbat cake which no mortal here may eat.

Cover the wine and cake with a cloth.

Accept this tribute, Wiccans who yet dwell beyond the veil! Watch over us and bestow upon us your blessing for the coming new year! So mote it be!

Everyone dances clockwise. When enough circle dancing has been done, we ground the energy by placing our hands on the ground.

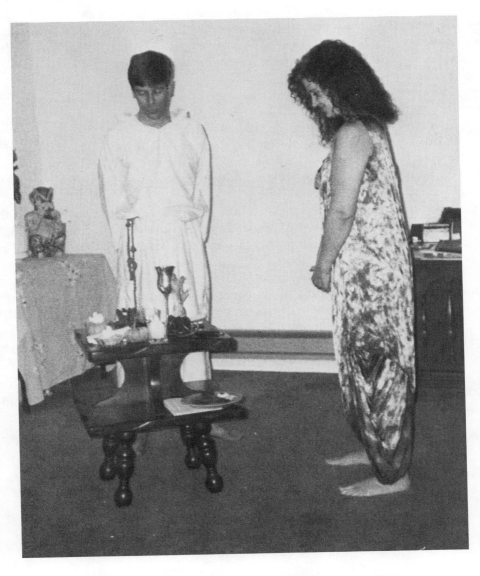

Osin and Morgan reflecting on the Samhain ritual after the rite had ended.

The quarters are then dismissed by going to each and stating:

Thank you for your presents. Hail and farewell. The rite is ended.

Then we usually have a small feast and discuss the ritual.

To most people who are familiar with the recent literature on Wicca, Paganism and magick, one of the first names that comes to mind is Scott Cunningham. Scott has been a practitioner of Wicca for more than half of his life, since a chance meeting with a girl who taught him the basics of the religion. It wasn't until several years and many teachers later that Scott decided to combine his religious beliefs and interest in magick with his chosen career as a writer. A list of his popular titles include Earth Power *(1983),* Cunningham's Encyclopedia of Magical Herbs *(1985),* The Magical Household *(with David Harrington, 1987), and* Earth, Air, Fire & Water *(1991). Here Scott gives us his method for casting a stone circle indoors.*

The circle of stones is used during indoor rituals, for energy raising, meditation and so on.

First cleanse the area with the ritual broom.

For this circle you will need four large, flat stones. If you have none, candles can be used to mark the four cardinal points of the circle. White or purple candles can be used, as can colors related to each direction—green for the north, yellow for east, red for south, and blue for west.

Place the first stone (or candle) to the north, to represent the Spirit of the North Stone. In ritual when you invoke the spirits of the stones you're actually invoking all that resides in that particular direction, including the elemental energies.

After setting the north stone (or candle), place the east, south and west stones. They should mark out a rough square, nearly encompassing the working area. This square represents the physical plane on which we exist—the Earth.

Now take a long purple or white cord, fashioned, perhaps, of braided yarn, and lay it out in a circle, using the four stones or candles to guide you. It takes a bit of practice to do this smoothly. The cord should be placed so that the stones remain *inside* the circle. Now you have a square and a circle, the circle representing the spiritual reality. As such, this is a squared circle; the place of interpenetration of the physical and spiritual realms.

The size of the circle can be anything from 5 to 20 feet depending on the room and your desires.

Next, set up the altar. The following tools are recommended:

- A Goddess symbol (candle, holed stone, statue)
- A God symbol (candle, horn, acorn, statue)
- Magick knife (athame)
- Wand
- Censer
- Pentacle
- A bowl of water (spring, rain or tap)

- A bowl of salt (it can also be placed on the pentacle)
- Incense
- Flowers and greens
- One red candle in holder (if not using point candles)
- Any other tools or materials required for the ritual, spell or magickal working

Set up the altar according to your own design. Also be sure to have plenty of matches, as well as a small heat-proof container in which to place them when used. A charcoal block is also necessary to burn the incense.

Light the candles. Set the incense smoking. Lift the knife and touch its blade to the water, saying:

I consecrate and cleanse this water
that it may be purified and fit to
dwell within the sacred Circle of Stones.
In the name of the Mother Goddess and the Father God
(If attuning with a specific Goddess and God, substitute their names here.)
I consecrate this water.

As you do this, visualize your knife blasting away all negativity from the water. The salt is next touched with the point of the knife while saying:

I bless this salt that it may be fit
to dwell within the sacred Circle of Stones.
In the name of the Mother Goddess and Father God,
I bless this salt.

Now stand facing north, at the edge of the cord-marked circle. Hold your magick knife point outward at waist level. Walk slowly around the circle's perimeter clockwise, your feet just inside the cord, charging it with your words and energy. Create the circle—through your visualization—with the power flowing out from your knife's blade. As you walk, stretch the energy out until it forms a complete sphere around the working area, half above the ground, half below. As you do this say:

Here is the boundary of the Circle of Stones.
Naught but love shall enter in,
Naught but love shall emerge from within.
Charge this by Your powers, Old Ones!

When you have arrived back at the north, place the magick knife on the altar. Take up the salt and sprinkle it around the circle, beginning and ending in the north, and moving clockwise. Next, carry the smoking censer around the circle, then the southern point candle or the lit red candle from the altar, and finally sprinkle water around the circle. Do more than carrying and walking; sense the substances purifying the circle. The Circle of Stones is now sealed.

Hold aloft the wand at the north, at the edge of the circle, and say:

O Spirit of the North Stone,
Ancient One of the Earth,
I call You to attend this Circle.
Charge this by Your powers, Old Ones!

As you say this, visualize a greenish mist rising and writhing in the northern quarter, over the stone. This is the elemental energy of Earth. When the Spirit is present, lower the wand, move to the east, raise it again and say:

O Spirit of the East Stone,
Ancient One of Air,
I call You to attend this Circle.
Charge this by Your powers, Old Ones!

Visualize the yellowish mist of Air energy. Lower the wand, move to the south and repeat the following with your upraised wand, visualizing a crimson Fire mist:

O Spirit of the South Stone,
Ancient One of Fire,
I call You to attend this Circle.
Charge this by Your powers, Old Ones!

Finally, to the west, say with wand held aloft:

O Spirit of the West Stone,
Ancient One of Water,
I call You to attend this Circle.
Charge this by Your powers, Old Ones!

Visualize the bluish mist, the essence of Water.

The circle breathes and lives around you. The spirits of the stones are present. Feel the energies. Visualize the circle glowing and growing in power. Stand still, sensing for a moment.

The circle of stones is complete. The Goddess and God may be called, and magick wrought.

The above casting of the circle of stones is from Scott's book, Wicca: A Guide for the Solitary Practitioner. *Next Scott shares with us a never before published Midsummer rite.*

This is a private rite, but others can participate; simply adjust the ritual. For best results, perform this during the day in a darkened room (close curtains and doors).

Items needed:

- One green candle (to represent the Goddess)
- One red candle (to represent the God)
- Your athame (a finger is an excellent substitute)
- Bowls of water and salt
- Censer and incense (recommended incense blend: frankincense, sandalwood and dried orange peel)
- Charcoal block

- Several small mirrors, and any large broken mirror fragments that you may have (use care in handling them)
- A large cauldron (substitutes can include a very large ceramic mixing bowl or some other suitable container—it need not be fire-proof)
- A piece of red or black cloth, wadded and placed in the bottom of the cauldron or bowl)

Scott Cunningham's Summer Solstice ritual using candles and mirrors (photo by Dan Campanelli).

- Four white and four red quarter candles and holders (explained later)
- One extra red candle with holder on the altar
  (if a group ritual, one red candle per attendee)
- Matches and a container in which to place them after lighting

Place one red and one white quarter candle each to the north, east, south and west. Place cauldron on center of altar, or on a table behind it at the same height as the quarter candles. Place mirrors and/or mirror fragments to the left side of the altar. Set up other tools on altar. Extinguish all artificial lights.

Light Goddess candle, then the God candle, then the extra red candle.

Light charcoal block and set in censer. Sprinkle with incense.

Purify water by touching it with your athame (or finger) and say while visualizing:

I now purify this living water of the Earth
by the power of the Goddess.

Bless salt by touching it with your athame (or finger) and say while visualizing:

I now bless this salt of the Earth
by the power of the Goddess.

Cast circle with athame (or finger) beginning and ending in the north, while saying:

I create this circle
of power, light and love
to be a meeting place
with the Goddess and God
on this day of Midsummer.

(Visualize and send energy out from your body to create the circle. Remember: the circle is actually a sphere of energy.)

Set down the athame. Always moving clockwise, sprinkle salt around the circle. Sprinkle water around the circle. Carry the red candle around the circle. Refresh incense and carry censer around the circle.

Approach the southern quarter. Light the two quarter candles there while saying:

Sunlight burnishes the land,
unhindered by winter's prison.

Light the two quarter candles in the west and say:

Sunlight spills upon the land,
unhindered by hail and sleet.

Light the two quarter candles in the north and say:

Sunlight blesses the land,
unhindered by drifts of snow.

Light the two quarter candles in the east and say:

Sunlight refreshes the land,
unhindered by chilling winds.

Now place the mirrors into the cauldron. Prop them on the cloth within the cauldron so that they catch the quarter candle's light. (Be certain that the mirrors reflect the candle's light.) As you do this, say:

How green is the Earth!
Warmed by the Sun,
strengthened by the God,
bursting with life and fertility.
Sunlight . . . Godlight . . . Lifelight . . .
blesses all below
through the eternal love of the Goddess.

Pick up the extra red candle on the altar. Standing in the south before the mirror-fire, walk slowly around the altar and cauldron. Hold the candle so that its flame is reflected in the mirrors. Stare at the reflected candle flames. Feel the warmth of the Sun, the coming of summer, the magic and mystery of this time. Say these or similar words:

I hail the birth of Summer!
Prevail, oh warmth of Summer!
Unfailing light of Summer!
You sail, oh Sun of Summer
Across the gleaming sky!
Above the Lady's Earth!
About the God's domain!
Within the hearts of all!

Pause for a moment, still gazing at the mirrors, then say:

Midsummer's come!

Set the red candle on the altar. Stare into the mirrors for a while. If you have acts of magick to perform, now is the time. Or, sit and meditate in the candle's reflections.

When the rite is over, take your athame to the north and undraw the circle by moving clockwise around it, gathering up its energy into the athame. Pinch out or snuff the quarter candles, then the red candle, then the God candle, and finally the Goddess candle.

Afterward, eat spicy foods and drink red wine or orange juice to further celebrate the coming of Midsummer.

Your rite has ended.

From the very buckle of the Bible Belt, Lord Galen and Lady Hesperia, High Priest and
Priestess of the Coven of the Eternal Harvest, describe for us their method of casting a very

traditional circle in a very unique way.

In our coven we begin our circle preparation in the latter part of the afternoon of the day of whatever sabbat or esbat we may be holding. In which we do such mundane things as ensuring the area of my home that we are using is cleaned as appropriately as possible. We hold all of our rituals indoors for two reasons, first, the lack of private ownership of land by any of our coven members and, second, methods of harassment that Pagans/Wiccans receive in this (Fundamentalist) controlled area of North Carolina. Then we start ritually preparing ourselves, by taking ritual baths, meditating and so forth.

At the appropriate time the person appointed to cast the circle will drive a small nail into the exact center of the room where the ritual is to take place (usually my living room), then we attach a segment of string exactly 4 1/2 feet in length to the nail, at the other end of the string is a squeeze bottle filled with salt (reason being for the belief of its symbolism of purity and protection). Then the person casting the circle begins to slowly cast the circle of salt in a deosil direction, beginning in the east, pouring a continuous unbroken circle of salt until they are back in the east. At this point they leave open a space in the circle of roughly 9-12 inches for the use as an entry point for the coven members. The same person will go to each of the cardinal points, north, east, south and west, and with the same bottle of salt will draw the alchemical symbol for the element representative of that direction. For Full Moon rituals and lesser esbats we use only the alchemical emblems as part of our circle construction, but on the more important festivals such as Samhain, Imbolc, etc. we draw the entire symbolism of the zodiac around the circle in salt.

Our circle is nine feet in diameter for the following reasons: first, 9 is a much recognized number of the Goddess by most traditional Wiccans; second, a 9-foot circle is a comfortable size for all of our ritual needs, and third, it fits nicely into my living room. Next, we set votive candles in the appropriate spots in the quarters: east/yellow, south/red, west/blue and north/green.

Next, we prepare the altar. The Priest and Priestess enter the circle to prepare to welcome the other coven members. Each coven member requests permission to enter the circle. We then grant that permission. At the moment the member enters the sacred circle, if a female, the Priest will anoint her forehead at the spot of the third eye chakra with blessed oil, in the sign of the pentagram, and state, "I anoint thee (their sacred name) in the name of Cernunnos and Cerridwen, may the God and Goddess bring you peace and joy." Then after everyone has entered the circle and taken up their respective positions, a previously assigned coven member takes the squeeze bottle of salt and closes the circle, while saying, "I close this circle in the name of the Lord and the Lady, may none leave it but for good cause!" Then the Priestess calls forth an assigned member of the coven and hands that person the coven sword and instructs the member to begin the circumambulation of the circle while pointing the sword at the salt circle and visualizing a pure white light emanating from the tip of the sword and going into the salt raising the circle's power as he or she goes along its perimeter. This is started in the east and ends in the east (deosil).

We then call the quarters in the following way. Starting in the east a specified coven member first lights the east candle then takes his athame and touches it to his heart, raising it back in a type of salute per se. While holding his athame high he says the following, "Oh guardians of the watchtowers of the east, we ask you to join the Coven of the Eternal Harvest in our rite, and to guard our Sacred Circle! So mote it be!" The same is done in the south, west and then in the north. After the quarters are called, another assigned coven member (we will call the summoner), beginning in the east, rings the coven bell three times (also three times in the other quarters, as a final gesture of ritual summoning).

The salt circle of the Coven of the Eternal Harvest.

After this is completed we consecrate the circle with the four elements, in the following way. Beginning in the east with a censer and burning incense the person doing the Air consecration makes three circumambulations, while saying the following, "I consecrate this sacred circle with the power of Fire." The same is done in the west while the person who is doing the consecration with water (that will have earlier been consecrated), gently sprinkles small amounts of water while making the three circumambulations. And, finally the person consecrating with the element Earth, will take a small dish of salt and gently sprinkle it around the perimeter of the circle, ending in the north. When the person who is consecrating the circle begins the circumambulations, they will start and end in the quarter represented by the element that they are consecrating it with. The person doing the consecrating will hold the candle, censer or whichever item they're consecrating the circle with high in salute to the respective elementals and say the following: "We have purified this circle with the power of Air/Fire/Water/Earth, and have made it sacred in the eyes of the Lord and the Lady. So mote it be!"

After all the circle casting and purifying is complete we direct our attention to the altar, and beginning with the left altar candle (representing the Goddess). We light the Goddess candle and say the following: "Lovely Goddess, we invite you into our sacred circle in the name of your love and wisdom!" After completing the lighting of the Goddess and God candles, we do an invoking pentagram in the air at a point above and between both the Goddess and God candles. Upon completion of whatever ritual celebration we are doing, we extinguish the God candle and say the following: "Mighty God Cernunnos we thank you for participation in our sacred rite, return now to the side of your lovely Goddess Cerridwen, in the name of your wisdom and strength!" We extinguish the Goddess candle and say the following: "Lovely Goddess Cerridwen, we thank you for your participation in our sacred rite, return now to the side of your mighty God Cernunnos, in the name of your wisdom and love!" Then we do a banishing pentagram above the altar once again at a point above and between both the God and Goddess candles. We now begin the process of dismissing the quarters. Once again a coven member beginning in the east will stoop down, extinguish the quarter candle with a candle snuffer, stand up and do a banishing pentagram for the east, and say; "Oh guardians of the watchtowers of the east, we thank thee for thy participation in and the guarding of our circle, as you leave us now do so in love and in light!" The same is done in the remaining quarters, with the same amount of reverence.

Then an assigned coven member goes to the east quarter, stoops down and with their hand breaks the salt circle and simply states that "This rite has ended."

Not everyone is able to cast a traditional circle in a traditional manner. Ron E., who described for us his method for creating an altar in a prison cell, now describes for us how he casts his circle.

Behind bars it is not possible to physically draw a magick circle on the floor indoors, or on the ground outdoors. For an individual behind bars a circle must be cast mentally by visualizing. For this reason, a magick circle behind bars is always temporary. Normally a person behind bars is a solitary practitioner and a magick circle for one person only is needed. The magick circle should be approximately three to five feet in diameter. I only know of a couple of prisons within the United States that have organized groups within them. Here at the institution that I am incarcerated there is such a group. However, we are not allowed to draw a magick circle within the group physically or practice any of our rituals. We all are solitary practitioners of our beliefs.

Casting a magick circle is done for the purpose of determining and also pinpointing the spot from which you are going to conduct your rituals and your activities. The magick circle draws a boundary for all to see and know as to what it is as well as who it is that is performing the activities or ritual. When you cast a circle, you are not actually casting a circle, but instead, you are casting a sphere. However, it is impossible to physically draw a sphere without more hands. So to attempt to would be impossible as well as unnecessary. As you cast a circle and it is closed, it becomes a sphere equal in all directions.

The use of color in casting your magick circle as well as using an item to signify the elements or watchtowers is also helpful. The following is a list that indicates such color usage. I have also given you a few symbols that are used to represent the elementals or watchtowers:

Name of Element	Corresponding Colors	Symbols Used
Air	White, Sky Blue	△ ◇ ≈
Fire	Red, Orange	△ △ ♌
Water	Blue, Aqua Blue	▽ ╳ 🦅
Earth	Green, Brown	▽ ✡ ♉
Spirit	Gold, Silver	⊕

I personally use a two inch by two inch piece of parchment with the symbol of each elemental on a separate piece. The symbol is placed in the middle, and I added the zodiac signs that correspond to each elemental to add more beauty to my personal activities. You can add color to these if you wish to add more to them. Here is a list that shows which zodiac signs correspond to which elemental symbols:

Name	Symbols	
Air:	Ⅱ Gemini, ♎ Libra, ≈ Aquarius	
Fire:	♌ Leo, ♈ Aries, ♐ Sagittarius	
Water:	♓ Pisces, ♏ Scorpio, ♋ Cancer	
Earth:	♍ Virgo, ♉ Taurus, ♑ Capricorn	
Spirit:	All	Example

Be creative and use your imagination when creating items to use in your magick circle. This really all depends on which type of circle you wish to draw or cast. The only element that stays the same is Spirit. It is always centered in the circle, as above, so below. Always start by placing the elemental symbols into their position in the east, going clockwise to erect the magick circle and going counterclockwise to banish a magick circle.

Remember, different sources of information provide you with different ways of invoking the element as well as banishing them. Certain sets actually use a particular calling sign for one particular one, while at the same time, that same sign is also used to banish another. Depending on how much thought and common sense you employ in your activities, you could wind up confusing yourself in the middle of things as well as confusing others. These may help to alleviate such happenings. Here are diagrams to show you the proper placement of the elementals for you magic circle, depending on the type of circle you are casting, whether it be a physical circle, an astral circle, or a spiritual circle.

In all actuality, the circle/sphere itself is closed to all without an invitation to enter, but it is not closed to observation from any who choose to watch. So by adding color and symbols to your magick circle, you add an esthetic beauty as well as a focal point to all for the efforts on your part to call upon and use. To focus the energies you draw upon, it also helps extensively in your visualization of your ritual activities. The glow of this particular source of power will then highlight each of the other specific ones within the magick circle.

Now that you have the proper materials needed, you are ready to cast your magick circle. Before doing so though, you may wish to meditate and think about what you are about to do. The correct positioning of the elemental symbols, or watchtowers, the type of ritual you are going to perform, and make double sure that you have everything that you will need to perform the ritual. There is nothing more disturbing than having to stop in the middle of a ritual because you forgot something. You are now ready, remember to start in the east to invoke a circle moving clockwise, move counterclockwise to banish a circle.

Greeting to announce yourself and your intent to invoking the gates of a magick circle. Be creative and change this to suit your needs. Say:

> *Lords and Ladies of the land, I* (your name) *call upon the element of* (the element's name), *I* (your name) *call upon you. Hear my voice and gather at this gate in order that you may bear witness to these rites I am about to perform. Come forth in a form that is pleasing to the eye and the mind as well as one that*

will not cause harm to any that have gathered here. Help me establish this point as the watchtower of the (direction) and the elemental realm of (element's name). So mote it be!

Substitute appropriate directional titles as well as elemental titles for where you wish to place the gates. Place *all* gates in a clockwise manner and take the gates down in a counterclockwise manner.

This is a three dimensional look at what a completed circle looks like with the elementals in place. This is where the theory of the sphere comes in. Notice that the circle looks somewhat like an atom, and you are the nucleus of it all. I hope this can help someone out there, especially those of us behind bars.

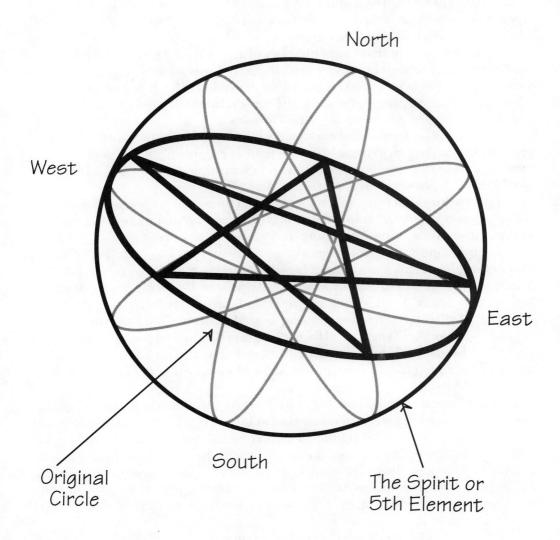

While many Pagans and Wiccans, by choice or by circumstances, are confined to limited space, others might find themselves bound to travel. Here, Wylundt, author of Wylundt's Book of Incense *(Weiser, 1991), and editor of* The Silver Chalice *, a lively and informative newsletter of the Magick Moonstone Coven, demonstrates for us how he carries his circle in his suitcase.*

Many occult practitioners are not fortunate enough to have permanent ritual areas, especially those in urban areas. Space is at a premium in the city and the cost of obtaining one (if it can be gotten) is prohibitive. And the thought of using a public park for rituals would make even the staunchest occultist cringe.

Because of this, most practicing Pagans, Witches, Magicians, and those in other "New Age" religions as well must depend upon the use of a kind of "Psychic Survival Kit." This kit is a bag, box, or suitcase which contains all of their necessary ritual articles. The contents of this receptacle will vary dramatically, depending upon the individual involved, their personal belief and/or value system, and whether they work alone or in a group.

I am fortunate, in that I am a member of an organized group. We take turns meeting in each other's homes for our rituals. Because we are a group, our "survival" bags are not as well stocked as a solitary's would be. Each person brings only what they will need personally, while the person in whose home we will meet in supplies the bulk of the necessary ritual articles.

All of this may be well and good; but what about the solitary and/or the person who has just begun to tread upon the path of Paganism? In this person's eyes, everything is of major importance! To carry everything that they feel is necessary would take a large trunk or several suitcases.

I sympathize with those solitary seekers out there. For several years, I was one myself. However, you will come to learn, as time goes by, that you will depend less and less upon your "tools" and more and more upon yourself.

I can imagine many solitaries saying to themselves right now, "I've heard that before, but it still sounds like a bunch of crap to me. I need my tools!" This article is dedicated to those of you who feel that way. Below is a listing of what I feel are "necessary" tools for the beginner and/or solitary Pagan.

First of all, you will need something to hold all of your portable ritual equipment. I use a cloth and vinyl travel bag. It has several zippered pockets and is large enough to hold all that I need, yet small enough that it is not heavy or bulky. It is also nondescript; it has no pentagrams, stars, Moons, or unicorns on it. It is what it's intended to be—a travel bag.

When "stocking" your bag, only put things into it that will fit. Swords, staffs, besoms, etc. may be pretty and nice to use at home, but they are of very little use when traveling. Leave them at home. I work robed, so for my "ideal" travel kit, I'd include one. Again, like the bag, it doesn't have to be gaudy, just functional. Its design and color is up to the individual (however, plaids and polka-dots are rather tacky). Stick to basics, like black or white. Any design is acceptable, but one you've made yourself is best; even if it is only a length of cloth with a serape type head hole cut in it.

With your robe, you'll need a cord. Curtain cords are excellent for this purpose. There's a lot of unnecessary debate over whether a cord should be nine feet long or the height of its user. It's my opinion that for a beginner and/or solitary a nine foot cord is more practical. It can be used for both holding the robe in place and for drawing a nine foot circle (when it is doubled).

Wylundt's circle in a suitcase (photo by Dan Campanelli).

The athame is another very important tool. In choosing one, you should never be rushed into buying one just because you need one. It has to "feel" right to you. Once you do find your athame (or it finds you), use it only for rituals and/or within your circle, and never use it to cut anything. Another point to remember is that in time you will probably "outgrow" your athame. You may some day come across another knife that appeals to you even more than your present one. This is fine, for it usually means that you are "growing" psychically.

A cup is also an important article to have, especially to those new to the Craft. Like your athame, the choice of style and material is left to the user. A suggestion, however, would be to have one that you can actually use. Remember that an expensive ornate cup may be nice to look at, but what good is it if you can't use it for fear of damaging it? For the beginner, use one that you are comfortable with; don't worry about its design or material as long as it appeals to you. For the "pros," even a paper cup will do in a pinch.

While jewelry and other adornments aren't exactly necessities, they do seem to set the mood. It does feel good to "dress up" for that special someone; and there's no one more special than the Gods. So, if you have an inclination for jewelry—go for it. One small suggestion: if you do wear adornments, don't use just your everyday things; have something special that you only wear within the circle. These special adornments will remind you of the peace, happiness, and magick you feel within your circle every time you handle them.

Wear as much or as little (or no) jewelry as pleases you. If you do wear jewelry, store it in a small cloth or leather bag so that it won't get lost or misplaced.

A working knife is also needed to cut herbs, carve symbols on candles, etc. within your circle. A regular kitchen paring knife is very handy for this sort of thing. Once you do use it within your circle, it should not be used elsewhere.

You will need a bowl to hold water for your rituals. It can be made of any material—from silver or crystal, to tin or ceramic. Do, however, try to stay away from using plastic or styrofoam. If working indoors, you will need a second bowl for pouring libations into.

You'll need water for your water bowl. Fresh spring water is the best choice, but bottled spring water is almost as good. You don't need to carry a whole gallon jug of water with you, a small container will do. Just be sure that it is sealed tightly and kept in an upright position.

Salt will also be needed. I prefer kosher salt because of its large course grains, but sea salt or even table salt will work just as well. You can use another bowl for your salt or, better yet, use a large clam or scallop shell. You don't need to carry a whole box of salt; a partially filled sandwich bag will hold more than enough salt.

You will need some candles. Carry a good supply of candles with you; but try to keep your use of candles to a minimum. The reason being that for every candle that you use you will also need a candle holder; candle holders are heavy and will take up a lot of space in your bag. Colored candles create nice effects but aren't necessary; neither are long "dinner" candles. Short white candles are the most practical and versatile.

Incense is another must have article. For the beginner, store-bought stick incense is the easiest to use. Later, as you gain experience, you can make your own incense. Incense tends to get very hot, thus creating a fire hazard. To help remedy this you will need an incense burner to burn your incense in and a small ceramic tile to place under the burner.

You'll want to have a good supply of matches to light your candles and incense with. Always carry two or three packs, just in case.

Always clean your ritual articles before and after each use. Most things, with the exception of your robe and the water, may be stored in your bag all the time.

Don't forget to bring something for "cakes and wine." Again the choice of what to use is yours. I've used everything from champagne and eclairs to spring water and Ritz crackers.

While it is desirable to memorize your rites and rituals, it is not always possible to do so. Bring a copy of your ritual(s) with you, in case it is needed. It will probably be dark and the lighting will be poor, so be sure that you hand print your rite, don't write it. And make sure to use large block letters and print your words dark and heavy.

If you have some pieces of good ritual equipment, such as silver, crystal or some handmade one-of-a-kind article, don't pack it. Leave it at home. Also try to keep everything that you do bring along as small and light-weight as possible.

I highly recommend making as many of your own ritual tools as you can. This will add greatly to their power and your personal identification with them.

Always remember that while your traveling kit may not be of the highest quality, it will be highly functional. Besides, the Gods aren't really looking for perfection from you, just sincerity—your most important tool is *you.*

A group of Witches practicing in France, who call themselves Wicca International Witchcraft* use some interesting names for the various aspects of the Goddess and the God, names that might raise a few eyebrows here, but perhaps our continental sisters and brothers in the Craft are a bit more open about the darker sides of the Lord and Lady than we are. They also use a most interesting material to physically define their circle, a material which can only help to enhance the magickal energy raised within. Here, in the words of Pierre le Corroller, an English-speaking member of the coven, is how it is done.

The altar is covered with red tissue and located in the north of the circle. So when we practice our rites in front of it, we are facing the north. The main symbol on the altar is the pentagram, the star, which is drawn on a lambskin or on a leaf of lead. We also have on the altar white or red candles, earth, water and a censer to represent the elements, a wand and a sword and our Book of Shadows.

This altar is used for all our rituals. In our main coven we have an altar as described and others dedicated to other divinities. The main altar is for Lucifer, the other ones are for Lilith, Diane, Astaroth, Belphegor, Belzebuth and the elementals, adorned with statues and candles. So we worship the Goddess under the names of Diane (Dana, Karridwen . . .) and Lilith, the two aspects of the Goddess, the God under the name of Lucifer (Lug, Phosphorus, Ra . . .).

During our rites we invoke also the 72 Genii of the Qabalah. This Qabalah doesn't represent a Jewish tradition but a much older one. These invocations of the Genii depend on the periods of the year and of the days. Astrology takes a great place for us.

We follow also the classical calendar for the sabbats: Imbolg, Spring Equinox, Beltane, Midsummer, Lughnasad, Autumn Equinox, Samhain and Yule.

Our rituals may take place indoors or outdoors, but always in a circle, a sacred place considered as intermediate between the physical and spiritual worlds. This circle is also a barrier for negative beings, larvae who must be dissolved with the sword, when the circle is opened.

Practically, we materialize this circle with a copper wire for indoor rituals. It does not have to be circular and the ideal is to encircle a whole room, which is especially a reservoir for magick with such a copper wire.

Every object coming into this circle must be consecrated, only initiates are allowed to penetrate this space and, following the Gardnerian traditions, all our rites are performed skyclad.

This physical circle must also be spiritually cast before every ritual, the wand is used for this with the whole coven inside the circle. This wand, a twig of elder bush cut during the Midsummer's night and with a copper wire inserted in its pith, is moved counterclockwise to cast the circle. We banish the circle with the sword used clockwise.

All our evocations are in Latin, for instance, before casting the circle: "Adjutorium nostrum in nomine Luciferis, qui faecit caelum et terram. Benedic Lucifer, Deus omnipotens, locum istum et sit in eo sanitas, victoria, virtus, bonitas plenitudo roboris it hale benedictio maneat super hune locum, nunce it in omnia saecula saeculorum."

As the circle may be formed by copper wire, so may it be formed at other times by other things. At Samhain the candles of the four quarters might be placed in jack-o'-lanterns while at Beltain the circle may be adorned with the flowers of May. At Lammas, wheat, corn, and barley might form the circle along with the tools of the harvest. In our own tradition here at Flying Witch Farm, just as Lammas is the celebration of the first harvest, the harvest of grain presided over by the Grain Goddess, the Autumnal Equinox is the celebration of the grape harvest presided over by the God of the Vine. As the Grain Goddess presides over physical life, the God of the Vine is the God of Death and Resurrection. It is at the time of the Autumnal Equinox that the Goddess and the God stand in perfect balance, as they did at the Vernal Equinox; but as the Vernal Equinox marked the shift in power toward the Lady and the light half of the year, the Autumnal Equinox marks the shift to the dark half of the year and its emphasis on the spiritual side of life. And so, at the Autumnal Equinox, Dan and I celebrate the grape harvest and all it symbolizes about the spiritual sides of life.

By late September the grapes have begun to be picked and crushed, and the autumn evenings begin to be a bit chilly so the circle is usually cast indoors, and as often as possible in the wine cellar where the yeasty smell of the must mingles with the damp earthy smell of the cellar itself. This location is also symbolic of the Underworld where spirit awaits rebirth. Here in the Underworld the individual is

The Autumnal Equinox circle of grapevine in the wine cellar at Flying Witch Farm (photo by Dan Campanelli).

transformed by the experience of being pure spirit, just as ordinary grape juice is transformed in the barrel to noble wine. There can be little doubt that in ancient times an initiation into a priesthood was arranged to induce what today is called a "near death experience." Today most initiations are simply a matter of taking certain oaths and being told certain secrets of the particular tradition, but individuals who have spontaneously experienced an NDE (near death experience) are transformed forever. In our own tradition this is the purpose of the Grail Quest, and as the Wine Moon waxes full and light and dark stand in perfect balance, it is this idea that is expressed in our ritual.

At sundown of the Autumnal Equinox, all has been made ready. The circle has been delineated with grapevines, still supple and pliant. Although the vine is associated with the God, it also produces little tendrils that form perfect spirals symbolic of the Goddess, reminding us that within the Goddess is the God, and within the God there is something of the Goddess. (In life is the seed of death, in death is the seed of rebirth.)

Within the circle an altar has been arranged on top of a wine barrel which itself seems to be the belly of the Mother of all Life. The barrel top has been draped with a purple cloth and decorated with bunches of wine grapes. On the altar, along with the other ritual tools, is a bottle of wine and the cup.

Just above the altar hangs an ancient terra-cotta head of Dionysus—God of Wine and of Resurrection. At an appropriate time during the autumn rites the bottle of wine is held aloft before the mask of Dionysus and consecrated with words such as:

> *Lord Dionysus*
> *God of the Vine, God of Joy*
> *you who have sought your mother*
> *in the Underworld and returned*
> *of you do we ask this blessing.*
> *That your spirit now enter this wine*
> *that it may be consecrated in your name.*
> *So mote it be!*

We replace the bottle on the altar and pause to wait for a sign that it has been done. When the sign has been given the bottle is held high again and the following words are spoken:

> *This wine is now consecrated to Dionysus.*

Then the blade of the ritual knife is placed, or held across the cup and the wine is slowly poured over the blade into the cup, while speaking words such as:

> *Blood of the sacrificial God of the Vine*
> *fill the Sacred Grail.*
> *Spirit of the Divine Child*
> *return to the Cauldron of the Great Mother.*

Then, take up the cup and say:

As the wine is transformed in the barrel
so are we transformed,
by the liberation of the Spirit.

We dip our fingers in the liquid and anoint one another making the sign of the solar cross on our foreheads with the wine, and then we each drink some of the wine saying:

Now do we drink the Wine of Pure Spirit
from the Cauldron of Immortality.

Finally, while holding an image of the cup in the eye of the mind, we sit within the circle of vines chanting:

In life is the seed of death
in death is the seed of rebirth.

It is not our intention to have an NDE within the circle during the ritual, but only to express magickally our desire to undergo true spiritual initiations as we walk the hidden path. Still as we sit quietly within the circle of vines by the flickering light of candles in the musty dampness of the cellar, the magickally imbued liquid begins to weave its spell, its radiance warms us, the face of Dionysus seems to smile down upon us, and we are changed.

When this ritual is ended, any wine left in the cup is poured out on the Earth. Since we work this ritual in a wine cellar where wine is spilled and barrels are washed out and where Dan has dug drains in the dirt floor, we pour the wine into these drains which go directly into the Earth. Any wine left in the bottle is still sacred wine consecrated to Dionysus, and is saved for similar rituals. New wine is then used for the blessing of the cakes and wine.

While some circles are made of practical materials, others are made of the stuff of Faerie tales. Opening a letter from a Wiccan friend in the Midwest one day, we noticed, on my lap, a tiny, shiny star of deepest red. Then suddenly a silver sliver of a crescent Moon appeared. The source of this glitter was the gift of Faerie dust in the letter. As we read the friendly message we began to know the magick of this charming gift.

My coven observed Samhain at our woodland home. For the ritual I covered the floor with white sheets to define the magick space, then cast the circle with Faerie dust (a combination of iridescent glitter and Moons and stars confetti).

The morning of clean-up faced a floor cover full of charged glitter. I could not just *dispose* of it. So I gathered up the sheets into a pouch safely containing the glitter and shook them out over the Moon circle in my herb garden! No amount of rain can wash away the glittered earth. When the Sun or Moon shines on the garden, firework sparks are struck from the confetti, and digging in the beds will be a pleasure with the Sun sparkling off each little bit of magick, and my thoughts dance to the future when we no longer live here and perhaps the new owners have a child. The child goes out the back yard to play where once there was a magick garden, and the Sun that always shone upon that garden space smiles so for the child . . . smiles and shines rainbow surprises from bits of glitter shaped like that very garden's night sky. What a thrill for that child! What an encouragement to tend the Earth . . . if only *that* particular patch!

When her own child was critically injured both physically and intellectually, in a near fatal accident, this Wiccan combined the magick of a mother's love with some traditional cord magick to bring about a healing. Noticing that a strand of embroidery floss is made up of several finer strands, much like brain neuron and synapse connections, she prepared a spoked wheel of embroidery floss in a symbolic color. At an appropriate time in the next sabbat ritual the "wheel" was spread out in the center of the circle between the coveners and together they made a re-weaving to repair the child's damaged neuro-electrical system, to help the connectors find new paths to previous abilities. "Weave and chant, weave and chant, did we." The finished weaving was left on the altar in a bed of silk and rose petals resting in a silver cauldron until the Moon completed Her cycle. And one cycle is all the time manifesting required. The child had a remarkable intellectual "brightening," and future letters told of her brilliant recovery.

While indoor circles have been delineated with such ancient and traditional materials as salt and stones, or such innovative materials as copper wire or Faerie dust, Mark Peters* takes innovation a step further and casts a circle for the Aquarian Age.

I have been a computer enthusiast for a number of years. In the past year I have become active in using the computer as a means of communication. There are a number of services that are available for a fee to computer users with the facilities to connect their computers into the phone lines. This type of application is called telecomputing and was demonstrated in the movie *War Games*. These services are called computer networks. Among other things these networks allow the users to talk to each other in "rooms." It is similar to a conference call except that one types rather than talks.

This media has a number of advantages. The first being that the user can meet people from all over the country on a live "pen pal" basis. Depending on the network the fees are cheap to moderate in price, compared to an equal amount of time on a long-distance phone call. The rooms can be made private. There is an opportunity to share ideas with people one might never meet otherwise.

Initially, when I joined I figured I would be the only Witch on the network, so I chose the alias of Wiccan. (Aliases, handles, screen names are generally used on networks, partly for fun partly for anonymity). To my surprise the system responded that the name was already in use. That began my search for others. Soon there were several of us that met on a regular basis. Naturally, when you get three or more Witches together you end up in a circle and where there's a Witch there's a way. Thus, occurred my first experience of being in a circle with a radius of over a thousand miles.

Since we are not physically with each other certain modifications were needed to make it work. Since this is not a voice media all the ritual lines are typed. This is a case where the thought is as good as the deed. Calling Watchtowers is fairly simple, determine which member is closest to that direction. For example, one circle included four people—one in Alabama, New Mexico, Colorado, and I was in Nebraska. One person is usually appointed the leader. This is determined by his/her knowledge of the Craft and speed of typing. That person would cast the circle and then indicate who is to speak next with stage directions. "KP turns to the east," the person in the east would then summon the east Watchtower and indicate when they had finished by "turning to the south," and so on.

Mark Peters of Wiccan 3 says, "Techno-Pagans do it on line!" (photo by Dan Campanelli).

Other conventions are used as well. An asterisk may indicate that the line is to be echoed by the coven: "So mote it be!" Abbreviations are used throughout: BB=Blessed Be!

The truly amazing thing is that it works so well. The power raised in a circle this size has to be experienced to be understood. I think that because of the nature of the circle we tend to actually have it on an astral level more than a physical level. Which to me seems more appropriate as a place between worlds. Perhaps the world of electrons *is* the place between.

One of the advantages of this type of circle is that it is done from the comfort of your own home. We each have our own computer nest where we feel relaxed and at ease. The cats are not disturbed by "strangers" coming into the house and the neighbors don't complain.

Interestingly, we all have cats and they tend to play a part in the process just by their presence. My cat, Gretchen, parks on the disk drive, because it is the warmest place in the house. Another of our members rests the keyboard in his lap with the cat.

We meet almost every Monday night on line. The majority of our meetings are not circles, but more along the line of discussion. During these, we try to have a topic and stay with it, but anything of interest is allowed. Some of the topics of past discussions have been past life recall, Craft laws, herbalism, origins of various Wiccan customs and local events that do not make the news. When all other topics run dry we talk about our cats.

Since most of our members come from varying traditions we agreed from the start to keep things somewhat generic. Most of the rituals are composed on the spot with only the theme agreed to beforehand. The theme might be a New Moon or a Full Moon, for example. Using an existing ritual is not forbidden, but it is not practical since it has to be typed in live.

The preparation for circle can be as simple or as complex as one wishes. Lighting some candles and incense is sufficient, but a complete altar can be laid out as well. When we are ready to begin each person casts his or her individual, personal circle. Then each of these is linked to form the large circle. The person leading the ritual might start by cleansing the circle with the elements. This may be done as a simple narrative: "HP casts out all evil with element of . . . " Or it could be done more as a ritual: "I consecrate and cleanse this water and bless this salt. With the elements of Earth and Water I banish all evil from this circle."

Perhaps one of the best things about the electronic circle is that it is always different. By having different people doing different things this alone adds variety. Add to this the fact that each of us tends to create rather than quote and you have circles that are always fresh and original.

Once the circle is cleansed and cast then the Watchtowers are called. This is a place where even the slow typists and bashful get their chance. Each of the Watchtowers is called in a different manner befitting the one calling. We have a Discordian that likes to join in our circles and his method is unique to say the least.

The next item would be the nights ritual. One person will lead the group through this. The ritual can be for whatever occasion is at hand, a lunar ritual, a sabbat, an invocation for help in overcoming a problem, and so on. If the ritual is to be done by two people, then they would meet prior to the circle to work out the details.

After the ritual, it is time for cakes and ale. A blessing is done and the cakes and ale are passed around. It has been a long standing practice on line to offer drinks to those with whom you are talking. It may sound silly, offering a drink to someone thousands of miles away, but it is a very friendly gesture and makes everyone feel closer. Since this is well established in the computer world, cakes and ale are a natural part of the electronic circle. Individually we can share in the gesture only or get something appropriate to eat and drink.

Once all the parts of the circle are complete for the night we close the circle. This is pretty much the reverse of the casting. The Watchtowers are thanked rather than summoned and so forth.

An item that is always of concern is finding or attracting like minded people. Depending on the network used, here are different methods. On one network we created a room just by naming it. The name of the room was visible to all. We experimented with a number of names before we found the right one. One of the first efforts was "Pagan Place." Unfortunately, this attracted those that thought it was some sort of computer orgy.

We had the best results with "Deosil." The Pagans and Witches would enter and say, "Merry Meet." Everyone else would say, "Hiya what's Deosil mean?" This way we could screen them out very quickly. We did run across a number of people that were not Pagans, but interested in Pagan ideas. As long as a person behaved politely he or she was welcome in the discussion. For the actual circles we would move to a private area where we would not be interrupted.

On the network that I use now we use other methods. This network handles the discussion areas differently. Instead of names for the public rooms they are numbered. However, this network allows name changes at will. To attract people here we can change the name we use to reflect something about the Craft. One might choose an alias like Besom, Deosil, Watchtower and so forth.

The upshot of all this is that Techno-Paganism is here to stay. If you get in a computer network look for other Pagans and make yourself visible to Pagans. Talking with others across the nation is very enlightening and educational. Talking by means of computer is relatively inexpensive. With a little imagination most anything can be done if you want to do it.

CHAPTER FOUR

Indoor Sanctuaries

Many thousands of years before the ceiling of the Sistine Chapel was adorned by the brush and the genius of Michelangelo, the ceiling of the cave at Lascaux was painted with the brush of another genius, possibly several, whose names long have been forgotten but whose powerful paintings have survived to this day leaving us with little doubt that this cave was, and still is, a sacred place, a sanctuary. Only a few thousand years later, a blink of an eye for the Goddess or the God, in the ancient land of Sumer between the sacred rivers the Tigris and the Euphrates, a land recently violated by the insanity of war, ancient Pagans erected ziggurats, at the top of which were chambers, sanctuaries, where the God and Goddess, Earth and Sky, Spirit and Matter were united. Later still, in a cave on the shore of the Bay of Naples, deep below the Temples of Jupiter and Apollo, the Sibyl of Cumae sat on her tripod stool and pronounced prophecies in a cryptic language.

While we generally think of ourselves as practicing our sacred rites in forest groves or moonlit meadows, it also seems to be in the Pagan nature to create or adapt enclosed places in which to perform our rituals and make our magick.

We will probably never know exactly what magickal ceremonies were performed beneath the painted canopy of the cave at Lascaux or the nature of the Sacred Marriage at the summit of the ziggurat or the identity of the Sibyl of Cumae, who in the womb of the Earth where life and death interfaced, learned the secrets of the future, but within the pages of this chapter we will be given a private tour of some of the magickal sanctuaries created by the Pagans of today, places between the mundane material world and the world of Spirit where ritual and magick can happen. And some will reveal to us as well, a secret or two of the magick they perform there.

Cindy Testerman is one Witch who came out of the closet some time ago, and she now has a small mail-order business called Visualization/Reality*, selling such occult items as Saxon wands and Tarot boxes that she makes and blesses individually during the correct lunar phases. Here she describes for us her magick room.

My magick room is a small space 8 x 8 feet. To begin to prepare it for my work, I first took out the ceiling to expose the rafters. There were two purposes for this. First is to allow more overhead room for the smoke from incenses to

A corner of Cindy Testerman's magick room where herbs, oils, tinctures and other magickal materials are stored.

travel to so as not to get too smoky too fast. Secondly, the rafters are a great place to hang drying herbs and flowers. The next step was to scrub the entire room with water and sea salt to purify it. Then, over a period of weeks the room was sealed and smoked or incensed with sulfur, frankincense, benzoin, myrrh, pine, copal. All to purify and remove negativity from the space. Then the room was painted white as well as the rafters and peaked ceiling. Three coats of paint were used. The room was again incensed for a few days to remove negativity and to purify.

I then planned the arrangement of the room by first using a compass to determine each direction. I wanted to work facing north so then I arranged my altar table accordingly.

Cindy Testerman's altar: a wicker table covered with a black cloth and dried herbs and flowers under glass, here prepared for crystal scrying.

The altar table is wicker which was cleansed with salt water, and then painted white. It was then covered with a black cloth. The top of the altar was then covered in dried herbs and flowers and a glass table top placed upon this. I used glass since it would be easiest to keep clean and free of soot, ash and wax and also because it is non-flammable. (During one candle spell I had incinerated my wooden pentacle.) There is something to be said in Wicca about practicability. The two chairs in the room are also wicker which were cleansed with salt water and painted white. I used black cushions and black and white curtains to finish my decor. (Maybe a Wiccan version of a popular magazine *Better Altars and Circles?*)

Then I had a book shelf built for the room and several wooden cubes that I could stack, rearrange, and add to as necessary. They were also cleansed with sea salt and water and painted black or white.

To stock my room I have included a selection of books for reference and a selection of catalogs for ordering (Pagan consumer and loving it!). My Book of Shadows is in a working binder. Herbs, oils, tinctures, charcoals, candles, candle-holders, stones, crystals, incenses (cones, sticks, lumps and loose) homemade oils, eyedroppers, matches, brooms, bells, posters, alcohol for tinctures, cheese-cloth, material, yarns, needles and threads, boxes . . . each item carefully dated and labeled, are here too.

To set up the altar I placed my God and Goddess white candles to the north. For the Goddess I have holey stones, jet balls, my wand, bell, and water. For the God I have crystal points and acorns, my athame, working knife, salt, incense and spoon. In the middle is my caldron and in front is where I place the supplies I will need for each session of magickal work. Hanging over my altar is a mirror, faceted lead crystal ball, and a three dimensional star, each was a gift to me.

The room is lit by both candlelight and/or electric light. I use colored light bulbs for color therapy or to intensify a particular spell I am working on. I also include a diffuser for aromatherapy and a boom box to play my tapes (mostly before and after my magickal work).

Once everything was in place I again incensed the room. Then I recon-secrated everything with a simple ceremony of dedication and blessing with the four elements . . . Earth, Air, Water and Fire. I usually perform my rituals sponta-neously and heartfelt and remember not what was said but instead the ways I was moved and felt and emoted.

Now I am cramped in my small room. Soon I may take over the entire house!

If you were to walk one day through the deep shaded forests and wooded hillsides that border the Delaware River in Pennsylvania's beautiful Bucks County you might encounter a man with snow white hair, twinkling blue eyes and a powerful physique, searching for rare or unusual plants among the ferns and wildflowers. Known as "Grandfather," to members of his Coven and others close to him on the Pagan path, this former fundamentalist has just recently found the joy and beauty of the Old Ways. Since finding his way back he has created an environment for himself in which both meditation and magick can flourish.

The wall in my den/sanctuary that faces north has in the center a map of the zodiac, and around it are individual signs of the zodiac and constellations which I have colored by hand. (Above this map is a drawing I made that represents Draw-ing Down the Moon.) Other colored cards are the Moon, 4 elements, the Sun, and a small zodiac. They are followed by the zodiac signs all in order of, Earth, Air, Fire and Water according to the elements. On the right side of the zodiac map is an Aztec calendar, and on the left is a map of the volcanoes of the ocean floor, both of which glow in the dark. Other interesting wall hangings include a chart of water birds.

On either side of the central zodiac map are bags containing sage and crystal points, the latter are to be left as gifts to show thanks for things received from the Goddess. Above the central map hangs the talons of a great horned owl I found killed on the road, and below hang pendulums and a necklace I made of acorns.

Below the north wall hangings, is a long shelf about 1 foot wide I use as an altar, which contains things that have meaning to, me. Center on the shelf is a

The north facing wall in the sanctuary of Grandfather, with a map of the zodiac in the center (photo by Dan Campanelli).

Grandfather's altar below a map of the zodiac on the north facing wall (photo by Dan Campanelli).

so-called artist's mushroom which I obtained 25 years ago from a fallen tree, to the right of it is a varnish mushroom which I glued on a base. These two mushrooms now support a knife or athame which I purchased in Virginia, and to the left is a cluster of amethyst crystals which just fit the curve of the mushroom. On the right is a cluster of quartz crystals that just fit the curve of the mushroom on that side. I then was inspired to add 4 acorns representing the 4 elements, and 3 star anise which give psychic ability. To complete my center piece I placed a small oil lamp on a bed of river sand on the artists fungus. Other pieces on this shelf are painted candles, ornaments I made with milky quartz crystals and turtella shells, half of a geode with a small figure of Merlin in it (that was a gift), a strange tree root for my stick incense, a candleholder which contains sage used for smudging, a plaque of Horus was given to me by a good friend, a mortar and pestle for grinding herbs, and a small basket containing natural objects that have special meaning to me.

In the corner of this shelf is a wooden box that once belonged to my great grandmother which I keep sacred objects in. On the box in a wooden bowl are two pods of *Datura stramonium,* used by shamans to induce trance. There is also a small totem pole from my grandson and a cedar box containing a deck of Tarot cards.

To the left side of this shelf is a terra-cotta censor, and a plaque inscribed with a seven-pointed star and the signs of the days of the week. Next to this is a bell which has been in our family for years and a goblet containing various bird feathers I found along the Delaware River. I use these feathers, including crow feathers, to visualize far below me the river and trees and other places the crow has been. Another hollow geode contains 3 pennies to be used for I Ching. Here too is a black candle representing the God and at the opposite end of the altar is a white candle representing the Goddess.

Below the altar or shelf are stereo speakers and a futon, which I purchased from an occult book store.

The east side of the room contains more objects that have significance to me, including a large stone I had always admired in my daughter's garden. One Yule she gave it to me as a gift. The stone has strange markings that have only begun to appear in the 2 years since I've had it. Objects on the wall include a snake chart, turtles, reptiles and frogs, snowshoes which I have used to camp out in the winter, a candleholder in the shape of the crescent Moon (I turn it according to waning and waxing of the Moon). Centered against the window is a totem pole which I carved when I was a Boy Scout, it represents a creature called a "wigget," which when an Indian was out in a canoe and had caught too many fish, the wigget would overturn the canoe with its wedge-shaped head to free some of the fish. Above the window is a shelf I built containing lanterns, 2 musical drums which I decorated with the signs of the pentagram, miniature corn representing the Goddess because grain is sacred to her. Above my totem pole is a mask of an Indonesian god which was a gift to me from the man I worked for. Above the Indonesian god is a shelf with tom-toms which I decorated and rattles from Bogata, Columbia, the jaw bone of a deer and the skull of a deer I found many years ago in the woods. There are several shadow puppets from Indonesia which were gifts that I placed around the window and behind my hanging prayer plants.

Each window in my home has an acorn in it as an ancient protection from lightning. The east side of the room also contains a drawing board, telescope for studying the stars and nature and a scale for measuring herbs.

The east wall of the sanctuary includes Grandfather's totem pole (photo by Dan Campanelli).

The south side of my sanctuary room contains my book shelves and my desk. The books are mostly on nature study, occult and related subjects, and Wicca. A large paper wasp nest, which I had watched being made, is over my desk, and a very small window used to watch the phases of the Moon.

To complete the south side I have wind chimes, and a shelf of magickal herbs, many I collected in the wild.

The west wall contains many more nature posters and charts of birds and animals, hand-colored enlargements of Tarot cards as well as a wing from a great horned owl above my door (the same one whose talons hang above the zodiac chart). I use this wing for smudging and at various Moon ceremonies. I feel that the wing has been truly honored. This wall also contains my sound equipment, CD player, tape deck, mixer and speakers which I use to make spiritual tapes of music and poetry.

Grandfather also has a beautiful wand in his room, which he cut from witch hazel after asking the spirit of the tree for it and cutting it very carefully and leaving a piece of silver at the base of the tree as a thank you. He let the wood season for several months and then inserted a quartz crystal in the tip, and cut a spiral all around it and added found copper wire as decoration. The wire is inserted from the base where it is held, to the quartz crystal which it contacts. This acts as an electromagnetic conductor for him.

His room is used for many spiritual and meditative hours and could be an inspiration to all of us on the path. Here Grandfather gives us a ritual that he uses to begin his meditation or magickal work.

First I put on a tape, usually something with chanting such as "O Great Spirit" by Robert Gass or Libanna or "Silk Road" by Kitare. Then I turn out all lamps and light the 3 candles on the altar, which represent the Triple Goddess or New, Full and Old Moon. The phase of the Moon at the time determines which candle I light first.

Then I light the incense stick which I have selected to suit the type of meditation or time of the month. I light the incense from the center candle. If there is no set requirement I prefer sandalwood. Holding the incense stick in my right hand and standing before the altar, facing north I inscribe a pentagram in the air repeating the word north, and circumscribing a circle around it clockwise while repeating the element Earth. I also meditate on the various correspondences associated with the north direction such as the color, zodiac signs, spirits, season, etc.

I then face east, south and west in order repeating the appropriate ritual at each. I complete the circle to north where I raise the incense stick upward and say, "As above" and then point it toward the Earth and say "so below."

With the incense pointed towards the floor I then circle the room three times in a clockwise direction while visualizing a ring of fire, the purpose of which is to keep in any power and to prevent any interruption from without. Ending again at the north, I then place the incense in a holder on the altar.

After this I may seat myself on the floor facing the altar and drum (tom-tom) to the music until I reach the desired alpha state. Then I proceed with my dedication or whatever work is intended. After I have finished I sometimes sit and play my recorder, allowing the music to come to me, somewhat like automatic writing. When so moved, I close the ritual by facing north and retracing the circle counterclockwise 3 times at the same time calling to mind any adverse things I want to be rid of such as bad habits, attitudes, etc.

Arriving back at the north, I face the altar, contemplating the three candles until I feel moved to extinguish them, leaving the center candle till last.

The above ritual may not be performed exactly the same way each time. Any part may be changed as the Spirit dictates. I have just begun a course in Tai Chi and am looking forward to incorporating it into my rituals.

The nature of the place where we choose to create magickal space can enhance the type of magick that is performed there. John Bullington of Michigan has adapted two different areas of his home to two entirely different types of magick, apparently with excellent results.

The place where I practice is a sectioned off part of my basement. Prior to its construction it was a storage space where a strewn group of belongings seemed to find its place. My need for a place to practice was small so I only needed a quarter of the space that was available. As my need grew I slowly cleaned and moved into the once idle space. In the long cleaning process and fitting the room to my needs I learned more and more about myself and the Craft.

I hoarded books on Witchcraft, herbs, crystals, etc. of the past and present. I found a good, dependable, and easy-to-understand book brand (Llewellyn of course!) to follow. I also found my favorite author who agreed with what I knew was right for me.

The room began to grow, the energies began to run. By just stepping in I could feel the peace and security. The room took an image of my inner self, and I dedicated it to Mother Earth. For the purpose of worshiping Her and all Her giving.

A predominant magick circle lies in the center of the room. It lies in a nine foot diameter with a pentacle another foot inward, pointed towards the north. A few feet from there is my altar, also pointed to the north. The rest of the room is used for relaxation, meditation, and storage for my tools. The decor is dark shades of brown, green, silver, and black. I like a natural setting, a tapestry of the ocean at dawn hangs on the wall and pictures of peaceful settings hang around the room.

Because this is a room in the basement, unfortunately, there are no windows. For that reason the amount of plant life in the room is limited to seedlings and mushrooms. All other greenery must be kept upstairs near windows. Also, all spells requiring the Sun, Moon, or stars must be performed outside. This is not always sensible because Michigan's climate is harsh in both degrees from extreme freezing to scorching heat waves.

My other indoor magickal space is my bedroom. All of my dream magick and some of my Moon spells can be done there. My bed faces north, it seems to give me the best results. A flat top of a high boy is my second altar. There is always quartz crystals, candles, incense, personal jewelry, and silver on it. My bedroom is decorated in different shades of gray and has a peaceful feeling to it. The bed has an old oak frame passed down through my family, like much of the furniture in the house.

Not all sanctuaries are on the material plane, there are sacred places of the soul that some are privileged to visit under special circumstances, and once the way has been discovered these individuals can act as guides for others. Steven Smith, who described his circle in a suitcase in the previous chapter, now gives us a guided tour of this sacred, inner space.

Many, if not most, Pagans and Witches live in either suburban or urban areas, and, as such, have no ready access to sacred spaces on the material plane. Of the fortunate few who do have access to a special place, the sacred place is usually not always readily available.

For anyone in this situation, an inner space is the next best thing. This inner space is created by the individual and can be visited any time there is a need.

To create this inner sacred space, a person should have at least a minimum amount of experience or training in pathworking, lucid dreaming, or creative visualization or, preferably, all three. I claim to be no expert of the above methods, so would make a very poor teacher. I will, however, relate how I've created my own inner sacred space.

The idea for a sacred space came to me, long ago, while taking a ritual bath, prior to performing a rite. While soaking, I pictured myself afloat in a shallow body of water; floating along with the gentle warm current. With eyes closed, I could almost "see" the small delicate waves as they broke gently upon my body. The waves pushed me slowly but steadily towards an unknown destination.

Up ahead there suddenly appeared what seemed to be a small island. On later "visits," I discovered it wasn't an island at all, but a peninsula leading to a strange and wondrous land. But that's another story.

On this first trip to this new and magickal place, I didn't get to stay very long. In fact, I just barely touched the shore when once again the current took my body in its gentle caress. I was returned once again to my own world—the bathtub in my home.

After this first visit, I was determined to return to this new and compelling land. In my eagerness, I took bath after bath. I got mighty clean, but that's all. The "island" seemed out of reach. I began to wonder if it was, after all, just a figment of my imagination.

I asked around and got a few nods and knowing smiles, but little else. It seemed that others knew of this strange realm, but were either reluctant or unwilling to talk about it. "When you are ready, the path will be there," was the only reply I managed to get.

And then, while preparing for another ritual, I once again returned to my island! This happened quite unintentionally and without even trying! Upon reflection, the answer came. I had tried too hard before. The proper method was to be open and receptive, not to struggle and strive to reach the "goal"; but let the "goal" come to me.

On this second visit, I once again only managed to reach the shore, as I had done before. I then tried to "take control" and the trip was suddenly over. Through trial and error, I finally figured out the way to visit this wondrous realm. The following explains how I did it. It should work for you as well.

The ritual bath wasn't necessary after all, though it did help. All that was really needed was the mellow peaceful frame of mind I was in while taking the bath.

When reaching out to this new land, be open and receptive. Don't dwell on your objective. Don't try to force your way into this place, you'll never succeed. Instead, let the sacred space come to you.

Every person's idea of what and where this sacred space is will be different. It depends entirely on the individual's personality and belief structure. Don't expect immediate results, success usually doesn't come until much later. At first, just be satisfied if you can actually reach your new realm at all. On succeeding visits, you can "help" the land come into existence by adding a tree, rock, or flower each time you visit. The images of these additions will have to be reinforced with each visit, until they become a permanent part of your land.

After a time, your realm will become real to you. Then the hard work begins. Within this land, you will begin to build your sacred space. This space will be an area within yourself that will be a special and safe place; a spiritual and holy haven. It will be out of reach of the mundane world and its troubles. Don't think of this space as a hiding place, for it isn't. Instead, look upon it as a place where you can come, at need, where you can rest and renew your spirit. A place to recharge your energies, rebuild your strength so that when you do return to the mundane world, you will be prepared to face any situation with determination, alertness, and confidence.

As I said before, each person's sacred space is different, as it should be. Your space awaits you. Will you help it to become an inner reality?

Let me tell you of my inner sacred space. It is a small abandoned Greek-like temple, set in a small natural clearing within an ancient forest. Its roof has long since vanished, and several of its pillars have toppled. Within and without its walls are several varieties of wildflowers. In the very heart of the temple is the statue of a long forgotten Goddess. There is a knowing smile upon her lips and love in her eyes. A flowering vine grows about her head, giving her a crown of natural beauty.

It is always spring in this sacred place, with every flower and tree in full bloom. Nearby runs a small babbling brook, which cascades over a fallen pillar, forming a little waterfall. The sunlight shines and sparkles upon this waterfall as it flows into a pond in front of the temple.

The air is always filled with the sounds of birdcalls, and the gentle breeze carries the fragrance of pine, herbs, and flowers.

Nothing of the mundane everyday world can be seen, heard, or even sensed in this holy place.

The world changes from day to day, but here each day is always the same. The sacred space will allow nothing profane to enter. Instead peace, love, and contentment reign supreme. It is a place the Gods call home.

With time and practice, you will come to realize that you carry this sacred space within you at all times. Wherever you may go, it is always close at hand. You may be tempted to stay there forever, but don't. That's not why it is there; not why you helped to create it. It exists to be visited only when needed, and then only for brief periods of time. For though the mundane world isn't always the most pleasant of places, it is your home. It is where you live; where you belong.

Let me leave you with the same advice I received so long ago. "When you are ready, the path will be there!"

The Silver Elves*, Zardoa Silverstar and Silver Flame here invite us, by written word and fine photography, to cross their threshold and enter into the realm of magick which they have created, the entire home in which they live.

Silver Elves' temple/bedroom/living room.

This is a picture of our temple, our living room and bedroom. Our magickal and spiritual philosophy differs in many ways from that of other traditions. Crowley, for instance, admonished his readers to keep their magickal tools separate from the mundane aspects of living in order to keep them pure and holy. We, however, do not separate our magickal and mundane lives, nor the spiritual and material. We live within the circle of our magick . . . to enter our home is to step within the aura of the accumulated Eldritch powers . . . as one crosses our doorstep they pass into elfland, they step into a different realm . . . thus in that sense we return to Crowley and tradition for we have created a spiritual world separate from the mundane world about us. In our typically elfin manner, we both do and don't simultaneously thus preserving the Tao in all things.

In the very center of the room is a copper table, we call this our mobile magick table, since when we have group rituals we lift this table to the center of the room and place our candles and ritual tools upon it. Above this table is our banner which has the combined Mars (male) Venus (female) symbol pointed up and thrusting through the horizon and directed toward the stars. This is in accord with our belief that we both come from and are headed back to the stars. It is our elfin destiny, we believe to create Earth in space where there will be plenty of room for everyone to "do their own thing." Thus in a way our living room, bedroom, temple is also our prototype space world where elfland shall exist wherever we can create it. When one enters our space they encounter life invigorating atmosphere quite different, we believe, from the often vacuous nature of the void of "modern culture." Our rituals are nearly always improvised, often we use songs or chants that we've used previously inserted at slow moments to keep things moving; however, we try to encourage spontaneity and find that the Spirit responds. So, too, our temple is not entirely an intentional creation but in many ways an accidental (magickal and often mysterious) gathering of mystical artifacts, statues and ritual pieces that we have found at discount prices at the flea market/swap meet where we work each weekend selling hippie, Gypsy, magickal clothes and doing Tarot and palmistry for $1 a reading. Many writers tell us never to barter for one's magickal tools, however, these elves being the "little folk" we are, simply cannot afford not to do so. In addition to the fact that it is the tradition of the flea market to do so and is expected of us. On the other hand we never bargain them lower than a truly fair price and occasionally give them more than they ask when they are simply being overly generous because they know we are the "card readers." Doing Tarot readings for a mere $1 brings rewards that most people wouldn't think possible, by charging little we get so much more.

Silver Flame with the mobile magick table.

Zardoa practices Wyzardry.

We also dream within the magick circle . . . a circle that is constantly growing, evolving and changing from week to week and in which the next magickal tool is most often a surprise . . . another piece in the puzzle that is the evolving reality of living elfland.

We do not use the word altar because of its religious connotations. While we elfin are a truly spiritual people we are not religious in the traditional sense of the word. Nor do we worship (whoreship) the gods . . . we believe worship to be an obsolete concept which is both inappropriate and degrading. Thus instead of altar we use the term "magick table" because a table is a place where one can eat and work, and we envision ourselves both communing and working in coordination with our "relatives," the Divine Forces of the Universe.

A magick table dedicated to Pan. Zardoa and Silver Flame kissing in picture at right.

Among the traditional divine archetypes that we relate to, Pan is a particular favorite, on either side of him and just in front are tree Ents which represent friendship to us because when we bought them at the flea market we only had enough money for one and as we were leaving the person ran up to us and gave us the other saying that they had been together so long that he couldn't see them separated. The little one in front of Pan we found later.

Our chalices are on either side between Pan and the Ents and in the front laying horizontally is the magic wand that Zardoa made for Silver Flame. All about the table are little figures of elves, faeries, and wizards, plus miscellaneous stones and rocks and bits of magick, each with their own story and power. Our magick tables always tend to accumulate more and more as time goes on.

When we do our rituals we often sing these chants in honor of Pan:

Hail, hail, hail to Pan
he's the Lord of the Forest

> *we're his merry band*
> *Hail, hail, to Pan's Queen she's the Mistress of*
> *Magick in the worlds unseen.*

and:

> *On his throne sits Pan*
> *he wakes the magick again*
> *on his throne sits Pan*
> *He wakes the magick again*
> *again, he wakes the magick*
> *Again, again, he wakes the magick again.*

Above the Pan table (although cut off in this picture) is a tapestry of Krishna and his lover, since Krishna is another Pan figure, a flute playing, frolicking "playboy." Note that Krishna is always shown as being blue and that he was an Aryan cult that came from the North, note also that the ancient Celts whose civilization extended from Ireland to at least Greece often painted themselves with blue "wode," could it be that Krishna was a Celt?

Also in this picture to the right you will find another picture of Zardoa and Silver Flame kissing, what could be more appropriate?

In the past five years we have created Pan sanctuaries deep in the woods up and down the coast of California from Alpine near the border of Mexico in the south to the Avenue of the Giant Redwoods in the north and many places in between, thus we feel that our Pan magick extends and radiates to and from these places, beaming Pan consciousness throughout the state. It's been said that the Great Pan died when Jesus was born (see *How the Great Pan Died: The Origin of Christianity* by Edmond S. Bordeaux), however, we think Great Pan is just sleeping and if we dance enough and sing to him with joyous voices he will awaken and return to us and together we will frolic through fields and forests with ecstatic abandon.

In the southeastern corner of our living room, temple, magick circle sits the Black Buddha the patron and protector of the Shadows, the ninja.

We have made a study of the mystical and magickal aspects of ninjiusu, including the finger intertwining mudras that the ninjas use for focusing and channeling their powers and utilize what we have learned in our own magicks.

While we are not ninja, we elfin share many qualities with the ninja. We are an elusive people who have learned through time to be both hidden and secretive ... yet we accomplish this by being both open and obvious. People upon hearing that we are elves simply do not believe their own eyes and ears. They think that we are joking and we share their laughter.

Around the Buddha are our personal and magickal swords. Above his head, on the shelf are a collection of menehunes (Hawaiian elves) since Hawaii is truly the meeting ground of East and West. To the sides of the menehunes are the masks which remind us of the necessity of presenting different faces to the world. To the far left of the picture is the Captain Kidd lamp with his treasure at his feet and a Buddhist lamp shade above him. A pirate might seem an odd figure for a

The Silver Elves' Black Buddha—guardian of the ninja.

magick circle but we call to mind that the Buccaneers (who were escaped slaves and prisoners) established the first democratic societies in the Americas.

The lamp shade brings to mind the scene in the movie *The Karate Kid* when Mr. Myiage "borrowed" a black belt for Daniel and when asked where he got it replied "Buddha provides." We are not thieves, nor do we condone theft, yet we have a deep compassion for the impoverished who are in their way "little folk" too. Since Captain Kidd's treasure is composed of bits and pieces of jewelry and foreign coins that were discarded at the end of the day at the flea market, we like to think of ourselves as treasure hunters and finders and trust this bit of magick will increase our luck in doing so . . . finders keepers.

At the very bottom of the picture beneath the Buddha you can see a ninja baby doll in honor of both our children, Solon and Elantari, who are intrigued by the ninja mythology.

We might also mention that the Gypsies (Romany) who originated from India (and whose mythos we relate to calling our shop at the market the Silver Elves Gypsy Boutique) worship the Virgin Mary in the form of Sara la Kali, the black virgin, another version of Kali the black Goddess of death and sexuality? Is she Kunoi chi? Female ninja? Note picture postcard of female ninja to left of Buddha.

In a fashion we might call this our magick to remind us of the four vows of the Wicca, calling for the courage and silence of the ninja and the knowledge and wisdom of the Buddha. Let us have the courage to be our elfin selves, let us prosper in darkness hidden from our foes as we are silent, let us act with the confidence born of knowledge and attain the wisdom to use our powers wisely so they will prosper and endure thus shedding light onto the world.

Opposite our magick table dedicated to Pan is the Dragon Magick table. We relate to a being we call the Rainbow Dragon (known in Australia as the rainbow serpent, in Haiti, as the rainbow snake, among the Aztecs as the winged serpent, etc.) who is part of a nearly worldwide myth of creation and whom we think of as Pan's mate and lover (note that the Chinese divine creator is named Pan-Ku or Phan-Ku).

In this midst of this magick is a *lamia*, a Greek word which our dictionary defines as meaning a witch, a sorceress, a vampire or a woman with the lower body of a snake. (Note that the vampires are drow . . . dark elves, who attain immortality by preying on mankind, while the elves of light choose an immortality of spirit—reincarnation. Mankind for the most part believe they will either die and go to oblivion or heaven or hell . . . as far as the elves are concerned, for the most part, they are welcome to do so.) Both she and Pan are mutant beings sharing both human and animal features thus representing the merging of the logical left brain activity with the spatial animal sensual right brain.

On this table are cobra candleholders (inherited from Zardoa's grandmother) and a cobra holding sphere which we call the Orbs of Healing reminding us that love and sexuality/sensuality can be rejuvenating. Above the lamia and to the left is a cardboard dragon of which we have four identical ones about our house both within and without. Also to the right on the picture is a dragon statue. To us the Rainbow Dragon is a more serious spirit than Pan, a fitting compliment to his festive nature. She represents revolution, transformation, transmutation, metamorphosis, the power of magick to instigate/initiate change and growth.

Also on this magick table is a statue of a wizard holding an orb of healing representing the concept "healing is as healer does." For the elfin this means, heal ... be sensual, be sexy, awaken the Kundalini (snake), revive the spirit and live forever (note the entwined snakes around the winged wand of the medical profession). Through the intertwining of Pan and the Rainbow Dragon the world is born, our elfland manifests here—now. It lives within us, around us, in our days, our nights, our dreams, our lives and it is spreading. As we elfin say: "Healing is contagious ... Pass it around."

The Silver Elves' lamia.

From the mystical realm of California's Silver Elves, we now visit a magick room in the Midwest which has an east facing window and we are invited to join ShadowCat as she performs a sunrise ceremony and recreates the ancient myth of Demeter and Persephone.

Yaaawn. Scratch. I squint at the clock to discover it is only 4 a.m. The light comes earlier now and affects my sleeping habits. Turning toward my husband. who is still lost to sleep and dreams, I decide not to rouse him from his robust snoring. I remember what day it is, Ostara, Spring Equinox. The Gods and my magick room await me. I took care of some of the initial preparations last night. The east altar was given its spring look, complete with white and pale green candles and a newly potted plant. The eggs were dyed, hot crossed buns were purchased from a local bakery (hey, I work and raise a family, there isn't always time to bake during the week), the seeds destined for planting were blessed and the request for a sunny morning was sent out to the universe.

I shiver out of my warm bed and my feet are the first to meet the morning's cold floor. My slippers are invisible in the gray light and my eyes are not cooperating with clear focus. Is it all worth it? Shouldn't I just crawl back into bed and curl up with Tom? No, the Gods should be honored on this day and there will be many more warm, sleepy mornings to enjoy with Their blessings. Aha, the slippers are found, my robe is drawing itself around me, and the smell of freshly brewed coffee meets my drowsy presence. As I lumber down the hall to the steps, a cat slips between my lazy feet. I stumble and my feet are out from under me as I ride down the steps on my bottom. Yeah, I'm awake now.

The crystal cauldron on the kitchen table, purchased one lonely Lupercalia when I had neither lover nor husband, reminds me of the cold task ahead of me. Before I savor my first cup of coffee, I must gather some snow for the ritual. Yes, generally speaking, Ostara in Minnesota is snowy. It is foolish to *plan* an outdoor ritual. While the rest of civilization may be celebrating the arrival of spring, we mark that the calendar winter has passed and the calendar spring is about to begin. You see, in Minnesota, we have calendar seasons and Minnesota seasons. As a more graphic example, let us turn our attention to Beltane for a moment. While Pagans in other parts of the country are running around skyclad and making merry, we Minnesota Pagans are still clinging to our parkas, just in case. Anybody who plans far in advance to go skyclad for Beltane in Minnesota is certifiable. Why? Well, one year we had 6 inches of snow on April 30th. So, we clever Pagans make adjustments and alternative plans.

I pull on my parka and Sorels (you betcha, women wear them here), then head out to the back yard to find some fresh, clean snow. It is too early for the birds to be singing and, except for two bunnies scampering across the yard, all is very still. The temperature is around 25 degrees, but without the wind and with the thoughts of spring, it feels good. Not warm, mind you, but clean and alive with the expectation of new life and green, but more importantly, the arrival of the warm winds of the south. In the growing light, I discover a lovely patch of snow just on the north side of the drift. I dig a bit and pull out a handful of fresh crystals and place them in my cauldron, then dash back to the warmth of my kitchen and the steaming mug of coffee. Kicking off my boots, I let my parka slip to the floor to add to the heap, there is still too much to do to worry about housekeeping at the moment. Ah, my first cup of coffee of the day, pure heaven. Some Pagans go on and on about their herbal concoctions in the form of various teas. That's real nice. However, I have been enjoying coffee since I was two years of age. It is part of who I am, and part of my heritage, which I honor. I love herbal teas, but not to open my eyes and clear my brain after a night of passion then slumber. A glance at the clock reminds me I have to work on my time magic skills.

Gulping down the last drops, I fill the air pot with coffee, then head upstairs to place the cauldron of fast melting snow on my altar. In defiance of the cold, I open the east window a crack to allow some of the clean spring air to flow into the room. A windless morning, I am not worried about keeping the candles in flame. The air pot of coffee and plate of hot cross buns are put in place for the feasting after the ritual. All appears to be in order. As a solitary, I don't have to fret the details. If something is forgotten, it doesn't inconvenience anyone to just go and get it. However, I prefer to be fully prepared and organized.

The time is slipping away as I prepare for my ritual bath. I strip off my red flannel nightshirt and undo my braided hair. As my long golden hair cascades over my shoulders and breasts, I am aware of my station in life. A powerful woman of 38 with well-defined muscles and soft curves of flesh; physical stamina and flexibility are as important to my magick as the strength of my thoughts and the focus of my will. The Mother—strong, voluptuous, grounded. I think of Demeter in this moment. Her sacrifice, Her victory, Her magick, Her power. As the last shadows of darkness slip away, I gather the lavender and salt solution prepared last night, enter the bath and begin to cleanse myself for the ritual. It is such a sensuous experience, the hot water, creamy soap, sweet perfumed scent. Demeter. After a final rinse of lavender and salt water, I towel dry and slip into my ritual robe. It is a very plain green silk, but it serves well for a number of magickal occasions.

Entering my magick room, I shiver in the cold air, but this too serves to remind me of the shift from mundane to magickal. The scent of the air is sweet with hints of the coming season. I sweep the room with my broom and light the incense, the one with the scent of rain. We have been in a drought for four years now, and I want this ritual to reflect the needs of the Earth at this time and place. The altar candles are lit, the salt and water blessed, the quarters silently called, the circle cast.

Sitting cross-legged on the floor facing the east, I close my eyes and look with my inner eyes. I am standing in a barren meadow, a soft breeze is blowing, the horizon is aglow in anticipation of the rising Sun. Concealed by an old oak, I watch as She walks through the dry, dead grass, calling Her name. Persephone. Persephone. She starts up the hill, silhouetted against the light of Dawn. Calling, calling Her name. Then, as the Sun rises atop the hill, a small form can be seen cresting the hill from the other side, then running toward Her. Demeter, Persephone, once again united. The sunlight follows Them spreading the joy. In Their shadow, the grass is made green again, new buds appear on the trees, all wildlife renewed, the birds sing, the wild flowers bloom. All is alive, fertile, joyful with the promise of the season. A Mother's unending quest of love, a promise kept. A Daughter's victory. Life renewed!

At that moment the Sun gleams through my window pulling me from my trance. At the same time, there is a knock on the door. (Nothing like a closed magick room door to arouse the curiosity of household members.) I cut an opening in the circle and answer the knock. It is my 13-year-old daughter, Genesis, who has just returned from the dark place of dreams, pillow folds still etched in her face and her eyes only partially open. I take her hand and pull her through the opening in the circle, then quickly close it behind us. (My children and feline friends are always welcome in my celebration circles.) "What are you doing, Mom?," she queries. We sit and talk about the season and about mothers and daughters. I see that the snow in the cauldron has melted and instruct her to pour the water into the plant. "Why?," she asks. "Because it is a symbol of one season flowing into another. The snow of winter nourishes the growth of new plants in the spring. All things in nature serve the Goddess and Her changing forms," I reply. Thanking the Gods and dismissing the quarters, I open the circle and extinguish the candles. We sit munching the hot cross buns and sipping the steaming coffee talking woman things: relationships with friends, boys, and menstruation. Genny shares her dreams of the night before, then requests a Tarot reading.

"What's going on? How come you're having breakfast in here?," a rumpled Tom wonders as he stands squinting into the morning sunlight. We giggle. It is our secret. Lovingly, I hand him a cup of coffee and a bun then steer him toward the kitchen. As important as he is to us, this is a time for Mother and Daughter. He gives me that infuriatingly knowing look and slurps his morning coffee. Life is ritual. Ritual is life.

Although it has never been formally consecrated as a sanctuary, or for that matter, ritually purified, the smaller of the two bed chambers on the second floor of the old stone farmhouse here at Flying Witch Farm has certainly become a sanctuary dedicated to the Old Gods and to the practice of magick. The room has acquired an atmosphere all of its own as a result of the intensity of the work that takes place within its walls, be it magickal or mundane, and visitors to the room are occasionally overwhelmed by it. The west wall of the room contains the chimney of the great cook fireplace in the kitchen below and provides a smooth white plaster background for the still-life subjects I arrange there for my paintings. Dan is a landscape painter and usually works outdoors on location so the paint studio end of the room is more or less mine alone.

My still-life subjects are illuminated by light from a window in the north wall. The light is twice filtered; once by the branches of an old maple tree, and once again by the waves and bubbles of the old window glass itself. The venerable old panes are surrounded by an assortment of charms and amulets: an "Eye of God" made by a friend in Arizona, a charm of beads and feathers made by another friend of the Tuatha de Dannan, a corn dolly and a braid of sweet grass. On the deep window sill set in the thick stone wall a variety of Indian baskets woven in sacred designs and pre-Columbian pottery that may have once held grave goods mingle with oak leaves, acorns and ears of raspberry corn regardless of the season. Here too rests a shaman's rattle fashioned from a gourd and sometimes used to summon the spirits of the four directions. The window itself frames a view of Hecate, our Flying Witch weather vane, pointing her broomstick into the wind atop the smokehouse, and our sheep grazing on the hillside beyond, their collar bells tinkling like wind chimes.

Just next to the window is the desk where charms are made, runes are cast, cards are read and magick is made. Along the back of the desk exotic boxes from distant lands hold magickal tools and object's of power. A red lacquered box from China decorated with gold butterflies contains a deck of Tarot cards, a photo of a dear friend at Stonehenge, and three ancient bronze coins brought by a friend from Beijing for casting the I Ching. Another box carved of Indian sheesham wood inlaid with ivory holds bits of thread, feathers and photos, all relics of charms that have done their work. A small inlaid box from the Middle-East holds beads of jet and amber, fetishes of turquoise and obsidian and stones of magickal powers. A tiny hand-painted box from India, bearing the likeness of an

The desk where runes are cast, cards are read, and magick is worked at Flying Witch Farm (photo by Dan Campanelli).

ancient scribe, contains Dan's dowsing pendulum of crystal and mine, a tiny brass bell.

Always on the desk, when it is not tied to my waist, is my bag of magickal objects and amulets, each in its own bag within. My pouch of runes is also in this bag, always ready to answer a question. Here too is our Moon diary divided not into days or months, but phases of the Moon. In this book all mystical experiences and all works of magick are recorded. Here too is a crystal ball and an incense burner.

From time to time the desk top might be cluttered with other things—herbs and oils, feathers, cords or stones for the making of charms or the casting of spells, or books, papers, notes and pamphlets for research or studies of ancient ways. Below the desk top are two drawers, one filled with objects of the mundane world—paper clips, rubber bands and pens but the other is filled with objects of magick—colored candles inscribed with runes and anointed with oils, sticks, cones and cakes of incense. In this drawer too resides the white handled knife used to inscribe runes, cut cords, harvest herbs and cut wood into staves and wands. There is also a stone round and white as the Moon, found between the tides, kept in a clam shell, and there is a small silver bowl filled with wishing bones, hazel nuts, locust shells, Faerie wings, and other wonderful magickal things.

Standing on the chair rail behind the desk are photos and post cards of Stonehenge and above that is a case containing pre-Colombian artifacts, some of which are of great magickal significance. On the bottom shelf of the case, among clay beads and loom weights is a cluster of spindle whorls from Peru. Such spindle whorls are often found in great numbers in sacred caves and apparently served a ritual purpose. Still today these little clay spindle whorls are storehouses of psychic energy, and they also suggest that the act of spinning was as sacred to the pre-Christian people of the New World as it was to our ancestors from the Old World—but we may never know. In the very center of the case is a "tajadera"—a bronze ritual knife, believed by some to be shaped like the sacred mushroom which it may have been used to prepare. To Dan and me its resemblance to the labrys of ancient Minos is stunning. Just to the left of the tajadera, is a clay Inca condor head which still bears traces of a painted red design. Lurking in the shadows far left on the shelf above is a terra-cotta Mayan jaguar mask. We had obtained the condor head first and when the jaguar mask was later placed in the case with it the two seemed to have a power struggle. Neither piece would stay in place, loud electrical "pops" could be heard coming from the case, and blue-white sparks could be seen. At this same time I had a very strange experience involving the jaguar head. I had washed my hair and gone into the studio to brush it dry. The last thing I remember is gazing into this case. The next thing I can recall is still standing there gazing into the case but with my hair completely dry. My hair is very long and takes at least half an hour to dry. Somehow, somewhere, I lost that half hour and all I can recall of the experience is that all time—past and future lives—seemed to be happening at once. When it was over, there I was gazing at my own reflection in the glass of the case, my face superimposed over the face of the jaguar, my eyes looking through its eyeholes.

Dan and I finally settled the problem with the jaguar and the condor by explaining to them both that if it was a matter of a culture clash they had both better try to get along or one of them would have to move in with the Egyptian pieces! Things finally settled down—eventually.

The two white figures above the tajadera are the Chancay Moon Goddess.

She is the spinner of dreams and the bringer of ghosts and nightmares. Dan and I have always wanted a figure of her but at antiquities auctions she was always way out of our price range. Then at one auction we bid on a lot containing fourteen items. We were the high bid and the lot, which sold for far less than one Moon Goddess usually costs, contained both figures!

Other objects in the case that are of special interest are small almost thimble-sized vessels used to contain grave offerings of copal, an Aztec terra-cotta seal with a perfect spiral of five rings, an ancient obsidian knife and, just below the tajadera, three small pottery fragments, the first three artifacts Dan and I ever owned. What is important about them is that they once belonged to a Brujo in Guatemala. Such fragments may have been buried by the ancient Maya as field offerings. When discovered by the descendants of the Maya they were considered as amulets. These particular pieces were discovered by the Brujo, in a jungle hut high in the mountains, when he was a very young boy. The hut was considered taboo by the other members of his tribe. These ancient pottery fragments eventually came to be arranged on the Brujo's altar among his other objects and tools of power. Today one of them still bears drips of wax from his altar candles, and all of them contain a portion of his magickal power and the blessings of his spirit.

Just above the case of pre-Columbian artifacts are two small paintings I did many years ago. On the left is a chiaroscuro painting of some amulets and ritual jewelry. On the right is a trompe l'oeil painting of Tarot cards, an old palmistry chart and several charms and talismans. The two paintings together are a sort of self-portrait.

Turning the corner, the east wall is bookcases from floor to ceiling. Appropriately, the entrance to this room is also in the east wall. Here are books on every subject that is of any importance to Dan or me. There are books on antiques and on the restoration of antique cars. There are books on Oriental arts and Eastern religions, on seashells, minerals, fossils, wild flowers, ferns, birds, birds' nests, and marine life. I even have a book on drift seeds. There are books on herbs, herb gardening, magickal herbs and even a book on herbals. There are shelves of books on archaeology, anthropology, mythology and spirituality. These books include the works of Joseph Campbell, Robert Graves, Sir James Frazier, as well as works on Wicca by Gardner, Valiente, Murray and Lethbridge and the more contemporary work of Buckland, Cunningham, Pepper and Wilcock. Here too are older volumes, the works of Shakespeare, Dickens, Malory and Tennyson.

Here and there among the books, whether new ones paperbound with graphic cover designs or ancient volumes leather bound and gilt-edged, are other things of interest to Wiccans and Pagans. Just to the right of the desk leaning against a book in the bookcase is a box made as a replica of an Egyptian sarcophagus.

Just above that is a reproduction of the Venus of Willendorf, who silently peers down between her pendulous breasts at my work desk. To her right (and out of the photo) is an image of the Horned God, a reproduction of a piece of Native American rock art pecked and painted on a slab of southwestern sandstone. Two shelves above these figures of the Lord and Lady stand some replica Greek vases and a figure of Astarte, her arms raised so that her mantle forms the crescent of the Moon. Elsewhere among the books a cornhusk doll with hair of auburn corn silk holds a besom prepared either to sweep or fly, a Tibetan prayer wheel still contains strips of paper inscribed with prayers, and a shadow puppet from Java, now dances in the light bringing with him secrets of the shadow world.

Centered in this wall of books is the entrance to the room and in an alcove above it stand a few ancient volumes, and a reproduction of the Venus of Lausel. Holding her drinking horn of thirteen rings she almost seems to breathe in the flickering light of a votive candle and the veil of incense smoke. From the shadowy cave of her alcove above the door she looks down upon the entire room blessing all who enter it.

On the south wall of the room hangs another case of artifacts, these from the ancient world of Greece and Rome, Egypt and Assyria, and even from ancient Britain. Many of the objects in this case were made to be magickal or religious objects and invested with magickal powers by priests or magicians over 2,000 years ago—they still contain much of that energy today. The large white object on the bottom shelf is a fragment of a ruined ancient Egyptian tomb wall. It is a piece of white limestone carved with figures making offerings to the deceased. The round object on the far right of the same shelf is a funerary cone bearing a prayer for the deceased. When it is held in the hands, one's thumb automatically falls into the thumb print left by the maker three thousand years ago. Between these two objects are two figures of Khunum, the ram-headed potter god, "shaper of gods and men," a bronze votive figure of Osiris, Lord of the Underworld, another bronze of the infant Horus, divine child of the Sacred Marriage of Isis and Osiris, a flat faience figure of Duamutef, one of the "four sons of Horus," which was once stitched into the linen wrappings of a mummy, a faience Ushabti (or Shwabati) figure made to magickally take the place of the deceased in the next world when called upon to do manual labor, and in the background a small bracelet of faience "mummy beads" collected by the "father of Egyptology" himself Sir Flinders Petrie.

On the next shelf up is a variety of small faience amulets worn by the ancient Egyptians to attract a variety of blessings. There are scarabs and Ujat eyes, tiny figures of Bes the dwarf god of happiness, and Anubis priest of the underworld, and there is a large amulet of the Goddess Isis suckling the infant God Horus, which Dan and I found at a garage sale for $7.50. This is the sort of find that dreams are made of, and that keep people going to garage sales.

In the center of the middle shelf is a "pillar type" figure of Astarte (the Greek name for Ishtar), which may once have stood on a family shrine in Phoenicia or been offered at a temple. On either side of her are other smaller Astarte figures, and two pottery vessels. On the shelf above that, far to the left, is a figure of the Etruscan Goddess Tanit, only slightly encrusted from almost 2,000 years on the ocean floor in a shipwreck off the coast of Tyre, and a little to the left of her is the figure of the Phoenician God Baal. Lurking in his shadow is a small bronze ax head from a Celtic tomb not far from London. On the highest shelf far to the left is a small Celtic amulet, a tiny head carved of stone, and on the right is an oil lamp from the ruins of Pompeii. Centered on the highest shelf is a hollowed head of Dionysus God of Wine, and of Death and Resurrection, that once hung over the household altar of a family in ancient Greece.

Although these objects are kept in display cases where they can be seen by anyone who enters our home, while at the same time they are protected from hands that would not appreciate their power let alone their great age, they are also taken out at the appropriate season of the year to be worn or placed on our altar, or incorporated into our sabbat rituals as we celebrate the Wheel of the Year.

Clutterbuck the frog sings and dances beneath ancient statues of the Goddess and the God (photo by Dan Campanelli).

Below this case is a pine cabinet that contains jars of magickal herbs and bottles of oils that sometimes overflow onto the cabinet top. Here too sits a bronze sculpture of a pair of mating toads. They gaze eternally into a rectangular Plexiglas pond which is the abode of Clutterbuck, a 7-year-old aquatic frog who sings his song and dances his water ballet for me while I work at my easel. Although he is not exactly a familiar, Clutterbuck and I have a very special relationship.

On the wall next to the case are some of the awards and gold medals that Dan and I won during the early days of our art careers when we entered our work in competition. They hang there not to remind us of those achievements and successes, but of the negative side of those early days and how far we have come since then with the blessings of the Lord and Lady.

This brings us back to the west wall of the room completing the circle and returning us once more to the mundane world. But here in this sanctuary where the smell of turpentine mingles with the smoke of incense, and the powers of ancient priests blend with our own, though pale by comparison, spells are cast, charms are made, words of magick are chanted, and the Old Gods are venerated.

For many of us who found our way back to the Old Religion in the late 1960s, one of the very few guiding lights along the hidden path during these early days of the Pagan revival was a little booklet called The Witches Almanac. *Sometimes it could be found right out in front at a bookstore, next to the cash register, but more often it was to be discovered hidden in a dark corner, ready to reward the determined seeker.* The Witches Almanac *was published annually, at the time of the Vernal Equinox, for nine consecutive years beginning in 1971 and then, when its cycle was complete, it was no more. But during those nine years,* The Almanac *drew to itself a loyal following, for its pages fairly exuded a love of life's magick and a reverence for the Old Ways. It is with great joy that we can say* The Witches Almanac * is once again available through Pentacle Press. Its authors are John Wilcock and Elizabeth Pepper. John now roams the world on his quest, while Elizabeth lives an observant life with her husband and her animal friends, on an island off of the coast of New England.*

To Elizabeth, life is primarily a voyage of discovery. Her altar is within, her sanctuary is her home and garden, her circles are drawn in the sand or formed by moving a candle. Here, Elizabeth shares with us the secrets of her indoor Witches garden.

The indoor garden of a Witch follows an old rule of keeping color and fragrance alive in the home during the year's dark season. I have an assortment of geraniums—white, pale pink and ruby-red—along with several miniature roses, a showy hibiscus, and an orange tree that bears tiny inedible fruit and white blossoms at the same time. For scent there's gardenia, sweet olive, and best of all, a rare night-blooming jasmine. The perfume of jasmine is indescribably lovely and its white flowers are in the shape of small stars. But the plants I cherish most are three sacred herbs of Witchcraft that can and will flourish as house plants.

Bay laurel (*Laurus nobilis*). I keep a bay tree under a skylight in my kitchen. It stands about four feet tall from earth to top branches in a 12-inch clay pot and is ten years old. The sweet bay requires only moderate light and water during the winter. I sponge the leaves with a solution of water and baking soda at Full Moon.

The old leaves fall only when new ones develop, so the tree is always green, a true emblem of immortality.

Laurel is an important ingredient in many love charms. A maiden of ancient Greece would burn dried laurel leaves with barley grain in an iron bowl wreathed with red wool at the time of the waxing Moon to bring forth her lover, either lost or as yet unknown. The tale of Apollo's amorous pursuit of the wood nymph Daphne (the Greek word for laurel) and her escape by transformation into the graceful tree is a product of the imagination of Latin poet Ovid. A genuine Greek myth would never link laurel with denied love.

Elizabeth Pepper and a friend in her indoor sanctuary garden.

Rosemary (*Rosmarinus officinalis*). The Latin name translates to "dew of the sea." My rosemary looks like a small fir tree and occasionally flowers of an exquisite blue-lavender brighten the gray-green needles of foliage. Seen under a magnifying glass, the tiny flowers outshine the most exotic orchids. Beyond its beauty and evocative piney scent, rosemary has a great variety of uses in magick.

Shakespeare's "rosemary is for remembrance" stems from an old tradition that the herb sharpens the memory. Medieval scholars wore a sprig in their caps when they sat for exams. Another tradition, one I must personally dismiss, holds that "where rosemary flourishes, the wife rules." It does. I don't. Rosemary figures in love charms, marriage and funeral rites, beauty preparations, and aphrodisiac dishes (add a pinch when scrambling eggs for two).

As its Latin name indicates, rosemary likes moisture. I give my plant strong indirect light, an airy cool atmosphere and regular misting of its branches. Its clay pot rests in a saucer lined with pebbles which I keep moistened. And I water whenever its surface earth is dry to the touch.

Myrtle (*Myrtus communis*). "The myrtle belongs to Venus and love" quotes an old herbal. In a 10th century romance, Ogier the Dane was the knight chosen by the enchantress Morgan le Fay to dwell with her on Avalon. To erase the memories of his past life, she placed on his head a garland woven of myrtle and laurel—the crown of forgetfulness. The herb has kept the lover's theme of "forsaking all others" for centuries.

My myrtle, seven years old and three feet tall, bloomed only once—tiny white puff and petals—but the profusion of delicate bright green leaves alone makes a handsome little bush. I was warned never to let the roots dry out. I've seldom been forgetful, but when I've lapsed, the uppermost branches drooped to remind me of my duty. The myrtle shares the same environment as the rosemary.

Large clay pots filled with earth and sweet smelling herbs will attract cats. Covering the dirt with flat stones protects the plants from the ravages of feline digging and scratching. I know. We have nine cats.

Caring for plants is in itself an exercise in love. It's not surprising that the most effective love charm I know is based on the power of winter herbs.

In the seventh day of the waxing Moon, enclose the dried crumbled herb of rosemary (Sun), sweet bay (Sun) and myrtle (Venus) in a fine white linen packet about the size of the palm of your hand. Carefully fold and sew three sides with red silk thread in even stitches. As you sew, concentrate on the gift of love, the giving as much as the receiving of human life's finest tribute. Keep this token in a safe and private place. Touch it from time to time.

Silver RavenWolf, editor of The Wiccan/Pagan Press Alliance *, gives us many inventive ideas for creating sacred or magickal space which can be anything from a spare closet to an entire house.*

There are two kinds of solitary Witches, those whose immediate family and friends know about them, and those who have kept their faith completely in the closet. Regardless of the type of Witch, she/he needs some area for sacred space, even if it can't be very large due either to people or physical environment.

Creativity is the hallmark of the solitary Witch. Since the sacred space is more presence than environment, a lot can be done with the most meager accommodations. Big bucks are not needed to entertain the God/dess.

To practice in a closet can be taken quite literally. Take that spare closet full of junk, clean it out, re-paint it (how about blue with stenciled stars and Moons or other magickal symbols), and hang a few shelves. If a table doesn't fit, buy one of those put-together cardboard boxes with two drawers.

If your house doesn't have any closets (don't laugh, mine doesn't), you will have to think of other alternatives. Of course, a separate room is ideal, but not everyone is fortunate enough to have a spare room lying around for magickal use. An attic or basement can be utilized by sectioning off an area with sheets of plywood, even blankets or flexible rugs hung on rope or clothesline can be used as a partition. For any area of the house use decorative folding screens. Paint one side to match the normal decor of the room. Paint the other side to harmonize with your magickal self.

The sacred indoor space of Silver RavenWolf in her dining room.

The bedroom dresser top is a popular place to create a sacred space. Many college students use this method. When I prefer absolute privacy, I too clear off my four foot dresser, Windex the triple mirrors, and set up my altar there. To separate the middle of the dresser for actual altar space, I found two tall (36") pillar candleholders at a thrift shop. Instead of using them as I had intended, I bought two large glass globes (the kind you put the snow scenes in), filled them with water mixed with India ink and sealed them. Each globe sits in a wooden base that fits nicely on top of the candleholders. Presto, a door between the worlds. In candlelight, this produces a tremendous effect, especially on Samhain with lighted pumpkins around the room for the quarters.

If no dresser is available, you can even take a large piece of cardboard and place it on your bed. A seamstress cutting board was the first thing I used to create sacred space. Just remember *not* to sit on the bed, especially if you have lighted candles!

A dining room or kitchen table is also a good place to set up a sacred area. I used to pull the table to the middle of the room, then thoroughly wax the top and wash down the floor in preparation for a ritual. The altar area can be sectioned off by your cloth and you have a working area on the side.

Hide-away work surfaces are very popular these days. Large leaves fold down on either side of a two foot table top in the middle. When set up, the work surface can span up to 8 feet. When not in use, the table can be wheeled into a corner out of sight.

The hutch in our dining room is also a popular magickal space that the entire family can enjoy. With the seasons, we change the theme. The main door of our home opens into this room, so it sets the tone and atmosphere for those coming to call. This room is also where I do my Tarot readings for interested seekers. I have a round table in one corner of the room that I can move out and place chairs about to perform this particular magickal function.

Wall altars are a very nice touch. Glass or wooden shelves can be purchased at a hobby/craft store. If you have chosen wood, be creative and stain, paint, or stencil them. To add to the mood, hang candleholders designed for wall use. Hurricane lamps can be an alternative to candles and truly add a beautiful, mysterious touch when electric lighting is not in use. If you are industrious, ceramic plates and tiles can be made or purchased, then glued in a pattern on the wall.

If you sew, large wall hangings are a beautiful and unique touch to the wall altar. Even a large quilt with a pentagram or star/Moon design adds personal flair.

Plain window shades can be spray-painted or stenciled with magickal designs and only pulled down during rituals. They can also be used in general protection of the home.

Many Pagan families use their mantle as a sacred space. Items from nature's bounty can be lovingly placed there, along with candles, lamps, crafts, statues, and plates. Paintings of the God/dess can be hung above the mantle, as well as wreaths, quilts, or other wall art. And, of course, walls themselves can become magickal with stencils and hand paintings. My dining room sports green leaves and black cats sitting demurely above the wainscoting around the entire room.

When completed, our living room will be surrounded by willow trees and wolves.

If you are an active Witch and just about everyone knows of your faith, you can decorate your entire home and turn it into a sacred place. From bathroom to basement, you can create an atmosphere of peace, magick and harmony—a sacred essence in itself.

Silver RavenWolf's wall altar in the dining room.

SECTION TWO

Outdoor Magickal Space

CHAPTER FIVE

Outdoor Altars

Here at Flying Witch Farm, in the dappled shade of a magickal rowan tree, libations of wine are poured and offerings of cakes marked with the solar cross are made on a tiny altar of stone, while on a wooded hillside high above a Faerie tale village in Germany a coven of modern Witches gather at an ancient stone altar in a sacred grove to perform their sabbat rites.

While some of us live in rural areas close to the ever-changing face of Nature, many more live in towns and cities, but all of us live in buildings, be they houses or apartments, log cabins, split levels or city condos, all of which were designed to "protect us from the elements." Yet as the sacred nights of the sabbat approach, we are drawn to do our rituals out of doors, whenever possible, just so that we can be affected by the elements.

As the ancient Britons did on the Salisbury Plain, we cast our circles where the Earth Mother interfaces with the Sky Father. We salute the four directions which symbolize the four elements and at the circle's center, where all things meet their opposites, we place our altar. Beneath a canopy of stars, bathed in palest moonlight, we dance the sacred round dance, our bare feet tread joyfully upon the Earth while our spirits soar.

While others bow and kneel in temples and cathedrals, insulated from the elements, we who follow the Old Ways choose to worship in green forests or at the ocean's edge. While others are uplifted by the voices of a choir or sermons preached from a pulpit, we on the hidden path hear voices in the wind, in forest, field, or city park, we Pagans prefer to practice out of doors.

At the center of outdoor ritual is the outdoor altar. In the following pages Wiccans and Pagans from many parts of the world and from many and diverse traditions tell us of their altars, describe for us how they were constructed, and share with us some of the secrets of their traditions.

Master herbalist Ellen Evert Hopman of the Crystal Springs Grove* in western Massachusetts is the author of Tree Medicine, Tree Magick *(Phoenix Publications, 1991), a book about the magickal and medicinal properties of the trees of North America and Europe. Known as Willow in the Craft, she apparently shares with all of us a love of Nature and the Mother's wild Children. On the following pages she tells us of her altar arranged in the Keltrian Druidic tradition.*

Crystal Springs Grove, Beltane 1990. From left to right: Windwalker Bear, ElkLynn, Dorothy Moonsong, Steinos (Henry Canby), Willow, Moon Dragon, Taig O' Misteil (not visible) and in the rear, Mathonwy Owens (photo by Mark Harubin).

We generally try to set up our altar outdoors. I can't even remember a ceremony that was done inside! Once we did a ritual when it was 20 degrees below zero and no one got hurt. The only real problem was that the water in our chalice was frozen!

The altar is made up of "found" materials which we discovered in the surrounding forest—some cinder blocks and an old door. (As you can see we value creative recycling!)

The altar is used for Keltrian style Druidic rituals and every implement on it is part of the rite. From the left you will see a tree branch. This might be used for asperging (blessing the congregation with earth, water, or smoke) or it may have tiny bells attached. In the latter case it will be used to call in the "little people" or to invoke the Druids of past, present and future. Next to the branch is a container of spirits or tree sap used in the communion blessing. The two large chalices are filled with water or spirits signifying matter and spirit. The bottle on the right side of the altar holds the water.

Left of center is a shell which we fill with water and use to invoke Mannanan Mac Lir, Son of the Sea. The feather is used to asperge the worshipers. Oak leaves are placed on the altar because we never do a ceremony unless in the presence of oak. (In the case of our grove that's slightly redundant since we are located in the middle of an oak forest!)

The Druids altar, Crystal Springs Grove, Beltane 1990 in western Massachusetts (photo by Mark Harubin).

The three small black cauldrons are filled with Water (the ancestors), Earth (the nature spirits) and Sky (the God/desses). The ubiquitous Druid sickle is present to be held over offerings or to use when herbs are to be ritually gathered. We generally have candles lit during the rite.

While altars like the one at Crystal Springs Grove might be set up just for the rites, some altars are constructed to be permanent. From a place called Elfane, in England, Ros Briagha gives us this description of such an altar.

The altar is physically composed of two lengths of yew wood, sacred to Hecate, Goddess of Life and Death and Rebirth, and placed on top of them a large block of stone, which was so heavy it had to be moved by sound as well as strength. The altar is placed in my field in the north of the circle, according to the Wiccan tradition, and is set forward from the banks of the circle. There is a space under the slab, between the yew pillars, where offerings are put, or items of Mystery, which are better in the dark rather than on full display on top of the altar. There is also space each side of the slab, on top of the yew pillars, where items can be placed, perhaps if they are considered to have more affinity with wood than stone. Finally there is the space on top of the slab itself, and this is where most of our altar items are placed. This design evolved itself in some ways, using the yew and stone that we already had, and is not based particularly on any traditional design. It stands approximately two feet tall by two feet wide and two feet deep.

This altar is used for all ceremonies and rituals that take place in the ring. I have another one inside for when I work in my house. One feature of Elfane is that it is an open space for Pagans to come to if they seek/need somewhere to work/celebrate in safety, without outside interference. So the items placed on the altar vary every ceremony depending on who is present. I usually place images of the Goddess and the God there, and salt to signify Earth, the element of the north, and crystals, also of Earth. The symbols of the other elements are usually placed in their respective quarters, by the stones placed there. There is also a candle, usually placed on or in the altar, though this depends on the type of working and weather conditions. I use outdoor candles quite a lot for ceremonies and one is often placed behind the altar, in the bank.

(I must say I find it quite difficult to write about a ritual, since a lot of my work is based on connection with the Mysteries and words, and to some degree actions are channeled intuitively as each ceremony progresses.)

The Ceremony of Dedication for the altar starts by going around the circle, deosil, and at each quarter invoking the presence and blessing of the elemental power associated with that direction (for me, the order is east—Air, south—Fire, west—Water, north—Earth):

> *Oh most ancient and mighty powers of the east, breath of life, bringers of speech and thought, wild winds and gentle breezes, breathe into our circle here, bring clarity and purity of thought and speech to all beings within this space.*

The invocations for the other three quarters are similar, with obvious changes in the imagery for each element.

The circle is then cast. This happens on several levels. On the physical, I walk around the circle deosil, asking for a protective sphere to cover the ring. On the etheric, I visualize and potentise a ring of blue fire, drawn down through me and flowing out of my staff or hand, sealed with a pentacle at each quarter. When this ring of fire comes to completion at the east, it becomes a glowing hemisphere over the ring with a mirror image reaching down into the Earth.

The altar is then approached and one by one the elements of Air, Fire, Water, Earth and Spirit are invoked and asked to confer their energy and blessing and purification on the altar:

> *Powers of Air, I call upon you to witness the placing of this altar. May it be purified by the Air elementals. Breathe through it and surround it always with the benison of your blessing.*

As each call is made, a symbol of that element is placed on the altar: incense for Air, a candle for Fire, a chalice of water from the stream nearby for Water, salt for Earth and a pentacle for Spirit.

Ros Briagha's altar of stone and yew at Elfane, England.

When this has been done, the altar is offered to the Lady and Lord, with humbleness, and dedicated to their honor:

Oh Lady, Maiden, Mother, Old Wise One, this altar is offered to you; we dedicate it to your presence, to hold the sacred symbols of our Faith in your love, our trust in the endless cycle of time, our awe at your glory and splendor, and our love for the Earth, Gaia, Mother of All Beings.

Oh mighty Horned One, Lord of Life and Strength, symbol of the willing sacrifice, Lord of the Dark Places beyond the grave, endless youth of springtime renewal, this altar is offered to you; we dedicate it to your presence, to hold the sacred symbols of our faith in your love, our trust in your promise of renewal, our awe at your power and fertility, and our love for the heavens, Pan, Father of All Beings.

After this, there is a period of meditation and an opportunity for others present to offer their own dedications.

Cakes and wine would then be placed on the altar and each in turn blessed and purified:

May this wine, made with love and reverence for the bounty of the Earth, be blessed and purified, filled with the energy of the Sun and Moon, Earth and stars, that it may quench our inner thirst for love and wisdom. So mote it be!

May these cakes, made with love and reverence for the bounty of the Earth, be blessed and purified, filled with the energy of all growing things, all that is green and fertile, that it may feed our inner hunger for truth and beauty. So mote it be!

The cakes and wine are then shared, first being offered to the altar, then to those in the circle, and finally to the Earth, in thanks.

The circle is then opened, going round once more, widdershins:

Oh most ancient and mighty powers of the Air, we thank you for your presence and protection in this, our circle. We take your blessing with us as we return to the mundane world and wish you merry meet, and merry part, and merry meet again!

This is spoken at each quarter:

The circle is open but unbroken.

Many of us who were attracted to the truths of the great religions of the East early in our quest were stunned by the similarities between Taoism and Wicca when we finally found our way back to the Old Religion of our own European ancestors. Now East meets West in Minneapolis, as Hilarion Lee describes for us the altar of the Green Crane Coven.

The Green Crane Taoist/Wiccan altar of Hilarion Lee (photo by E.J. Allen).

This altar is the central piece of an indoor temple, but is portable and may also be used outdoors as either altar or icon, as it contains some elements of each.

Indoors, it is 30 inches in diameter and stands 37 inches high. It rests on a steel and cardboard salvaged industrial barrel which has been spray-painted silver. For outdoor use, it has screw-on legs 14 inches high, making the outdoor height 15 1/2 inches. When used as an icon outdoors, it is usually leaned against a tree with the altar set below it.

Minnesota is highly variable in climate. When weather permits, Green Crane prefers to hold its rites outdoors in one of two large public parks. When this is not possible, rites are held in the indoor temple which the priestess maintains in her apartment.

This altar is used in all of Green Crane's rituals, and also constitutes the physical surface on which all rituals taking place in this temple are enacted. Both the priestess and the 3 other groups sharing this space all use the surface—however, each group has a complete set of tools and the temple is made up differently according to the group working it and the symbolism each uses. Thus, while Green Crane may or may not elect an altar cloth, all other groups working within this space will use at least one.

The Book of Shadows of the Green Crane Coven (photo by E.J. Allen).

This altar was created from an unfinished coffee table by the priestess of Green Crane over a 2 year period of time. The design of the Cranedancer above the world emerged shortly after the forming of this Taoist-Wiccan group, and was a part of the first iconographic design specially created for the group, a color crayon drawing for a harvest ritual. When this design was transferred to a plywood disc, the piece was used as a north icon in the temple of the Green Crane Covenstead. When the priestess moved, the configuration of the new temple precluded this, and the most reasonable new location was as a new central altar. (The former altar surface, a larger marble slab, was deconsecrated.) The design was not yet complete, and a vinyl altar cloth was adopted to protect the work in progress.

Objects on the altar in the photo, which shows the altar in use, are two brass candlesticks with dark green candles, a wooden bookstand containing the Green Crane 1st degree Book of Shadows (Crane has 5 books, some of which are reserved to initiates), God and Goddess statues (behind the bookstand and hard to see), a coil of green macrame cord used in initiations, and the priestess' athame.

As set up for a ritual there would also be a green glass teacup full of sea salt, a small green glass full of water, a chalice and a copper censer full of cedar shavings. Most of those would rest behind the bookstand and thus be invisible from this camera angle. The reason for this placement is both symbolic and pragmatic—there's more room on that side of the bookstand—and it is also appropriate for the lesser ritual tools to cluster about the icons of the God and Goddess, at their feet. Thus implicit in the altar layout is the belief that all power descends from the Lord and Lady.

All ritual tools are kept in a shrine in the priestess' study when not in use. No offerings are made at this shrine, but it has occasionally served as a meditational focus.

Winters in upstate New York are bitter, and the cold wind that blows in off the lake preserves the snow cover well into spring, So Brigid Hagan who lives here must wait until winter departs to see the stone altar in her herb garden.

I have an outdoor altar which is in my little garden in back of the house. It is three flat stones (two sides and a top) which I place in the dirt every year (around May) and put plantings around to designate its space and as a gift to Nature and beauty. In the rest of the garden I always plant cosmos, my favorite flower. Around the outdoor altar I've planted and trained myrtle . . . and usually have rosemary, basil and other herbs planted nearby. I used to come to that particular spot to sit and meditate long before I set up an altar there . . . so it must have been a power/ sacred spot naturally and I was drawn to it. This year, I had hidden a blue votive candle under the altar, just so it would be there when I came out to pray and meditate. Lo and behold, a spider had spun her web right across the "door" of the altar! After I'd inspected it a bit, I decided to leave everything as it was, I didn't take anything down/apart this fall . . . snow and winter came so fast, I didn't have a chance. So everything is probably just as I left it!

In April of 1987 I learned two upsetting things: my mom had a carcinoma (mole) on her leg and my daughter Debbie had dysplasia (pre-cancerous cells in her cervix), both were scheduled for operations. I purchased a big, fat rose-pink candle and a big blue ("Virgin Mary blue") healing candle and placed them both in the center of my altar.

One evening, alone and quiet, I cast a circle by lighting a stick of incense and making a circle which included the altar, a chair and myself in the middle. I asked that all healing powers be with me because I had a request for them. I took my athame and carved Debbie's and Mom's names into both candles and their astrological signs (Debbie is Gemini and Mom is Leo). I took my special oils, and from the bottom of the candle up towards the top, I slowly anointed the candles, asking that healing thoughts and vibrations surround my mother and daughter. That we were Maiden, Mother and Crone, that we were One and the Same with the Goddess. I breathed deeply and closed my eyes; I "saw" the afflictions healed with loving pink and healing blue colors.

Brigid Hagan's outdoor altar.

I lighted the candles and turned off the lights. I asked that all love and healing powers begin to swirl (the beginnings of a Cone of Power). I started them from around my feet in a clockwise motion . . . just like a little tornado of love and healing "twirling, and swirling, and whirling around, healing my daughter, healing my mother! Around and around, faster still, the healing will reach them . . . it will! It will!" I envisioned the beautiful lights and colors going faster and faster around, and then . . . I sent it out to them! I sat still grounding myself and thinking and meditating—asking for this or better, according to free will for the good of everyone and everything concerned . . . and rested a bit. I then took two pieces of pink note paper and wrote "Blessings to Mom!" and "Blessings to Debbie!" on them. I tucked one under the blue candle and one under the pink candle and left them there. I opened my circle and ended the ritual/spell.

Both are healthy today. Whether my work had anything to do with it isn't important. It was the focus and the intent that helped the course of events.

The garden of Brigid Hagan.

Gerina Dunwich is a solitary Witch, astrologer and poet. She was born under the sign of Capricorn with Taurus rising. She edits and publishes Golden Isis Magazine * *and* The Age of Aquarius *and is the author of* Candlelight Spells, The Magick of Candleburning, The Concise Lexicon of the Occult, Wicca Craft, *and* Circle of Shadows. *When we first contacted Gerina, she was living in Salem, Massachusetts, a town famous for Witchcraft. The altar that Gerina uses for both indoor and outdoor rituals has an origin that sounds like a Hollywood plot. Gerina tells us the story in her own words, and also shares with us how she consecrates a healing crystal.*

The altar I use for many of my rituals is both unique and practical. It is an antique silver tea tray which I use as a portable altar in both indoor and outdoor solitary Goddess-worship and spellcasting. It is approximately two feet by ten and one half inches.

The idea to use the tray as an altar came to me several years ago when I found it while rummaging through an antique shop in Salem. As soon as I laid my eyes upon the dusty old tray I felt curiously drawn to it. It seemed to somehow possess a strange, mystical vibration which attracted me. When I inquired about the tray, the owner of the shop told me that it was almost a century old and originally belonged to a woman who lived in Salem. I asked her if there was anything strange or unusual about the past owner of the tray, and she gave me a strange look and said, "Yes, as a matter of fact. She had a reputation in Salem as a Witch!"

When I use the tray as an altar, I usually place it on a chair or a folding TV stand. Often, I simply place it on the floor, cast a circle around it, and then sit with my legs crossed before it.

To use it as an outdoor altar, I venture out into the forest behind my house and search for a good spot (such as a large, flat rock or a tree stump), and then place the tea tray altar on top of it. (The tray not only serves as an altar, it is also used to carry all of the ritual tools.)

To consecrate it, I light incense and a white candle (which I place in the center of the altar). I sprinkle a bit of sea salt and a few drops of fresh rainwater on the tray, and then bless it in the name of the Goddess and Her Horned Consort.

One of my own personal rituals that I perform is a crystal consecration ritual to cleanse a crystal of negative influences and charge it with healing power. The following is an outline of the ritual.

Begin by lighting two white altar candles (one on each side of the altar). Place a small bowl or cup of fresh rainwater and a dish of sand, soil, or salt on the altar. In the center of the altar, place a censer containing any of the following incenses: frankincense, myrrh, nutmeg, patchouli, rose, saffron or sandalwood. (I personally prefer using stick or cone-type incense; however, you may use powdered incense on hot charcoal blocks if you prefer.)

Take the crystal in your right hand and pass it through the smoke of the incense as you say:

By the power of the Goddess and by the ancient and mystical element of Air, I consecrate and dedicate this crystal as a magickal tool of healing.

Gently place the crystal in the dish of sand, soil, or salt, and say: "By the power of the Horned God and by the ancient and mystical element of Earth, I consecrate and dedicate this crystal as a magickal tool of healing."

Sprinkle a few drops of the rainwater on the crystal and say:

By the power of the Universe and by the ancient and mystical element of Water, I consecrate and dedicate this crystal as a magickal tool of healing.

Once again, take the crystal in your right hand. Move it in a circle around the flame of each candle as you say:

By the power of love and by the ancient and mystical element of Fire, I consecrate and dedicate this crystal as a magickal tool of healing. May this crystal stone of power work for my good and for the good of all. So mote it be!

After the consecration ritual has been performed, cup the crystal between your hands and allow it to harmonize with your aura and spiritual consciousness. Breathe gently upon the crystal as you direct your thoughts and intentions into it. The charged crystal will respond to the energy of your will.

Glen and Geri of Spokane, Washington practice a tradition that Glen received orally, although he admits that he has added much to it from contemporary authors. Here they describe for us their unique altar and share with us some of their hereditary tradition.

While nothing can truly be original, I have tried to avoid material that I have seen elsewhere in print.

Our altar is portable, used both indoors and outdoors, weather permitting. I liked the idea of a round altar from Raymond Buckland's books, but I constructed it pretty much my own way. We use a stump at our lake site. The altar table is two feet in diameter because the hardware store carries these in stock, with a lower tilted shelf, used to lay our Book of Shadows upon. The lower shelf makes it easy to read from books, notes and when outdoors keeps the Book of Shadows off the ground. Our Book of Shadows seems to lose its personality when touching the ground and must be reconsecrated, incensed and blessed before rituals go right again. The altar is made of wood with no metal. The joints are glued and pegged. The altar has standard greetings to the Goddess and God on the sides and is covered with an appropriate table cloth for the ritual to be performed.

We observe the eight sabbats and Full Moon rituals, also special healing rites when needed. While we once knew several original word-of-mouth rites, they have been intermixed with the works of Buckland, Cunningham, Reed, Fitch, Weinstein, Sherwood, and many others so that to say they are original would be untrue. There are a few chants I remember from my youth:

Hail, hail, fire and storm,
far off Spirit, still unborn,
far away, across the seas,
blessed Spirit, speak to me!

Hail, hail, ice and wind,
far off Spirit, come within,
far away, across the seas,
blessed Spirit, let me see!

This was chanted (monotone) each stanza nine times while gazing into the bonfire until a vision or inter-voice answered the question asked. A profound answer is usually accompanied by a sign, such as a double shooting star or chills down your back followed by immediate warmth all over (flush).

When we conduct rites outdoors we use the fire pit in conjunction with the altar or at times the pit by itself for meditation. The pit is used to burn blessed wood or smoke producing chips only—never for trash or cooking of any sort. The pit is one third of a 55 gallon steel drum buried. The drum is lined with fire brick and several circles of stones complete the pit above ground. The stones were chosen for feel, I cannot really explain how.

Our altar layout is a rather common one. In the center is a woven dish containing a steel, nine-inch pentacle so that the steel will not touch the table. A brass cauldron, glass subject candle, wooden framed black mirror, or similar focus point sits at the center of the pentacle. North of it is a brass candleholder honoring the "One." To either side of that candle are the Goddess and God candles. Other tools include a censer, goblet of offering wine, offering plate, offering (dependent on season), bell, magick knife, candle snuffer, blessed broom and, during healing rites, a violet healing ribbon. Candles of appropriate color are used to mark the four cardinal points.

Glen and Geri's altar table and fire pit.

The circle is cast in pretty much the standard format most authors have described. The only main difference is that when we call quarters we use intonations—similar to those found in Enochian magick. The dissimilarities may be due to the fact that mine was an oral tradition, with family roots in northern Spain and the southern France region of the Moors, until I discovered books on Wicca.

We have a small private shrine which would be inappropriate to take pictures of, but I have included a picture of a talisman which we have.

One talisman is in my wife's sewing room. It found her when she visited her sister, who lives in Denver. Her sister is something of an artist, owns her own studio. After a ritual cleaning, censering, and blessing of the room, the talisman was hung in its place upon the west wall. The room maximizes natural light and although small (10 x 9 feet) it is a gathering point on cold winter mornings.

A good luck talisman made by Geri's sister.

Another talisman is in my den. It was constructed by me about 14 years ago to prevent the entry of "Dark Magick" into a house or room. It protects all of our religious tools and candle making equipment from possession by other spirits when we are not around.

My wife also arranges seasonal hangings. These were changed five or six times a year until your book *Wheel of the Year* found us. All used material is placed in a sacred spot near our gardens. The materials are thanked for the use of their powers and returned to Mother Nature/Goddess.

Our circles are temporary, cast every time by the laying of a white cord of organic origin, in a nine-foot diameter circle. Four candles of appropriate color mark the cardinal points or watchtowers. This space is for my wife and I. The casting and consecration are not original enough for merit. They're the same words most contemporary authors use in slightly different order. Although my mother is the foundation of my organic gardening experience, she never held much with any religion and my father died in 1962 when I was a boy. I never made any written records of my father's teachings or beliefs.

When Dan first had the idea for this book, we both hoped that we would contact someone, group or solitary, who performed their rites at an ancient site, thereby creating a link with the ancient past. Dan always gets what he wishes for. Our wish was granted by Buck Cashel, a career soldier stationed in Southern Germany. Here Buck eloquently describes for us the beauty and powerful magick of this ancient and sacred place.

Ours is a most unusual, yet comfortable coven of Witches, though purist Wiccans would hardly call it a proper coven at all. What our family consists of is a fluctuating number of American military and European Wiccans and Pagans who worship the Goddess and God, work magick and celebrate the year's cycles in a small grove of trees on a hill overlooking an "Old World" type, small Bavarian village called Steinheim. This grove is off a seldom used road accessing farmers' fields and vineyards. It is completely surrounded by young evergreen, oak, birch and a sprinkling of various other sorts of 20 to 50-year-old trees. However, in its middle stands a healthy, strong oak of considerable age. It takes perhaps 30 full steps to cross the length and 15 full steps, the breadth of our quiet hollow. Few local Germans visit our grove in the woods overlooking their town except for an occasional old person after an afternoon of sunny contemplation. Within this natural sanctuary is a sacred spring which pours out cold, clear water from the heart of the hill, down into three descending pools, until it flows into the woods below. There, it joins the Murr River on its course to the sea. When entering the grove, we always ritually wash in the three pools (for the Maiden, Mother and Crone) before walking barefoot across the grass due south. Halfway across the clearing, we come to the great oak: the acorn of his grand-sires from centuries back when wise folk could speak with the trees. Those days may, perhaps, be over or at rest. But, during our worship of the Goddess and God there, this venerable tree often takes pleasure in joining our music with the clapping of his many hands. At the extreme southern end of this quiet place is the focal point of our fellowship—a second century Pagan altar cut from a single block of stone, dedicated to Diana and the Horned God. This sacred stone measures about 1m 50cm (high) x 1m x 1m. On the south side of the stone, there is a convex image of Diana attended by her nymphs. On her left, facing east, the Horned God stands majestically, despite the wearing and smoothing of 1,800 years under the open sky. Most rituals are conducted upon this altar as has been done since the time of the wandering tribes across Europe. However, various other rituals are done before the great oak and the three-pooled spring. Rather than memorizing a set formula for rituals of purification or the raising of energy, we Witches feel free to celebrate our rites with more spontaneity. For example, on a Full Moon, we have been known to gather in the grove and discuss a particular matter in need of magickal attention. Everyone focuses their whole being on the need, often holding the centrally concerned member. Then, we form a circle around the individual, who is then holding the great oak. We invoke the Goddess and God and the Guardians of the Four Towers to add their strength to the task. Then, we dance clockwise around the person and the great oak with appropriate, prearranged chanting. We also call upon the great oak to draw power from the earth through his roots and let it spiral around the person in need, until this combined tornado of power is at its peak. At the proper moment, the priestess or priest will drop silently to the earth, followed by everyone else. At that moment, the working power is released to accomplish its purpose. Afterwards, we give an offering to the oak in thanks for his help. And an offering is always left on the stone altar.

Though we read from a common Book of Shadows the rituals practiced upon this holy stone are as diversified as the group or individuals attending there at any given occasion. Yet, our common practice and understanding is in the beauty of working with mostly organic, natural tools. In casting our circle, for example, it is not uncommon to have individuals take upon themselves the spirit of the four elements and walk the circle with power-hand outstretched to earth. This has proven as effective as scattering salt and drops of water. Often the only tools resting on the altar itself are Goddess and God figures (or candles), a central candle and an incense burner. Yet the results gained from such simplicity are often staggering. The most powerful tools available to any follower of the Goddess and God are found within the worshipers themselves: a love for the Lady and Lord and each other, and spirits focused on a given purpose to effect positive change. With these two things we invoke the presence of the deities and the Four Keepers. With these we dance and sing and raise the energy to work the works of our Craft. When we are lost in such worship around the stone, beneath the Moon and stars or Sun, the spirits of generations gone before us join hands with us within the circle. Sometimes their shadows can be seen blending with our own. Always, they are felt. Perhaps that is why Steinheim (translated as "Home of the Stone") is a power place on the Earth. Or, perhaps, this has always been a place where the Earth has focused her powers, and that is why craftsmen lovingly placed the altar there many centuries ago. For whatever reason of their own, the Lady and Lord have chosen to grace us with their presence at Steinheim. I, myself, have seen the Horned One standing physically beside the oak while I was in solitary worship. Therefore, a sister made the banner of Herne pictured behind the altar, in memory of the moving occasion. Another midnight several of us saw the Goddess descending from the Moon to our assembled Circle. These contacts, if for no other reason, make Steinheim a sacred shrine. We understand that time and space are not linear, but multi-planed, often intersecting. With this truth, we have been able to use the altar as a porthole or door to time and go between worlds and across time. What we also learned in this is that when we magickally open these doors toward the four cardinal points, others from the other "side" can come and go as well. One night, a brother welcomed a staff bearing spirit who

The ancient stone altar in Steinheim, Germany where contemporary Wiccans still honor the Old Gods (photo by Buck Cashel).

had worshiped on the same spot many ages ago. When the Druid returned to his "side," he left his wooden staff to rest across our altar for our brother's joy and use. Our brother still treasures this beautiful gift today.

One mid-day, while worshiping and meditating before the image of the Horned God, an unusual, mammal type animal that I had never seen before crossed the grove. It demonstrated no fear as it gracefully walked past me, paused at the altar, and moved on into the woods. Having grown up in the country and being well-acquainted with four footed creatures, I could only ask myself, "From what world or time did this animal come?" It would not surprise me if the whole grove did not slip in and out of this world at times. The church bells of the village below sometimes cannot be heard within the grove at the appropriate strike of the hour, though they work perfectly well and are heard all over the surrounding countryside. No doubt, the skeptic or those who are unfamiliar with our faith will tend to disbelieve these accounts. But, all religions must have their "doubting Thomas" to provide contrast to those of great faith. What I would say to the disbeliever is to try this life for yourself before rejecting it in ignorance. This faith is not for everyone, though everyone can grow in their humanity through it.

After every rite or working of magick, we enjoy a feast of cakes and ale. Usually, we share a loaf of that delicious, fresh German bread with butter and honey or jam and seasonal fruit and local wine. There is always plenty to leave as an offering on the stone. This food, we quarter and place on the quarter points of the altar. We even make a ritual of the gift, giving back to the Mother and the creatures under her care. On any day or night, one might walk into the grove to find such food left for the Mother and Father and their charge.

Also, within the grove of Steinheim is a 2m (high) x 1m x 1m rough-cut stone pillar on which once an image of Diana stood. None can say at what moment of fear and ignorance the zealots of the newer faiths pulled her image down for destruction. But we do not feel a great loss in this, because the Mother herself fills the whole grove. She can be felt with every breeze, every brush from the wildflowers and grass underfoot, in the coolness of water and stone. She is everywhere today, and more than alive. She can be found there by the searching pilgrim or the innocent child. She is there as the maiden, reclining with young lovers beneath the hot sun. She teaches wisdom to the mothers with children who stroll past the place, looking for a respite from the house and its chores. She walks unseen as the crone beside the old people at days end. And she is there for us after nightfall, giving us power to work and comfort to live and joy and love to share. All people receive a blessing within this little grove with its ancient stones. Why is that? It must be so, anywhere She and Her Consort are lovingly remembered by humans, animals, birds, stones, trees and water. There, the air whispers Her name to the listening ear. And, no one leaves that place untouched.

CHAPTER SIX

Outdoor Shrines

On a sun-baked butte high above Chako Canyon three slabs of stone lean against a cliff face. Guarded by rattlesnakes this cliff towers above the canyon floor, and here in the shadows of the three carefully placed stones once a year on the Summer Solstice, an ancient mystery is revealed. As the sun reaches its height of power a serpent of sunlight slowly penetrates the spiral carved into the stone of the cliff by the ancient tribe of Native Americans known as the Anasazi. In utter silence this shrine to an unknown Sun god held its secret for over three centuries until it was discovered, and recognized by artist Anna Sofair.

Far from the heat-shimmering desert of New Mexico, among the green hills of England and the Emerald Isle, here and there are springs or wells sacred to an ancient goddess. Near many of these wells archaeologists have discovered ritual offerings such as coins, and most interestingly, the trunks of pine trees with the branches removed. These tree trunks could have been Maypoles placed in wells sacred to the Earth Mother as a symbolic Sacred Marriage, or they may have served as ladders to and from the Otherworld. We will never know. However, the one thing that these ancient shrines have in common is their pure, natural simplicity. A stone, a tree, water flowing from a rock, in a place quiet and serene, these are the places we Pagans are likely to call our shrines.

Kati-ma Koppana* of Helsinki, Finland has been a contributor to Circle Network News *and has published* Snakefat *and* Knotted Threads, *based on a chapter from a yet unpublished manuscript on Paganism in Finland. She describes for us here the natural beauties of her shrine to the ancient Nature deities of her country as well as some of the traditions of her faith.*

Kivikko is Helsinki's last wilderness, a long, high rocky area forested with pine, spruce and mixed deciduous trees, mostly birch and rowan. A mass of wild violets and anemones edge the paths in spring, moving on to tansy and other summer glories. White-tailed deer, hare and squirrels live alongside birds like crows and summer songsters.

At the beginning of World War I a wide system of fortifications were blasted into the rocky areas around Helsinki. Kivikko got trenches, storage spaces and a number of caves, usually full of water.

One day we were walking up from the path and found a small, about 8 feet by

10 feet, rectangular area, quite tidy and having two small spruce equidistant along the back wall. It was very quiet in there, unusual as two highways run around the area. Ferns grew in between the stones and violet plants were making seeds. Opposite the back wall on the higher side grew a rowan which bent down with her ripening fruits. One stood looking at the spruce and the names "Mielikki and Tapio" sprang to mind, the Goddess and God of the Greenwood.

A shrine in Helsinki, Finland dedicated to Mielikki and Tapio—Goddess and God of the Greenwood (photo by Kati-ma Koppana).

Later I went up there with my friend and priest Tapio and we worked hard clearing up the floor and building an altar between the spruce.

The altar is very basic, using the stones lying around we made it so there were flat stones to stand our ritual equipment on. Some lumps of quartz were brought from a nearby place and tucked in here and there. In the wall above the altar grew a lovely fern, a natural image of verdant Nature.

Later Tapio went along and constructed a circle of raised stones to put our fire cauldron on. Because the forest gets so very dry during our long hot summers we only have a small fire in a cauldron to reduce fire risk.

The last job was to cut away dead twigs and tidy up the ground. The trees seemed to know what we were doing and understood that it was for their good.

This shrine is dedicated to Mielikki and Tapio but is also used for the annual ceremony on April 4th in honor of the Skyfather Ukko and Earthmother Rauni. The rowan is sacred to Rauni—she is also the Lightning Goddess and rowan trees have been considered in many Nordic countries to be a protection against the house being struck by lightning bolts.

Ceremonies to Mielikki and Tapio are very minor ones, but it is in this place that we communicate with them and leave small offerings of grain for the mice and birds.

The Ukko ceremony is a larger one and usually several members of the grove attend. During the Ukko ceremony there is a juniper wood tankard full of home-brewed beer on the altar. In ancient times this feast was one of beer drinking and merrymaking. After the rituals people would go off into the forest for the more physical side of celebration. It was a fertility festival and one of the very few, if not the only one, mentioned in Finnish writings. Finnish was written down relatively late and Mikael Agricola mentions some gods in the preface to his Finnish translation of the Psalter in 1551. Among them was Ukko, also Rauni, and indications of the rites.

We usually bake a barley cake which is broken and shared, the rest being left as an offering. On the altar we often stand a little reproduction of the Thor statue in Reykjavik. As he was a thunder god he is suitable since Ukko is one too. Either ancient Finns never made statues or they crumbled away in the acid soil.

The offerings are made after a prayer or two and the beer and cake consumed. The fire is then lit and we circle around it singing or chanting God-names:

> *Oh Ukko Skyfather and Rauni Earthmother, we call to you to accept these offerings. Give us good weather and bless the crops this year. Give rain in those places in the world where they need it and stay your hands in those places where they have floods. Bless this place and us here and also our brothers and sisters not present today. Mielikki and Tapio, please bless this forest with your presence and keep it safe from developers. So mote it be.*

> *Not all shrines are in wild places. Our Wiccan friend from the Midwest, who sent us the gift of Faerie dust from a magick circle, has created a garden shrine to the Goddess which*

she describes for us here.

My artist husband built a low trellis over a bust of Diana, and this becomes overgrown with moonflower vines. She sits on a large flat stone at the northern "compass point" of the main herb beds, and so faces a clear southern vista. The Moon Circle/Goddess Shrine is at its finest in spring. As our yard is situated, the summer Moon shines fully on the Moon Circle, setting blue-white Faerie fire to the white moonvine trumpets, the ring of silvermound artemisia and the white marble star. The stones we chose to surround our beds are from our local wilderness area. It is pipestone, basically, with a fair amount of quartz in it; so it also shimmers when it catches moonlight. I know a photo could never really show all this, but it's just as special by day.

A small rose-colored stone is surrounded by white quartz. This is a natural "bowl" I found. I burn incense in it. In the overview, the marble star is clear. Its points touch an eight-foot diameter circle of quartzite stone. The stone circle is outlined (innerlined?) in silvermound artemisia, which makes a silvery, feathery ring in full leaf. Between the star points grow mini-carpets of mother-of-thyme. At the center, around the sundial stand, there is lady's-mantle. As I've said, the moonvine trumpets bloom over Her trellis. Last fall I added tulip bulbs to flank the wooden trellis that now replaces the first wire one. I couldn't help myself—they ranged in color from red-purple to deepest black and had as names Demeter, Isis and Queen of the Night! What could I do? They belonged in a Goddess shrine! (If the nurseries who develop and name garden bulbs ever do key in to the Pagan pantheon, my friends, I am doomed!) From this spot you can *just* spy the farthest edge of stone marking the main garden beds. That line is part of a square 16 feet on a side, with the Moon Circle/Goddess Shrine full center.

Not all shrines are created by Pagans, some create themselves. Glen Moyer of Catawissa, Pennsylvania describes for us his shrine to the Triple Goddess.

My shrine to the Goddess created itself in a way. It consists of a large (30-35 feet, it's difficult to estimate since it's in the middle of a grove of similar trees) three-trunked pine tree. I discovered this "shrine" by accident as I was walking in the woods around my home near Catawissa. It had been raining hard for almost two weeks in a row so many new streams had been created. Those new streams caused me to take a detour from my normal path and cut through the woods in a direct line to the house. I soon found myself facing a semi-circle of pine trees, the largest and westernmost of which looked as though it was three trees stuck together. Though only the top five feet of it bore needles it was still an impressive sight.

Something inside me called it "Ancient Mother" even though my logic said that a pine tree is more suited to the God than the Goddess. It was my heart that prevailed in this matter. From the view in the picture it is hard to tell but the trunks grow in a triangular pattern and go in order from smallest to largest (left to right), from the Maiden to Crone. Due to the angle needed to fit all three in without interference you cannot see the other trees in the semi-circle, there are seven in all ("Ancient Mother" is the fifth). I immediately buried a tiny quartz crystal at its base and thanked the Goddess for the opportunity to see something so steady and strong, especially after seeing all the damage from the floods. I was so absorbed by the presence of the tree that I was surprised to find that my home was in plain sight from there.

The Triple Goddess shrine "Ancient Mother" of Glenn Moyer of Pennsylvania.

After that I began to leave a monthly offering at the tree in honor of the Triple Goddess. The offering usually consists of three apples, one for each aspect, and some powdered herbs appropriate to the season. (I'm sure the deer come and eat the apples, but the earth takes them back eventually.) I generally leave the offering on or around the Full Moon. The herbs I use are:

Spring: lavender, mint, and sage
Summer: cinnamon, frankincense, and coriander
Fall: chamomile, iris, and violet
Winter: patchouli, fern, and mugwort

I chose these herbs by using the elements associated with the seasons (Air, Fire, Water, and Earth according to the above list). I used the quick reference charts in the back of *Cunningham's Encyclopedia of Magical Herbs* (Llewellyn, 1985).

I also use these recipes for incenses on occasions where nothing else seems appropriate.

John Bullington who shared with us his two indoor sanctuaries, now describes for us his naturally created outdoor shrine.

A semi-permanent space is set outside away from the houses in a circle of trees. This space is perfect for summer rituals and spell casting. It's thirteen feet in diameter with a huge bolder in the center which I use as a temporary altar. In late summer, with the scents of my flower and herb garden on the wind, some of my most enjoyable times are spent there.

I have two gardens, which are littered with all my favorite plants. One is for herbs the other is all flowers and other flowering plants. In summer there is always a fresh supply of greenery to be used. Late fall begins the collecting, drying, and storage of everything that will keep until spring. Now the gardens are relatively small and overcrowded but an expansion is being planted to better accommodate my needs.

Often times my cat joins me in seasonal rituals. Since she is one of nature's creations she helps me remember that we share this planet we live on with all other life forms. Practicing with a familiar as I see it has begun to die out. A lot of focus centers on either coven rituals or solitary ones. It seems that we're forgetting our animal counterparts! Some of my best spells have involved the blessing of my familiar. A cat, dog or even bird can be someone's best source of encouragement. Although they're not for everyone, there is one for every person.

Truly a Witch space can be a fourth of a basement room or the entire space of the stars that shine on the Earth. Any space can be magickal with the right time and energies put into it. Wicca can be a part of everyone's life in little ways. It's our responsibility to put that energy to work for us in ways that have boggled men's minds for centuries!

For anyone who does not know who Selena Fox is, she is founder and High Priestess of Circle Sanctuary*, an international Nature Spirituality center located on a sacred Nature preserve near Mt. Horeb, Wisconsin. As part of her work as a Wiccan priestess and healer, Selena teaches, writes, networks, leads rituals, and does spiritual counseling, shamanic *healing, and private consultations. She also is an activist for environmental preservation, feminism, world peace and religious freedom. She travels throughout the United States and other countries presenting workshops, rituals, and seminars, and is author of* Goddess Communion Rituals and Meditations. *Here Selena tells us of the powerful magick of a sacred tree and the work that was done to save it.*

Selena Fox making an offering at the Witch Tree (photo by Dennis Carpenter).

Rising out of the rocks on the shore of Lake Superior, the Witch Tree radiates magickal power and strength. Sacred to the Chippewa (Ojibwa) peoples, this four-hundred-year-old cedar tree has been honored throughout its life. Native Americans traveling in birch bark canoes, and later French-Canadian voyageurs as well, offered tobacco at the base of this sacred tree and asked for safe journeys over the unpredictable and dangerous great lake. Today, travelers by land as well as water visit this tree, also known as Ma-ni-do Gee-zhi-gance, or Spirit Little Cedar Tree.

Some visitors continue the tradition of making offerings and prayers. My husband Dennis Carpenter and I offered tobacco and small crystals when we visited during the summer of 1990. We were glad to see offerings there from other recent visitors. The spirit of the Tree is very strong. Being at this place of power was energizing. It also is inspiring, and in this century, artists from all over the world have come to connect with its essence and portray it in paintings, photographs, sculptures, writings, and other art forms.

Several years ago, the land on which the Witch Tree resides was put on the real estate market and was at risk for development. People from the area organized as Friends of the Witch Tree and began raising funds to buy this site and preserve this landmark. They were successful in their efforts and purchased the land. As part of the preservation plan, the property was then donated to the Lake Superior Band of Chippewa Indians on the Grand Portage Reservation to become a permanent part of the tribal lands.

Among those joining the preservation effort were Wiccans and other Nature religion practitioners from many paths. Magick was worked on behalf of the Tree at the Tree as well as at other places, including the Pagan Spirit Gathering at Circle Sanctuary.

The Witch Tree is located at Hat Point near Grand Portage, Minnesota. It is in the northeastern most tip of Minnesota near the Canadian border. The site is open to the public and has no admission charge. From the small parking area adjoining the highway, it is about a ten minute walk along a narrow Nature trail through the woods. When visiting, wear sturdy footgear and bring along a cape, jacket or other wrap—even in the warmest part of summer, Lake Superior breezes can be chilly. Remember to bring along an offering to honor the Tree.

Patricia Menzel Tinkey, who told us earlier how she solved the problems of practicing magick and performing ritual in a small apartment now describes for us how she created an outdoor shrine in the same environment.

Thankfully, our apartment is on the second floor and we have a lovely porch. After reading your book *Wheel of the Year*, I discovered that, even though we are lacking in much space, I could have a small shrine outside where I could go to address my Lady and talk with Her in Her space.

So, I went on a quest to find three appropriate rocks. I found four and I just couldn't decide which three to use so I incorporated them all. They are sitting on an old wooden grill stand along with a spring pot of flowers next to and above. A small votive candle is below the top rock, along with an offering of amethyst and quartz crystal. This is my shrine. It is specifically consecrated to Isis. This is where I can be with my Lady and where She can be in Her element.

Even a Pagan with limited space and funds can have a comfortable spot in which to practice his or her Craft. All it takes is a little imagination and a commitment in your heart. The first altar has been in use for six years; the larger one since the coven began a year ago; and the shrine is brand new, having been designed in May 1990. I am very happy with all three, and wouldn't, at this point in my life, have things any other way. With so many people living in the city, not being able yet to afford a real house, and still wanting desperately to have some kind of permanent, personal altar, I feel these are the best to work with. (Also, see Chapter One, Indoor Altars.) The steel shelves have turned out not only to be functional for kitchen use but also for Witchin' use. And, perhaps these photos will help inspire someone else into trying what we have done and enjoying the Craft even more.

Patricia Menzel Tinkey's outdoor shrine takes up a one-foot by three-foot area on her back porch.

In a similar environment Gloria Rivera, who earlier shared with us the consecration of her wonderful wand, has created sacred space on a suburban deck.

Living in a somewhat populated area I can't have an elaborate outdoor shrine or ritual area. However, I created a shelf that my husband secured to the house. It's about three feet long by one foot deep. It has a very simple altar layout of feathers, a candle, a small cup of water and a geode to represent the elements.

Above the altar is a masonry plaque of a woman picking grapes from a vine. Below the altar there is a long container with purple impatients growing in it and on each side of the container is a clay pot with English ivy. I'm hoping that the ivy will climb up the cedar siding of the house and frame the altar and plaque.

Since the plaque has a feeling of nature and fertility about it I have blessed it as an altar of growth. Ivy is very much a Goddess plant and she lends her abundant growth tendencies to the area. This shrine is situated in a way that both Sun and Moon energize it.

Gloria Rivera's outdoor shrine on her deck.

When I want to have a ritual outside on the deck it is usually very low-key because there are other houses nearby. My neighbors are able to hear me sneeze when I'm out there so I'm sure they would be able to hear me chanting to the Goddess and God. I also know that I'm pretty visible in candlelight so I keep the flames to a minimum and depend on the moonlight for sight.

Even though I don't have major rituals outside very often, I'm glad that I have this outdoor shrine. There is something very special about performing even the quietest ritual under the Moon and stars, and the shrine makes just sitting on the deck a more magickal experience.

Hex artist, Nan Conner* of Exton, Pennsylvania now describes for us the magickally intuitive way in which she came to create her shrine, and one of the wonderful mystical experiences she had there.

The red maple tree shrine of Nan Conner of Exton, Pennsylvania (photo by Anastasia Kean).

My personal shrine is located on the north side of a red maple tree. It has developed over the years because I feel drawn to the tree. The first year we moved into our house, I salvaged a four-foot segment of a railroad tie and used it to bank up dirt on the downhill north side of the tree. This made a small patch for flowers, and I've planted iris bulbs, crocuses, violets and columbine. It's one of the first spots to show spring colors each year. The railroad tie works well for a seat, to weed or just for contemplation.

I began building altars on that spot a few years back, mostly consisting of a pile or arrangement of stone which would be noticeable only to me. At that time, I was still largely an "underground" Pagan, so I was trying to accomplish my goals without being noticed. As it turns out, I underestimated the notice people would take of the ordinary herb garden which took up the front yard. More than one person has wondered what I was "up to."

This year, the shrine has evolved another step. Near here is a large field, each year planted in corn. This past winter it was sold for development. I felt the need to walk these acres before the bulldozers, building and concrete covered the land. Since the field is near the local school, I began taking my children to the playground to play, and then we would wander the land, watching crows and tracking deer, and saying good-by. It was on the first of these trips that I started coming home with pockets full of quartz stone. The spring field was bare at this point, and quartz "littered" the landscape. Bright white quartz in all sorts of shapes and sizes. I didn't know why I was bringing it home, except that I knew they would soon pave the field, and it all would be gone.

It became a habit for me to carry a bag with me, and I carried home more and larger stones as the summer wore on. The pile on the front porch grew, but still I had no idea why. I don't remember what finally made me think of the tree, but it was perfect.

So I began, tearing out the old gray stones which held back the dirt and replacing them with large chunks of quartz. Then I ringed the south side of the tree in fist sized pieces of quartz in a circle a foot wide. Then I began to fill in this circle with smaller pieces of quartz. It became a ritual for me, walking the fields collecting the stones, then bringing them home, and placing them one at a time in just the "right" spots. I was surprised how intense the experience became, hunting for the right stones, then deciding on the exact placement. It was as if some instinct guided me.

During this time I also found an oval blackish stone which became my "Primal" Goddess stone. At first I was going to paint some symbol on the rock, and dedicate it to a particular Goddess, but in the end I left it in its natural state. To me, the Goddess *is*, and my altar is inclusive of all of her aspects. I also found some flat white quartz rocks to serve as a small altar. On the exact northern point of the tree trunk is a small alcove formed by the root system. To me, it is almost a womb-like space, or a small cave. It is just the right size to hold my Goddess stone, and I also put in small offerings I find: special pebbles, or small feathers.

It's a cool night, and taking my tools, I go and sit by the tree. I don't need to light candles because the stars are bright, the sky clear. Taking my clay bowl, I sprinkle dried sage leaves in it, then put a match to them. The smoke offering fills the air, then drifts into the night. Taking up my drum, that I have named Tree, I begin to softly drum. Not loudly, but softly like a heart beat. My mind stills. I set Tree on the ground, and holding my piece of jet in my hand, I lay on the earth under the branches of the maple tree. Relaxing, I let the weight of gravity pull me to the earth. I close my eyes, and let my mind free.

I am small then, standing at the entrance of a cave, which is at the foot of the tree, giant now by comparison. Gently I push aside the offerings there, and make room for my entering. It is dark, the walls of the cave are rough bark. I am stepping forward, into darkness, thick and soft. Then I am falling, flowing down like water, a river flowing down. Down, spiraling, sinking down. I am sitting, resting on a sandy shore. The ocean is before me, the waves crashing against the shore. I have been here before, this night-filled beach.

To my left, an altar is set up. Tall thick white candles which burn, and do not blow out in the wind are on either side. I stand before it, and look at the objects. A medicine bag, beaded and fringed. Feathers and stones. Other objects I can't focus on. In the center is a mask. A strange mask, human and animal, both at the same time. I have been shown this before, but never clearly.

It is carved, the face long, human and animal. It has horns, long and twisting, like an antelope's. But the colors are fanciful, rainbow-striped. It is playful, and terrifying looking, both at the same time, like some primal jokester. I pick it up. Long ribbons trail from the horns. They blow in the wind. Holding the mask aloft, I face the ocean. The wind whips past me, my clothes blowing around me, the ribbons on the mask twirling, streaming in the wind.

"What is the meaning of life?," the voice booms across the darkness. The answer comes from me without thinking. "Art," I yell back, holding the mask higher, laughing into the wind. Do I get to wear the mask, my mind asks silently. I have asked this before, and the answer is always the same. "No, not yet," the answer comes. "But take it with you this time. Create it then, as it is in your heart, bring it to your mind, and then to your hands. When this is done child, we shall see. We shall see."

Dan's and my good friend, Gary T. Niall*, of the Tuatha de Danann and priest to Kat Clark, who told us of her traditional altar in Chapter One, is in the process of converting a suburban back yard into a Pagan sanctuary. In this chapter Gary tells us of his experiences in creating the Lady Shrine.

The northeast corner holds the Lady Shrine. The centerpiece of which is a six foot high statue of "The Shy Maiden." Behind her is a crescent of five wild cedars. Filling the spaces between the trees will be small trellises with moon flowers growing on them. At the maiden's feet is a small stone altar made of natural stone (not shaped by human hands or tools). The top is three sided and relatively flat, supported by three smaller, round stones, one under each corner. The stones with which this altar was constructed were a much cherished gift from Dan and Pauline Campanelli. Around the altar and statue grows a patch of flowers and herbs. Echoing the layout of the cedars is a crescent of the silvery leaved "dusty miller" plant; the arms of this crescent extend from either side of the pedestal which supports the Maiden. Before the altar are three round, paving stones forming a final crescent. The stones provide a solid area on which to stand (there being a very thick layer of cypress mulch) and also serve as a handy place to leave baskets containing offerings too large for the altar. Finally, the shrine is framed on either side with pussy willow bushes.

We made the Lady Shrine a part of our Beltane celebration, even though the ritual itself was held indoors. The High Priestess wore a crown of ivy during the ritual, and this crown was later placed on the head of the "Maiden" where it remained for several days to honor Her. Also, flowers which had graced the altar were placed at Her feet as an offering.

The devotional practices used for our Solar Grove (see Chapter Eight) can be easily adapted to the Lady Shrine. They could be performed on the nights of New and Full Moons, instead on the eve of Sunday. Or you may wish to place the vigil candle out on the eve of Monday (Moon day), which of course is Sunday night. Use three candles, white or silver for the Maiden, blood red for the Mother and black for the Crone. Libations of wine and fruit juice are appropriate, as are offerings of fruit, grain, vegetables, flowers or incense. My priestess, Kat, keeps a chalice on the altar to collect rainwater. After each storm she pours some of the water as a libation to the Goddess and anoints the statue with the remainder.

View of the Goddess Shrine of the Tuatha de Danann (photo by Gary T. Niall).

Kat then shared with us the lovely ritual she created to dedicate such a shrine, circle or grove.

While the area is being prepared, special care should be taken that the lives sacrificed by necessity (weeds, bugs, earthworms, or whatever microcosm you are disturbing/removing) are respected. It is best to verbally or psychically explain your intentions to the plot of earth being cleared, developed or changed, thanking all for their contribution to the intended sacred place. As much as possible, project the image of the completed grove to the weeds as you pull them, the worms as you uncover them, the webs as you remove them, etc.

If possible, when all is cleared—but before any planting commences—it is customary to leave an offering of thanksgiving to the soil. Some tribes of Native Americans use the sacred meal of blue corn; various Celtic traditions require an offering of three copper coins. You may wish to leave a crystal. a special possession, a cup of wine, some sweet cakes, or even honey. The important element is that it is an offering that has relevance to you, that "feels right."

When the sacred area is planted, arranged or landscaped to your satisfaction, or is ready for its intended use, the dedication may be done. The following is written as a solitary rite, but can easily be adapted for group use by assigning its ritual actions/readings to various participants. You might also have individuals read poems, lead chants, or compose music for the occasion, or request that each person make their own offering or bestow their own unique blessing upon the shrine.

Celebrant takes into the shrine the symbols of the four elements: a green candle for Fire, incense or a sage bundle for Air, a cup of spring water/juice/wine (celebrant's choice) for Water, and any Earth symbol for which the celebrant has an affinity. This may be blue corn meal, corn kernels, herb or flower seeds, wheat flour, or whatever you wish.

The celebrant stands in the center of the area. (If it has been fitted with a stone or natural altar, the celebrant stands before the altar, no matter where it is located.)

The celebrant lights and elevates the candle.

Celebrant: *May the sunshine and the moonlight*
meet as one in this place.
May morning calls and night whispers
join in one voice.
May rock and sky, rain and root
branch and bud and stem
touch in stillness, grow in peace,
continue on in beauty.
May the Old Ones take their rest in this shade
and glory too, in the brightness,
and may we, their children, greet them here—
joyful in their presence.

The celebrant walks around the area deosil, as best as possible, carrying the candle. If it is not possible to move freely at the shrine, the celebrant turns towards each direction (east, south, west then north) elevating the candle. It may then be placed on the altar, or set in the ground, to either burn or blow out naturally. (If safety is a concern, celebrant may extinguish the candle.)

Next, the celebrant lights the incense or sage bundle, and elevates it.

Celebrant: *May the winds of winter*
cloak you in purity,
and may spring set its
greening rain to blow.
May summer breathe
in your swaying branches,
and the leaves of autumn
tap their brittle dance across
your cooling earth.
May every wind
from every quarter
bring its music here,
ring like bells in early morning
and bless us with their song.

Celebrant again moves around the area deosil, incensing or smudging the area (or only the four directions if necessary).

(If you intend to include a wind chime at the shrine, this would be an opportune time to mount or hang it, so that it can begin its own song. If you have others sharing your ceremony, you may ask them to jingle strands of small temple bells as you incense/smudge the area. Temple bells may be strung in an outdoor shrine/grove/circle as an offering, after the dedication.)

Celebrant next elevates the water/juice/wine.

Celebrant: *We offer libations to the hidden, the deep,*
the watery heart of this place,
the springs that echo in buried rocks
which speak to diviners alone,
the rains that howl across the night,
and all the dews of all the mornings
past and yet to come.
We drink to you, and celebrate
your mystic ebb and flow.

The celebrant pours a libation and then takes a sip from the cup. (Libation can be poured onto the soil, or onto the altar top if appropriate.) The celebrant next may walk deosil around the shrine sprinkling the perimeter with the cup's contents, or pour a libation to the four directions. If others are present, the celebrant may choose to pass the cup so that each may sip or pour their own offering. No matter what the ritual action taken, the last draught is always offered to the soil in the name of the Old Ones.

Finally, the celebrant elevates the Earth symbol.

Close-up of the Goddess Shrine altar: smudge stick of sage and cedar, ceramic goblet, and candle (photo by Gary T. Niall).

Celebrant: *We bless this earth*
　　　　　with its own sacred self,
　　　　　the holy, the fruitful,
　　　　　the soil of life.
　　　　　May all who desire
　　　　　find nurturing here,
　　　　　a home for the spirit,
　　　　　a cradle for the heart,
　　　　　a unity of body and soul.

　　　Celebrant sprinkles the ground with corn, seed, etc. by either walking deosil around the area or by casting it in the four directions. The celebrant returns to the altar, or the center of the sacred space, and elevates their arms, palms upwards.

Celebrant: *So come Sidhe* and Gentry,*
　　　　　Old Ones of our ways.

---

*Sidhe: pronounced "shee," a name which means "hill" and denotes the ancient Gods of Ireland (or "Tuatha De Danann") once they withdrew from the world of men and took up residence in beautiful, subterranean palaces beneath the hills of Erin.

Bless this shrine called to life
by love and humble hands.
May all that walks, that crawls,
that rises to the skies,
may all that thrives in sand and soil,
or lies motionless in being,
find here the weave of many threads,
a web of life, and welcome.
This shrine is now blessed as sacred Earth.
May it be a meeting place
of love of peace,
and of unity of mind.

Celebrant (and any participants) meditate for a moment before leaving the shrine.

Cakes and ale and merriment should naturally follow! Blessed be!

CHAPTER SEVEN

Outdoor Circles

The magick circle is a place between the worlds, between the mundane world of men and the wonderful world of the spirits. It is here, within the circle that the two worlds meet and magick is made to happen.

It might be marked with the flaming grins of jack-o'-lanterns at Halloween, baskets of dyed eggs at Eostre, colorful gourds or baskets of plump juicy grapes bound to be crushed and fermented in oak barrels at the Autumn Equinox, or it may have cast itself over night as a Faerie ring of mushrooms to be discovered in the dew-soaked grass on a misty morning in May.

Circles may be drawn in sand with a wand of driftwood, to be washed away by the incoming tide, or they might be a ring of silent stones erected by a vanished tribe whose rites and rituals only the stones themselves now know.

A circle may be cast by magick only to be banished when the rite is done, or it may be made to endure long after our final rites have been performed.

Artist and writer Weland Ergwald* of Hartland, Michigan shares with us his experiences in creating a stone circle which, as his photo clearly shows, looks like one of ancient origin. His purpose in telling us why as well as how this stone circle was built is to let others new to Pagan ways know that they too can find bright blessings by walking the hidden path.

Some experiences in life transcend time and space to become the focus of our existence. Stonehenge was that experience for me. From the first moment I saw a photograph of the towering monoliths, I was enchanted. With hungry delight I devoured books and photographs and traveled in spirit to the place and time when men and women set up these megaliths and stood with reverent joy in the circle. When I had the good fortune to see a movie of Stonehenge, I was determined to construct a somewhat more modest stone circle myself.

Now, years later, a second marriage, and a move to the country has brought my dream to life. We live in east-central Michigan, where 20,000 years ago the Goddess commanded a glacier to push megatons of stone down from Canada. Limited only by my strength and the capacity of my wheelbarrow, I began to duplicate the designs of ancient sages.

My first success was a stone alignment from the northeast corner of our land. A large "heel stone" of about 180 pounds was erected to match the midyear Sunstead. A second stone of about 100 pounds was set at the edge of our large garden and aligned with the heel stone and Sunstead. On midyear's morn, I arose at 4 a.m. and, dressed in my white robe, stood at the station stone and felt my heart quicken as the fire of Apollo shot through the trees on the horizon.

"Arise, oh Sun," I cried. He did.

At first our neighbors were curious. "What are the stones for?," they asked. "For your friendly neighborhood Druid," I joked in reply. It wasn't long before the power of the spirit in the stones became manifested in our garden vegetables—the plants flourished like the Elysian fields. And this was in the 1988 drought! Yes, we did water it for an hour and a half every other day. The neighbors watered too, but it was our garden that passers-by stopped to look at. I enjoyed showing them the family of birds nesting in our six-foot tall tomato vines!

The leaves of our cabbage spanned 47 inches. We dug potatoes six inches long. Each tomato was a handful. Ears of corn averaged 12 to 14 inches long. It was a good year for those who love the Goddess.

We had moved here one year before, so this plot of earth had not been a garden until the previous spring. We use only organic methods, fertilizing with cattle dung, allowing the birds and lady beetles to devour harmful insects. I had performed no rituals because I was not yet a Pagan. But that day was fast approaching.

I had become disenchanted with mainstream religion, and loved nature, myths, and ancient lore. I was steeped in romantic visions of the golden age of Celtic and Arthurian pre-Christian legends. Then two events came together in my life that could only have been directed by the Goddess. I received in the mail a copy of Llewellyn's *New Times*. I had often said to my wife, "I have this strong feeling there is something I should know that would make life happy and fulfilling for us, but I don't know what it is. Oh, if only a book would just fall out of the sky into my lap with the answers!" (The Goddess was listening.)

The second event was a new family who built a home in the field next to us. They have studied the Old Wisdom and use it in their lives. When I told them of my desire to happily join the community of Pagans and study Wicca, they gave me the encouragement I needed to answer an ad to form a Pagan association in this area.

Now that I had demonstrated the power of the stones in a simple alignment on midyear Sunstead, I had the conviction and doubled desire to construct a stone circle. At the south end of our land, there is an unbroken sweep of meadow 100 feet by 200 feet, sloping to the south and east. Growing in the center is a pear tree rising from an ancient stump that had been cut down to ground level ages ago. I paced out the dimensions in early evening moonlight and lay in bed that night dreaming of magickal circles.

The next week was spent lugging four stones around the meadow and placing one in each of the four quarters to determine the best location. I first chose an eighty-foot diameter for the circle, as I had plenty of space. It was obvious the pear tree would be located very near the center of the stone ring. I gazed up into the daytime sky trying to imagine the position of the Moon.

Hmmm ... tree branches thrust their twiggy fingers into my view. I moved the stones a little east so the tree was behind me as I faced the moonrise. Hmmm

... I feel very exposed out here in the open near the road where anyone driving by might wonder if I were play-acting or if I had merely gone mad. Hmmm ... I moved the stones back west, skirting the back of our land. Now the tree was blocking the moonrise. No, I would not cut down the pear tree. It had survived one attempt to end its existence long ago. It was once again tall and fruitful. It deserved to live.

Hmmm ... so it went for three days and nights. I went outdoors near midnight and walked around inside the circle-to-be, feeling the glow of moonlight and dreaming of Pagan friends and I enjoying rituals together here. It was so peaceful and stimulating. But if I couldn't decide exactly where the center of the circle should be, it would remain just a dream.

Finally I had to admit the obvious—my circle was too big. I reduced it to a forty-foot diameter. Now it all came together in a rush.

I found a flat stone for the altar the very next morning. After loading it into my wheelbarrow and trucking it home I went searching again. The very next stone was a short pillar, flat on both ends, to hold up the altar. I located some larger stones in the ditch along our road and began extracting them and wheeling them to the spot where the circle was to be.

Weland Ergwald's beautiful circle of stones in Hartland, Michigan.

All afternoon I panted and heaved stones averaging 150 pounds from that clay bank into the wheelbarrow and trundled up the driveway, up the slope, and dumped them on the grass. Then I would flop down and catch my breath. That day I moved two tons of stone, measured out the distance from the altar, and dug shallow holes evenly spaced around the circle to stabilize the upright stones. I finished assembling the circle just as the Sun sank into the western woods.

As I dragged my weary frame into the house, my wife (bless her) didn't mention the rock garden I had promised all summer to build for her.

After a shower and change of clothes I went outside and walked around the stone "henge." Yes, it was worth the aches and stiff joints. Now I felt a real kinship with that community of Pagans who labored so long ago to erect a stone circle that has survived the eons since the Neolithic period to inspire us today.

My circle contains 29 stones, one for each night of the lunar cycle. There are 24 stones equally spaced around the circumference. Two stones make the altar and pedestal. One stone to mark the Samhain moonrise, and two stones to mark midyear and Yule Sunstead. Because the Sun has not reached his standstill point yet, I am adjusting these two stones each week until Sunstead.

The southeast edge of the circle passes under the branches of the pear tree, but the altar is far enough away to give an uninterrupted view of the Moon as she drifts across the sky. To the east and northeast, where Moon and Sun rise, there are trees across the road blocking most of the horizon. However, Samhain is only ten days away, and the leaves are falling already and clearing the view.

The four quarters are marked with the largest and most interestingly shaped stones. The cross-quarters are marked with the next largest stones. Two average size stones are placed between the quarters and cross-quarters.

The first night a thunderstorm came rolling in from the northwest. I took out my medieval two-handed sword and plunged the point into the earth next to the altar and performed the ritual to invoke the energy of the storm into the sword for use in future rituals.

The stone circle is dedicated to the Goddess, and the surrounding meadow is dedicated to the God. On the evening of the next Full Moon I will sweep out the circle with a broom, pour slightly salted water over each stone to purify it, and then invoke the elements to witness the dedication by pouring a measure of white wine on each stone while reciting poetic chants in praise of the gifts of the Goddess and God. Cakes, grain, and apples will be offered, then left around the altar in sharing with the abundant wildlife with which the Goddess has blessed this neighborhood.

Two days after the stone circle was completed our friend from the neighboring farm dropped in to visit. I was anxious to know how she felt about the obvious addition to our yard.

"Oh, yes," she said, "I noticed your circle." I held by breath for her next comment. "I have a friend who is a shaman," she continued. "She would love to come over here and dance around your circle in the moonlight."

Ros Briagha who told us of the altar of yew and stone in Chapter One now describes for us the construction, or rather the planting, of a sacred circle of trees, mentioned in the Celtic Tree Calendar, that surrounds that altar at Elfane in England.

Down the end of my field, separated from the animals by a wooden fence, is a space we have set aside as sacred. At its center lies the ring. This was created in several stages:

1. The firepit was dowsed in June 1981 and dug out ready for the Solstice. It is approximately 4 feet across, standing about 1 foot high, and has an inner space for the fire itself and an outer ring of turf, with large pieces of local white quartz at each of the cardinal points, and logs, useful to sit on round the fire when scrying or meditating. Beautiful wild flowers grow on it in the summer, and in the dark of winter the white quartz gleams like frozen snow.

2. The banks were created between Solstice and Lammas 1981. Turfs were taken from around the firepit, out to about 8 to 10 feet, and a ditch dug outside, and the banks were built up with this material, and using wooden stakes to hold the turves firmly in place. There is an entrance way in the east, with a bridge of elm wood laid there across the ditch. The banks are about 3 feet high, 6 feet wide at the base tapering to about 3 feet around the top, so it is possible to walk around the circle on the banks. In each quarter there is a marker stone, around 2 feet high, that came out of the ditch. The altar stands forward of the bank in the north and merges back into it.

3. The Celtic Tree Circle. Over the course of the years, usually at one of the eight sabbats or at Full Moon, the trees of the Old Celtic Tree Calendar have been planted round the ring. Many were trees rescued from death, and all have flourished here. I will describe each in turn (deosil from the east).

Willow: This tree is in the east, outside of the banks, and beyond the ditch, and by one of the eastern marker stones. It is a weeping willow, rescued from the local supermarket's rather pathetic garden section, a bare twig with one last green shoot, dry as a bone. It is now a graceful gentle being, draping each person as they touch the stone and delicately dancing in the wind.

Hawthorn/Mayblossom/Whitethorn: This is the first tree on the banks and was one of the first planted, at Spring Equinox, Ostara 1982, along with four others. It came from another place in the field and is beautiful in spring, white with flowers, then red with berries in autumn.

Oak: This one was also planted in Spring Equinox 1982. It was heavily pruned by our goats two years in a row and I feared for its survival, but it came back strongly and is now a golden glory in autumn, a column of dead leaves enduring well through the winter.

Hollies: These are on either side of the south stone and are both different varieties of holly. The first planted is a variegated one, yellow and green, rescued from the same supermarket, and now a glossy 5-foot high beauty. The other was given to me by a friend in 1987, and is deep blue-green, with blue berries and lovely flowers.

Hazel: This tree was brought by a friend who saw it half-uprooted after a hedge had been badly cut. It has sent up many side- shoots and bore its first nuts this year.

Magnolia: Definitely not a traditional tree for the Celts, this one found its way in by this wise; a friend was staying at my house while I was away and rescued the tree from a garden center. He offered it to me, as he had no garden, and asked where to put it. I suggested he ask the tree and so, at 2 a.m. at exact full of the Moon, he took it out and was led to the ring, where he planted it in between the hazel and the apple, in the southwest. It will be beautiful in the spring when its heady scent fills the air and the pink hearts of the great white blossoms show themselves.

Apple: This one came from a friend as recompense for her goats eating my trees. It was rather slow to take off, having been chewed itself, but is now growing strong and brown, tight buds curled with promise for the spring, the first few fruits this year tasting of the Apples of Avalon.

Sloe/Blackthorn: A dark, spiky tree, this one came from beside the stream that runs and sings at the bottom of the field. It went in 2 years ago and has grown quick and strong, edged with sharp deadly thorns and tiny bitter fruits that transform a plain spirit into the nectar known as sloe gin, ideal for warming cold winter nights round the fire in the circle. It stands beside the west stone.

Elder: Over the last two years I have been rebuilding Elfane and finally moved back in at Winter Solstice 1988. Two friends visited and together we planted the elder as a symbol of birth and rebirth and an omen of hope for the child they were expecting, and for the reborn Elfane, my new house.

Yew: I used to visit Greenham Common a lot in the early 1980s and did various ceremonies there, working magickally to aid the women and the Earth in getting rid of the cruise missiles. After one such ceremony, I was led to a tiny yew, valiantly struggling to grow between two silver birches, in the middle of a major walk-through. I dug it up and took it home, where it grows on the north facing slope, still tiny but holding in its tight grained heart the promise of still guarding that space in 1000 years time, when only the stones are left to keep it company.

Birch: The birch was planted by a friend called Aida Birch, who lived at a place called Birchgrove! It was planted Ostara 1982 and now towers above me, dwarfing the tiny yew beside it, about 17 feet tall. It is already silver on the trunk and covered in delicate catkins in winter, a fitting backdrop for the altar.

Rowan/Mountain Ash: Another one planted at Ostara 1982, this is a slim, dove gray tree, with soft, sweet smelling flowers in spring, and bright orange red berries in autumn. It has grown strongly, like the birch, and, on its other side, the ash.

Ash: The last one planted at Ostara 1982, this one has grown very strongly and is much bigger than another ash planted at the same time in another part of the field. It was cut to grow in two main limbs, a Y-fork, to represent the Horned One; it also has a strong flavor of Odin/Wotan!

Alder: This tree is due to go in this winter (1989-90), the last tree (I think!) coming up from the stream to join the others. It will be planted by the second east stone, where a friend's placenta from her home-birth was buried.

So, that is the ring at Elfane, a place where many people have come over the years to celebrate life, mourn death, and honor the Old Ones. Long may it prosper!

Over the years there have been many changes at Elfane and this has been reflected in the ring. It has become a part of the landscape, growing quietly, with its own serene beauty. Over the last few years I have been away a lot, partly because of the re-building of the house and partly being away working. The ring has a life of its own now, and when I do go down there, which is becoming more frequent again, it takes very little to evoke and tune into a very powerful presence. I always take down seasonal offerings when I go to the ring, to add to its own seasonal beauty. Often I put layers of thick sweet smelling hay on the floor which becomes a golden carpet in the light of the fire. Or sweet smelling herbs which give off their perfume when we dance.

Bel and Ros at the ring/circle at Elfane, England.

The ring is used at various times; these usually include the Eight Festivals of the Solstices, Equinoxes and cross-quarter days. Also the Full and New Moons, and various important astrological times. Sometimes I both purify with the elements *and* cast the circle, others I may simply walk round the circle, mentally/magickally waking the ever-present energy. I have given details of my way of opening a circle in the section on the altar.

There have been all sorts of interesting results to the ceremonies performed here. I think every person who has been in the ring for a ceremony will always remember it—the breath of the wind, the light of the fire, the rain that has freshened, but rarely prevented, many a rite, and the solidity of the earth and stone—and above all, the grace to go "between the worlds," to that inner magickal space that is the doorway to the Mysteries.

On a slightly smaller scale hex artist Nan Conner has constructed a circle of stones in her back yard. Here she describes for us not only her circle, but how she explained to her five-year-old daughter what it means to be a Witch.

The red maple is special, and I've always been drawn to it. During the summer, my children and I spend our time out under it, sitting on a large blanket spread out on the earth. We hang wind chimes on the branches, and this year we made a solar cross out of maple branches and gold yarn. After each summer storm, we go out and gather up all the broken branches to use for making wands, rune sticks, and other projects. The fact that we now orient our magick circle to this tree was just a natural extension of our other activities. I had been considering it for use as a sacred space—something artistically planned with torches and banners and markers for the points of the circle. In the end, it was simple need which turned it into our family's sacred space.

Watching television with my children one morning, one of the shows featured the stereotypical evil Witch, green skinned and wart nosed. This generated a discussion between my five-year-old daughter Tegan and myself.

"Mommy is a Witch," I informed her. We had talked about this before. "Nooo," she replied with five-year-old wisdom. "Mommy doesn't have green skin or a big nose or turn people into animals like on TV." I thought of Ana, a friend of mine who Tegan was fond of.

"Ana is a Witch also," I mentioned. Oh, she liked Ana. Ana has a red car. That was OK then. At this point, I pulled out a copy of *My First ABC: A Primer for Wiccan Children* by P. Scott Hollander, and together we looked at and talked about the pictures. This is a picture of a Witch. This is a kind of robe Witches wear. These are some tools Witches use. Witches make circles to worship in. The questions poured out. Can we wear robes? Can we make a circle? Can we have wands? Can we do it *now?* I had no idea of how to explain the complexities of circle making to a five year old, so I made it up as we went along. No robes at this point, but we did have maple branches for wands. Taking Tegan's plastic bucket, we collected small stones to mark out the circle. Using the tree as our focal point at the north corner, I marked out the other quarters in a rough six-foot circle. Tegan then helped me fill out the rest of the perimeter of the circle with more stones. Taking our wands, we entered the circle. I drew out the circle on the the ground, Tegan following behind, doing the same. I chanted:

Around and around, around and about, good stays in, bad stays out.

We then faced each of the quarters, saluting each:

Hail to the north, the element of Earth.

Hail to the east, the element of Air.
Hail to the south, the element of Fire.
Hail to the west, the element of Water.

Then back to the north:

The circle is now made, a place set apart for us to worship.

We then sat on the ground, facing the tree, and talked about whatever came to mind.

Nan and Tegan's magick circle at the red maple (photo by Anastasia Kean).

The circle is a special place, I explained. It's where Witches come to worship and to celebrate the seasons. That direction is the east, and that's where you see the sunrise each morning. Each day, the Sun goes across the sky, and then sets in the west over in that direction. Ahead of us is the north, where the tree is. A tree is a special thing because it exists in three places. Its roots are deep in the earth, its trunk is here by us, and the branches reach up into the sky.

This is the Earth, I told her patting the ground. The Earth is where everything comes from. Seeds grow in it, we live on it, and when things die, they go back to the Earth. She remembered the dead mouse we had buried, and how I had told her the mouse was now part of Mother Earth.

"But if the Earth is the mommy," she asked, "Who is the daddy?" To her, all families are like hers. They have a mom, dad, brother and sister. I told her about the American Indians, and how they believed in the Sky Father. The Sky was above us, the Mother Earth below us. We need both things for us to live, and plants to grow. The Earth holds the seeds, and the Sun and rain come from the Sky to help the seeds grow.

While we sat, a moth came and landed on the tree. I pointed it out and talked about cycles. Moths lay eggs, which become caterpillars, spin a cocoon, and hatch as new moths. These moths then lay eggs. Seeds have a cycle: from seed to plant to flower to seeds again. Each year is like that, turning in a circle. Now was the Summer Solstice, then would come Lammas, then the Fall Equinox, and on through the year. Did she remember Yule last year? Did she remember the Yule before that? All the festivals are like that, each coming after the other, year after year.

Then we were finished. It was getting hard for her to stay in one place, so it was time to close the circle and say thank you. We faced each of the quarters:

Blessed be the north, power of Earth.
Blessed be the east, power of Air.
Blessed be the south, power of Fire.
Blessed be the west, power of Water.

Tegan followed behind me, solemnly intoning "Bless that bee," at each quarter. I figured she had the right idea—bees are sacred, after all. Facing the tree again, I explained, "The circle is closed now. Blessed be the Mother Earth and Father Sky." Together we packed up the stones and put them away.

The next morning, Tegan got her bucket of stones, her wand, and going out to the back of the yard, made her own circle near the mugwort hedge. She stood in the center, and raising her wand to the sky, called out her own mysterious words of power. I watched from a long way off. When she was done, she gathered up the stones, put them away, and went off to play.

We now do various seasonal activities in that space. For Summer Solstice we put the cauldron under the tree and filled it with herbs and apples. We collected a batch of vegetables and prepared them while sitting under the tree. We then had a vegetarian barbecue. We talked about the harvest, and made little straw men to hang with the Sun wheel for Lammas. When Lammas does come, we've saved corn husks from the summer picnic to burn as offerings in the cauldron.

I don't plan the activities too far ahead at this point. Each season brings its own instinctive celebration. But one never knows. I might get those banners made one of these days.

Not all circles are made of such enduring materials as stones and trees. When sunny days bring heat and humidity to Flying Witch Farm and the afternoons buzz with the sound of cicadas, when the cows in the meadow across the road hide in the shade by the stream and the fragrant leaves in the herb garden wilt beneath the noonday sun, Dan and I usually take one day off to go to the shore, cast a circle in the sand and honor one of the many sea deities.

Here, in this magickal place between land and sea we can walk the beach for hours gathering gifts from the Gods—the spiraled shells of sea snails cast ashore and the magick holey stone revealed at our feet by a receding wave, the little gray nicker nut that warns of danger by changing color, and the coffee brown sea bean that protects against evil magick.*

A circle at the Jersey shore, with an offering to Aphrodite (photo by Dan Campanelli).

When the time is right, and this might mean waiting for the tide to turn because an incoming tide is better for magick dealing with growth or prosperity while an outgoing tide is better for rituals of banishment or ending a negative situation, or just when it feels right, we cast our circle in the sand. This might be done with an index finger, athame, wand, or a wand of driftwood given by the sea, such as one I once found.

*For more information on sea charms see *Wheel of the Year* (Llewellyn, 1989).

At the center of the circle a stone might be placed to serve as an altar, or an altar can be formed of wet sand. Dan and I usually bring a small stone just in case we can't find one that's suitable.

At the shore where the Earth meets the sea and both are caressed by cool breezes, the one element that obviously seems to be lacking is Fire. For this reason we bring with us some votive candles. We've also gathered driftwood for a real fire, but most public beaches do not permit fires. This seems strange to me because what can possibly catch fire at the beach? The oil slick on the water I suppose. At any rate, if fires are not permitted on the beach, we use candles for the element of Fire.

For the element of Water a found shell filled with sea water has served the purpose, and a joss stick stuck into the sand is always a good representation of the element of Air. For Earth a cluster of wave washed pebbles has been used, or a shell filled with sand. We do not usually use a pentacle because ours is embroidered onto the center of our altar cloth, but at the beach it seems appropriate to use a sand dollar which has a natural five pointed star etched in the center of its circular shell. However, these are not easily found at the Jersey shore. They're there, just not easily found, so Dan and I usually bring one with us.

Other adornments, symbols, and offerings depend on the nature of the God or Goddess we intend to honor. Poseidon is the Greek counterpart of the Roman Sea God Neptune. Aside from being God of the Sea, Poseidon is also the creator of the first horse, and so when honoring him we mark the four quarters of the circle with a horseshoe. We have one horseshoe that we take with us to mark each quarter with a hoof print and then use the shoe itself as a symbol of the God in his aspect as Poseidon on the altar.

We always bring white wine with us as an offering to the Goddess of the Sea who is the Moon Goddess herself, and in her aspect as Aphrodite, Goddess of Love and Beauty, seashells, the most beautiful seashells that can be found, are traditional offerings. The seashells of the genus *Cypraea*, popularly called cowries, which have apertures resembling the female genital area, were offered to this Goddess of fertility at her temple on the island of Cyprus.

When Dan and I recently cast a circle on the shore at Sandy Hook to honor the Goddess Aphrodite, we adorned the circle with sweet scented rose petals which were immediately taken by the sea breezes and scattered on the surf. We also brought with us a lambis shell, one of the most beautiful of seashells, and placed it on an altar of stone in the center of the circle. After a long meditation we poured the offering of wine as we intoned the words:

Aphrodite, born of the sea,
I offer this shell unto thee.
It's perfect beauty, like your own,
gracious Goddess born of foam,
it's all I have to give to thee,
grant that I may blessed be.

As we ended our ritual and gathered our tools we noticed up the beach a group of school children with a teacher gathering specimens of marine life with nets, studying them and then setting them free. Rather than having the children inadvertently disturb our altar, Dan took the beautiful lambis shell we had brought as an offering and tossed it into the waves. Then we left our circle in the sand to be reclaimed by the sea. As we walked up the dunes to the upper beach we looked back at the children in the surf and smiled at their excitement over their discoveries. We wished that we could be there when one of them discovered the beautiful lambis from the warm tropical seas of the South Pacific. We hoped perhaps it will stimulate some of these children to learn more about the creatures of the sea and to protect the watery realms of the Sea Gods.

Elizabeth Pepper who, along with her colleague John Wilcock, produced The Witches Almanac, *and who lives on an island off the coast of New England casts her Imbolc circle in the sand. Here in that magickal realm between land and sea, at the time of an incoming tide and a waxing Moon, Elizabeth might perform the "Water of Well-Being Charm," which she shares here with us. She copied this charm from a Book of Shadows compiled just after the turn-of-the-century, but it is undoubtedly much older.*

On Candlemas Day go to the seashore after the tide turns from ebb to flood. Collect from the ninth wave a jar of sea water. The count begins at your discretion. It can be the first wave to touch your feet or a breaking crest you see at a distance. Counting the waves by sight is often confused by contrary currents or eddies so it is far easier to close your eyes and depend on the sound of each wave as it hits the shore. Scoop up the water from the ninth wave in one fluid motion.

Elizabeth Pepper on an island off the coast of New England.

Now stand quietly and draw in the surging energy of the sea and wind. You will sense the right moment to dip water from the jar with your fore, middle, and ring fingers—one at a time in that order—to lightly touch your forehead saying:

One for courage.
Two for patience.
Three for luck.

You can perform this rite on any major sabbat that falls within a waxing Moon, but it is said to be especially effective at Candlemas. Keep the sacred water in a safe and dark place to use throughout the year whenever necessity arises.

Elizabeth, whose element is Water (Sun and Moon in Scorpio with Cancer rising), also shares with us a method for seaside divination. Living on an island she is naturally within walking distance of the beach.

Whenever I have a problem to solve I walk there, enter a semi-trance state, choose three objects—whatever catches my eye—and read their message upon my return home. Sometimes I'm baffled, but more often than not an answer comes through quite clearly.

Not all circles in the sand are cast at the seashore. Buck Cashel who told us of his coven's experiences with the Old Ones at an ancient altar in Germany was transferred from the Faerie tale village of Steinheim to Saudi Arabia early in 1991. Here in the Arabian desert, not far from the Iraq border, did Buck and his coven cast their circle in the sand.

This picture was taken on the front lines during the war just a day or two before the "ground war" started and we rolled into Iraq. The site of the picture was about 6-8 miles from dug-in Iraqi positions. In fact, we were within artillery range there . . . in the "neutral zone" or "no man's land" between Iraq and Saudi Arabia.

On this particular occasion, I was coming off "stand to" which is when all the soldiers mount the berm that surrounded our site . . . and much like the old Celtic forts of Europe.

The stone altar faced west. And, while on that site, I would go and worship there every sunset that was possible. For tools, I had my athame (a black-handled, double-edged Mark II fighting knife by Verber) to cast the circle. And I had a brass bell for summoning the four spirits of north, east, south and west. I had salt and water (precious elements in the desert), but I seldom lit candles for obvious reasons. In this picture I believe all I had was an offering of flat bread and fruit on the altar. Before the altar I had arranged round quartz stones into runes to effect specific requests or wishes such as protection of comrades and victory in battle.

The desert was the realm of the God . . . a wasteland of sand and rock and sky. He rode the heavens unhindered by clouds. The spiritual atmosphere was electric and powerful and strong, though many of our fellow Wiccans as well as I felt overloaded by it all. (Later the *joy* of walking on grass under trees was *total.*) Anyway, ritual was simple as privacy was unknown. No skyclad circle dancing during Desert Storm, unfortunately. But it worked and it was good. Removed from TVs and cars and climate controlled rooms, running water, etc . . . worship was a perfectly natural act. One didn't have to "call down" the Moon because she filled the sky. The Father and Mother were everywhere.

Ritual usually consisted of casting a circle in the sand, inviting the four spirits of the elements. Welcoming the Mother and Father and meditating. To be truthful, the main focus of the meditation was having successfully accomplished our mission and getting back with family and friends. It must have worked because no Wiccans I know of fell during the war. Really, we all came back stronger in spirit and love for the Goddess and God as a result of the experience. Sure, we did some magick and some unusual experiences occurred (seeing spirit folk and such) but the Desert Storm experience was more about learning to walk closer to yourself and to the Goddess and God. Though we worshiped openly (because of necessity), it was a very personal and individual thing.

At first, the "Christian" believers got up-in-arms about Witchcraft being openly practiced. But, in my case, I called my platoon together and explained what it was all about. I didn't have any more problems with it. What a time . . .

Buck Cashel at his circle on the Saudi/Iraq border just days before the ground war of Desert Storm.

In stark contrast to the shimmering heat of the Arabian desert, the cold snowy winters of Kenmore, New York provide an excellent environment for a most unusual circle. Breid Foxsong, editor of an exciting and informative newsletter called Sacred Hart **, tells us of her Imbolg circle.*

My Imbolg ritual begins on the afternoon of January 31st, when I begin preparing the outdoor circle area. One advantage of living and working in a part of the country with *real* seasons is the variety of materials available to work with. A winter celebration should have winter symbols, and what better symbol of winter than snow?

I start by making a snowball, rolling it to clear a 9-foot circle in the snow. When it is between knee and mid-thigh high, then it is rolled over to the northeast where it will be shaped into the altar. A mound of snow is piled at each quarter. The rest of the snow is packed to make a low ridge around the circle for a visible boundary. On the ridge are placed paper bag luminaries. With their dim light and lack of warmth, they are well suited to the season, and they won't blow out. To make luminaries, pour 1/2 inch of sand in a paper bag and put a votive candle on the sand.

With sword in hand, I begin with the snowball that will be the altar. I carefully carve a flat top, and spaces for each of my ritual tools. A large flat stone will hold the incense burner in the east so that it won't melt into the snow immediately; carved cavities keep the cup and candle from tipping over. For my Imbolg ritual, I prefer to work with all crystal or glass altar tools, because they look like icicles. When the top is how I want it, I start on the sides. Each side should be smooth and any dirt that was collected with the snow should be trimmed off. Once the sides are smoothed, I carve the symbols of each quarter into the appropriate side. I then run my bare hands over them to smooth and to make ice form. As I do this, I concentrate on the element and character of each quarter; focusing and condensing it so that my altar is made of each element. Frozen water, the heat of my hands as Fire, the Earth beneath and the Air surrounding it, all coming together under my hands.

My coven prefers having a bonfire at each quarter for warmth. When I work alone, I make the watchtowers out of snow and dress warm. Freeze in beauty, that's my motto.

To make the watchtowers at each quarter, I start with a pile of snow. Now my artwork looks more like Picasso than Michelangelo, so I don't try for more than suggested shapes. Earth (I always start in the north to ground) is a round smooth ball with a tree sketched in charcoal. Air is also round, but lumpy, decorated with swirls of blue water color from an old ketchup squirter full of blue water. If I've managed to find any spring flowers—daffodils or crocus usually—I stick them in the top of the watchtower, around the candle. Fire is as irregular and spiky as it will stand up to, with icicles sticking out like tongues of frozen flame. If I've had a chance in the last two or three days, I've made colored icicles. It's easy to do if you have access to already formed icicles. Take water colors and slowly drip them down the icicle. If you do this over a couple of days, the icicle changes to the desired color. Water is in the shape of a cauldron. I often put an empty #10 can in the center and pack the snow around it. After the snow's frozen, I can either lift the can out, or fill it with colored water.

My consecration ritual is simple, since most of the work goes into preparing the area. My tradition doesn't cast a formal circle on High Days; we simply bless the area. The altar is blessed and consecrated using either an icicle or athame, saying:

> *Bless this Earth in the name of the light. May strength*
> *shine forth from me and bring light unto others.*

*Bless this incense in the name of the light. May knowledge
shine forth from me and bring light unto others.
Bless this flame in the name of the light. May faith
shine forth from me and bring light unto others.
Bless this water in the name of the light. May love
shine forth from me and bring light unto others.*

I then bring each element to its watchtower and say:

Spirits of the _____ (east, west, etc.), *I bring this gift.
Join me in my rites and celebrate the season!*

As I move around the circle and light each candle (13 in all), I say:

The children of light greet you with light.

When the candles are all lit and the watchtowers called, I normally greet the
Lord and Lady with song. I try and write a new song for each ritual as my gift to
them, greeting them by aspect and phase. A typical Imbolg song might go something like this:

*Lady of starlight, Lord of the flame,
I greet you by moonlight, I call you by name.
Maiden of candles, child of the night,
come be my partners, in this Holy Rite.
Oh join me, I pray you, come join in the ring.
By the candle I call you, to dance and to sing.
Lady of starlight, Lord of the flame,
I greet you by moonlight, I greet you by name.*

I don't make candles at an outdoor ritual. Instead, I prefer to make them at
the Full Moon closest to Imbolg, so I can cast the circle in the kitchen.

The thermoses of hot mulled wine or cider are brought out now and we bless
them and drink. Libations are poured, usually by making runes in the snow with
the hot drinks. Dyed, peeled eggs are eaten in silence, while we meditate on the
gift of life that they have given us, and what we plan to do with that gift this year.
Four eggs of different colors are saved to be buried in four different directions
later as thanks.

Thanks are given to the Lady and Lord, and to the watchtowers for joining
us. As I snuff out each light, going widdershins around the circle, I say:

The children of light will carry the light.

The ritual ends in silence. The altar is packed and the area cleaned up without breaking that silence. If the ritual has been done in a public area, the altar is
broken and the circle destroyed so as to not cause problems or sacrilege later. If
in a private place, the altar and circle are left to melt and go back to the Earth on
the next sunny day.

Wife and husband Amethyst and Degan of Colorado are professional horticulturists and have spent the last ten years managing garden centers. They have also contributed numerous articles to Sacred Hart. *Here Amethyst shares with us her knowledge and suggestions for a circle of flowers that first appeared in* Sacred Hart. *It should be an inspiration to anyone who has a little room.*

Creating magickal space with floral color will give you some of the most powerful triggers you could have in a circle. Tending your magickal garden will give you a spiritual lift that can become habit forming. You will find that you cannot help but dwell on the aspects of a quarter as you work. As a coven garden, pun intended, it will create a level of bonding you can't even suspect until you experience it. And I don't just mean with the other people in your group; remember that the plant life is just as alive as you are, and if you want active participation from the plant kingdom all you have to do is open up and ask.

Basic guidelines for the creation of your magickal garden will include the use of both annuals and perennials as well as ornamental grasses for added interest. Annuals bloom all season long, but last only one season and must be replaced each year. Perennials come back each year, but have specific blooming periods. They are usually planted with some thought in mind as to what blooms when, so that when one perennial has finished blooming another has just started to take its place. The Ortho book *All about Perennials* contains an excellent list on the subject. Plantings should be done with the tallest plants either at the back or in the middle of the grouping. Graduate all other plants by height from there. Annuals will usually go in front of the perennials. The annuals will screen the perennials as they fade. The plant lists I have included are just to get you started. Check with your local county extension offices for more plant materials that would be suitable for your area.

This is not an article about astrological correspondences. I do not give a bat's whisker for the astrological correspondences of plants when I am planting outdoors if said plant cannot survive in the so-called correspondence. Ferns may well correspond to the east according to at least one of my references, but if you plant them there they will become "fry babies." Picture, if you can, a plant becoming animated enough to jump up and down and do cartwheels to make a point. This is the impression I get from ferns trying to tell me they belong in a northern exposure if they are going to thrive. If you want flowers, you need *full* sun, or at least an area that gets more sun than shade. Though limited, there are plants that will work. But that would make another article.

My color correspondences are those of my religious discipline. If they are not exactly the same as yours, I will be taking you through the full color spectrum before we're through, and you can adapt this information to your discipline.

The north is probably the most challenging to landscape with flowers, because its colors are green and brown. There aren't too many green or brown flowering plants. Gladioli do come in several shades of green, the bells of Ireland are green and there are bronze mums, but they need an unshaded northern exposure; one that gets full sun from the south all day. Scented geraniums and herbs are predominantly green. They would do well in a sunny northern quarter. Ornamental grasses are another choice. Lady's-mantle (*Alchemilla vulgaris*) needs part shade and has chartreuse or yellowish- green flowers. With a shady northern quarter you can plant ferns and hosta which are primarily grown for their foliage.

At this point, I must digress. I can' t see the north on any level of mind without trees. Considering the crucial importance of planting trees in a time when for every tree planted in the urban forest, four die, and when I know that we need one-third of the Earth covered in trees for life to survive and we're down to forty percent now, my first planting in the north would have to be one or more trees. My ideal north quarter would include at least one tree shading several varieties of ferns and bordered with ornamental grasses like fountain grass which comes in a variety with a feathery pink head and can attain a height of four to six feet, orchard grass which gets to be about a foot tall and is striped green and white, and lastly some lady's-mantle.

White or yellow can be used in the east. I prefer to save the yellow for the south and use it in combination with the other hot fiery colors corresponding to that quarter. An entire garden done in white or just a quarter of one as suites our purpose, can impart a dramatic sense of purity, peace and centeredness. This will be the place to go when you need some refreshment.

White Annuals

Hollyhock (*Alcea rosea*)
Spider Flower (*Cleome hasslerana*)
Sweet William;
    China Pink (*Dianthus sp.*)
Annual Baby's Breath
    (*Gypsophila elegans*)
Balsam (*Impatiens balsamina*)
Moonflower Vine (*Ipomea alba*)
Lobelia (*Lobelia erinus*)
Snapdragon (*Antirrhinum majus*)
Dahlia (*Dahlia hybrids*)
Transvaal Daisy (*Gerbera jamesonii*)
Candytuft (*Iberis sp.*)
African Daisy (*Arctotis stoechadifolia
    var. grandis*)

Sweet Pea (*Lathyrus odorata*)
Sweet Alyssum (*Lobularia maritima*)
Busy Lizzie;
    Impatiens (*Impatiens wallerana*)
Stock (*Matthiola incana*)

Poppy (*Papaver sp.*)
Annual Phlox (*Phlozx drummondii*)
Verbena (*Verbena x hibrida*)
Flowering Tabacco (*Nicotiana alba*)
Geranium (*Pelargonium x hortorum*)
Petunia (*Petunia x hybrida*)
Pansy (*Viola x wittrockiana*)

White Perennials

Yarrow (*Achillea ptarmica*)
Aster (*Aster*)
Harebell (*Campanula*)
Delphinium (*Delphinium*)
Foxglove (*Digitalis*)
Iris (*Iris*)
Beardtongue (*Penstemon*)
Speedwell (*Veronica*)

Marguerites (*Anthemis*)
False Spirea (*Astilbe*)
Chrysanthemum (*Chrysanthemum*)
Bleeding Heart (*Dicentra*)
Baby's Breath (*Gypsophila*)
Peony (*Paeonia*)
Phlox (*Phlox*)
Shasta Daisy (*Chrysanthemum*)

A sample combination of annuals might include hollyhocks at the back of the area because they will be the tallest, followed in descending heights by nicotiana which has star-shaped flowers and a wonderful scent, geraniums, petunias and sweet alyssum. The perennials are trickier for me because I would eventually include them all in the east quarter, but I think I would start with baby's-breath for its airy looking qualities and its ability to tie divergent flowers into a cohesive mass of blooms. Shasta daisies would be next just because they're long-lasting and fluffy, another airy quality! When you start your quarter gardens, they will be longer on annuals and shorter on perennials because it takes a couple of years for the perennials to reach their full size. Eventually, as you add to your perennial collection and it matures, you will have more perennials than annuals and less work because you won't have to plant as many each year.

Masses of red, orange and yellow flowers will make your southern quarter the place you will find yourself gravitating to when your energy levels are low and you need a boost. This quarter has the widest selection of colors and plants. Choosing just the right arrangement for the various colors is going to be half the fun. You might try graduating the colors to resemble the conformation of a flame.

Red Annuals

Hollyhock (*Alcea rosea*)
Ornamental Pepper
   (*Capsicum annum*)
Coleus (*Coleus x hybridus*)
China Pink; Sweet William
   (*Dianthus sp.*)
Blanket Flower (*Gaillardia puchella*)
Snapdragon (*Antirrhinum majus*)
Cockscomb (*Celosia cristata*)
Dahlia (*Dahlia hybrids*)
California Poppy
   (*Eschscholzia californica*)
Gazania (*Gazania rigens*)
Transvaal Daisy (*Gerbera jamesonii*)
Monkey Flower (*Mimulus x hybridus*)

Poppy (*Papaver sp.*)
Petunia (*Petunia x hybrida*)

Scarlet Sage (*Salvia splendens*)
Pansy (*Viola x wittrockiana*)

Stock (*Matthiola incana*)
Flowering Tobacco (*Nicotiana alba*)
Geranium (*Pelargonium x hortorum*)
Moss Rose (*Portulaca grandiflora*)
Nasturtium (*Tropaeolum majus*)

Zinnia (*Zinnia elegans*)

Red Perennials

False Spirea (*Astilbe*)

Blanket Flower (*Gaillardia puchella*)
Avens (*Geum*)
Daylily (*Hemerocallis*)
Iris (*Iris*)
Dahlia (*Dahlia hybrids*)
Cardinal Flower (*Lobelia*)
Peony (*Paeonia*)
Beardtongue (*Penstemon*)

Hardy Chrysanthemum
   (*Chrysanthemum hybrids*)
Cranesbill (*Geranium*)
Christmas Rose (*Helleborus*)
Coral Bells (*Heuchera*)
Blazing Star (*Liatris*)
Bee Balm (*Monarda*)
Poppy (*Papaver*)

Yellow and Orange Annuals

Hollyhock (*Alcea rosea*)
Pot Marigold (*Calendula officinalis*)
Coreopsis (*Coreopsis tinctoria*)
Dahlia (*Dahlia hybrids*)

Blanket Flower (*Gaillardia puchella*)
Transvaal Daisy (*Gerbera jamesonii*)
Balsam (*Impatiens balsamina*)
Stock (*Matthiola incana*)
Poppy (*Papaver sp.*)
Moss Rose (*Portulaca grandiflora*)

Marigold (*Tagetes species*)
Mexican Sunflower (*Tithonia rotundifolia*)
Verbena (*Verbena x hibrida*)
Zinnia (*Zinnia species*)

Snapdragon (*Antirrhinum majus*)
Cockscomb (*Celosia cristata*)
Cosmos (*Cosmos sulphureous*)
California Poppy (*Eschscholzia californica*)
Gazania (*Gazania rigens*)
Sunflower (*Helianthus species*)
Sweet Pea (*Lathyrus odorata*)
Monkey Flower (*Mimulus x hybridus*)
Geranium (*Pelargonium x hortorum*)
Gloriosa Daisy (*Rudbeckia hirta var. pulcherrima "Gloriosa Daisy"*)

Nasturtium (*Tropaeolum majus*)

Pansy (*Viola x wittrockiana*)

Yellow and Orange Perennials

Yarrow (*Achillea ptarmica*)
Basket-of-Gold (*Aurinia*)
Calliopsis (*Coreopsis*)
Leopard's Bane (*Doronicum*)
Avens (*Geum*)
Daylily (*Hemerocallis*)
Poppy (*Papaver*)
Black-Eyed Susan (*Rudbeckia*)

Golden Marguerite (*Anthemis*)
Chrysanthemum (*Chrysanthemum*)
Foxglove (*Digitalis*)
Blanket Flower (*Gaillardia puchella*)
Sunflower (*Helianthus species*)
Iris (*Iris*)
Beardtongue (*Penstemon*)

This may seem like almost too much to choose from, but for me, after spending the last ten years working in greenhouses, the choices are simple. Some plants tend to shout their exuberant love of the sun. Starting with the red flowers in the rear, I would use Mexican sunflowers—they are closer to a red-orange than a yellow. Blanket flowers, Oriental poppies and day lilies or red and red-orange would be next, followed by zinnias in shades from red to orange. Zinnias, like marigolds, pop like firecrackers when they bloom; you can almost hear them. Gazanias would follow in height and color. For the shortest plants, I would use yellow marigolds and then yellow celosia. This approach to color will limit you in the number of varieties of plants you will be able to fit into your color scheme. Another approach would be to use all of your favorite plants, graduate them by height, but mix your colors thoroughly.

Achieving a western quarter that is truly blue and not purple or violet may prove to be an interesting job. There are few flowers that are a true blue. Growers refer to blue, purple and violet flowers as "blue." You may want to buy bedding plants that are in bloom to be sure of the color of the plants that you purchase. This may not be possible as in the case of some perennials like delphiniums, but luckily plant tags are becoming more accurate all the time.

Blue Annuals

Floss Flower (*Ageratum houstanianum*)
Morning Glory (*Ipomea*)
Love-in-a-Mist (*Nigella damascena*)
Blue Sage (*Salvia farinacea*)
Pansy (*Viola x wittrockiana*)

Bachelor Button (*Centauria cyanus*)
Edging Lobelia (*Lobelia erinus*)
Petunia (*Petunia x hybrida*)
Wishbone Flower (*Torenia fourneri*)

Blue Perennials

Harebell (*Campanula*)
Cranesbill (*Geranium*)
Virginia Bluebells (*Bertensia*)
Wild Forget-Me-Not

Delphinium (*Delphinium*)
Iris (*Iris*)
Creeping Phlox (*Phlox*)

Nothing says peace and tranquillity like a solid mass of delphiniums. Average height is four feet, but under optimum conditions they can reach seven to eight feet or more. Irises come in several shades of blue from pale-blue to indigo. Bachelor's-button would make a delicate transitional plant from the more solid forms of the background plants to the dainty forms of the smaller foreground plants. Harebells could work in combination with the bachelor's-button. Petunias now come in a true blue and are next in height followed by ageratum, azure blue pansy, cranesbill and lobelia.

The center of your magickal garden space can be done in several ways. Leave it open so that you have room for an altar and lots of dancing space, plant it in a solid mass of purple and violet blooms or combine altar space with flowers. For a solid mass of flowers, put the tallest varieties in the center and graduate heights from there. With an altar in the center, either plant short varieties on either side of the altar or plant on all sides of the altar leaving paths between patches of flowers to get to and stand in front of the altar. Even, balanced spacing will look best for this. The listing of annuals and perennials for this section is short because you will be using the same varieties of plants as in the blue listing with a few additions.

Purple and Violet Annuals

Canterbury Bells (*Campanula medium*)
Rocket Larkspur (*Consolida ambigua*)
Globe Amaranth (*Gomphrena globosa*)

Heliotrope (*Heliotropium arborescens*)
Sweet Pea (*Lathyrus odorata*)

Purple and Violet Perennials

Aster (*Aster*)
Coneflower (*Echinacea*)
Globe Thistle (*Echinops*)

Lupine (*Lupine*)
Phlox (*Phlox*)
Speedwell (*Veronica*)

For a central area done in solid blooms, I would use delphiniums in the center followed by iris, purple coneflower, aster, heliotrope, petunias, pansy and lastly creeping phlox. To surround an altar in any fashion, stick to the medium to short varieties of plants, and the plants with more compact forms like the coneflower, heliotrope, petunia, pansy, phlox, Canterbury bells, amaranth and aster.

My lists of annuals and perennials came from Ortho's *All About Annuals* and *All About Perennials*. They are an excellent resource for any gardener. But my favorite book on gardening is Dorothy Maclean's *To Hear the Angles Sing*. If you can get past angels being a Christian construct and remember that Ms. Maclean is talking about plant devas, this is the most important gardening book any Pagan could own. Highly recommended reading before you start your spring gardening.

May the Shining Ones of the plant world join you in your endeavors this spring and enrich your lives as they have mine.

In a time when more and more groups are becoming "eclectic," one group, the Coven of the Spiral Castle* in Miami Shores, Florida is strictly Celtic in its teachings and practices.

Lady Dannaea in a "God position," displaying wand and athame.

Initiates of their tradition work with Faeries of both Celtic lands and those of their local environment. The coven is an artists group that places an emphasis on Celtic artistic styles. Lady Dannaea tells us of their work.

The fundamental goal of this tradition (and therefore this coven) is the practice and ongoing pursuit of the ancient religions of the Celtic peoples. We define "ancient" to mean the Celtic traditions before the Viking invasions. The elders of this tradition strive to eliminate all Anglo-Saxon influences.

This is obviously one reason why a working knowledge of a Celtic tongue is necessary for first degree initiation. The second reason is the sacred and astrally powerful quality of these languages.

Our covens consist of a High Priestess, High Priest, and initiated Witches or uninitiated "Pagans." We also have the conventional three degree system.

This leads me to a *very* important point: the structure that I have described in the preceding paragraph is *not* ancient, pre-Anglo, Celtic, and therefore, it is Neopagan as opposed to Pagan, as we profess to be. Any Celtic researcher would know this. The understandable question would be, "Then why do you practice this Neopagan degree system and circle form?"

The answer lies in the practical considerations of teaching potential members in the United States, and in communicating with the American Pagan and Neopagan community.

Firstly, there is a pronounced gap between the knowledge (and often abilities) of the native born Celt and the native born American. Most native Celts have roughly the same level of knowledge and training, and at higher levels than most Americans. Among Americans it is not uncommon to have novices that are nearly experts on Celtism alongside novices that know absolutely nothing about our sect of Paganism. The existence of multiple levels in one Coven necessitates the existence of a degree system on this side of the water. Also, American Pagans tend to have a greater desire for a clear hierarchy than does your average Irishman, for instance.

Secondly, and more succinctly, it is easier for American and English groups to relate to a group with some sort of "conventional" order. Also, unfortunately, there are those who feel that if there is no hierarchy there is nothing "genuine" and, therefore, nothing worth listening to—and we do like to be heard.

The Gaelic word "sidhe" (pronounced "shee") means "fairy folk," and so we are sometimes referred to as a Celtic Fairy Faith. This covers a major aspect of our sect and my Scottish relatives, to cite one example, cared very deeply for these folk. In fact, all the Celts worked heavily with the fairies for centuries, especially during the more magickal, religious eras just before the Byzantine era, around the time of Arthur. Thus, one could well say that our elders have a lot of experience. We have a training system that develops the Witches' abilities to communicate with, and perhaps more importantly, to understand the fairies. A strengthened connection with the fairies, coupled with training from a group belonging to this sect, and a certain amount of astral power (which a person is born with, and that exists as a result of having developed this ability over many lives) results in very wholesome, strong, healing and telepathic powers.

One cannot be admitted for training unless one regularly practices some art form, whether it be dance, music, writing, painting, or some other artistic craft. The process of creating works of art transmutes energy through the subtle-body centers, balancing the person who is constantly being fine tuned and sensitized as a result of his/her training with an experienced group.

Let me say one more word about our coven structure. Later on in the studies of the training group the knowledge and abilities of our members becomes a bit more uniform, and the presence of the initial structure and hierarchy lessens. In initiate covens it is nearly non-existent, with all females acting as high priestess and goddess, and all males acting as high priest and god.

Lady Dannaea (High Priestess) and Lord Endrion (High Priest) of the Coven of the Spiral Castle now give us a Gaelic dance-chant from their circle:

A Bhandia o' na daoine mhaith,
Beannai' mid do oi' che dubh ag' la' niamhrach.
Baili' mid i rince biseach—
Ta sé cosuil leis an corrai'
I gcoim na talu' n do-mharaithe.

I wrote this rhyme-chant for coven use, and what follows is a reasonably accurate translation (Gaelic does not translate very smoothly into English):

Goddess of the Faerie folk, we bless your dark
night and your lustrous day.
We gather in this spiral dance, which is as the
movements in the womb of the Earth.

Lady Dannaea with sword (symbol of the power within a coven), altar, and circle border showing inscriptions in all the Celtic languages, with sacred symbols.

There has been much interest recently in the Native American sweat lodge ceremony, and when we first received the following description, Dan and I were uncertain to which of these chapters on sacred spaces the sweat lodge belonged. We finally decided that the sweat lodge is most definitely an outdoor circle, and furthermore, that the similarities between this Native American ceremony and the casting of a European Wiccan circle are stunning!

A student of shamanism, Robin Marie Linster is also a chiropractor who uses a holistic approach to her own experiences at a sweat lodge ceremony.

Returning to the womb of our Earth Mother is the overwhelming emotion as one enters the Native American sweat lodge. A ceremony for purification, the sweat lodge acts to rejoin us with humanity and melt away the armor we create as we walk through this lifetime. The structure is circular, constructed of pliable branches and covered with tarps or animal hides. The door is kept low to the ground so that entering and exiting become birthing experiences. Inside the lodge is a central pit which will hold the heated rock. Before entering the lodge, prayer bundles (pinches of tobacco wrapped in one of the colors of the directions) are made requesting the guidance and gifts characteristic to that individual direction. These will be placed inside the lodge and ceremoniously burned at a later time. The making of the bundles marks the beginning of an incredible journey that disregards time. Once the ceremony is started, all light is gone save the glow of the Stone People. All of the elements come together in this sacred space to support the expansion of consciousness and demonstrate the synergy of the life forces on this planet. Fire and rock combine to produce the heat for our cleansing. Water is poured onto the Stone People who share the wisdom of time with us through the steam. We perspire, replenishing Mother Earth and at the end of each of the four rounds, the door is opened to welcome in father Sky and release our prayers. Each of the four rounds acknowledges one of the four directions and, in doing so, allows the participants to experience life through different vantage points. As the sweat lodge progresses, one becomes engulfed in the present moment. Even the most skilled of observers cannot inhibit total participation because there is something which innately calls to one's Spirit—a sense that, at this moment, *we are all related.*

The circle as the Mother Goddess, the welcoming of the Sky Father, birth and re-birth, the offerings to the four directions, and the four elements; the stones (Earth), the Fire, the Water and Air (the steam) all have an ancient and familiar ring to those of us who follow the ways of Wicca.

Greta Marchesi, a high school senior, does not follow Wiccan ways, but she does attend sweat lodge ceremonies, and shares with us here her experiences.

As one of the many and varied beings who has been conceived and nurtured on the blood and bones of this planet, I have long felt a silent but pervasive spiritual and physical bond with the land and all that it sustains and proffers. However, as an Anglo-American with a predominantly Christian religious upbringing, I have long found myself devoid of an outlet to explore these compelling forces within myself. Recently, a family friend who had left his position in the medical world several years ago to explore his Lakota-Cherokee roots invited my

A dome-shaped structure of saplings is the frame of the sweat lodge (photo by Rudy Marchesi).

family to participate in a traditional Lakota sweat lodge. To my own surprise, the Native American cleansing ritual of the sweat lodge brought me, with an almost alarming immediacy and lucidity, face to face with the ever-present but hitherto formless visage of my own physical and spiritual American heritage.

On a purely technical level, the sweat lodge can be seen as a particularly hot and muddy sauna. However, functioning on a purely technical and intellectual level was to become for me, despite my resolve to remain detached and objective, an unreality.

Participants sit on a packed dirt floor beneath a low, dome-shaped structure of saplings and heavy blankets. In the center of the floor is a sunken pit approximately three and a half feet in diameter, and my group arranged ourselves in a circle around this pit. Prayer-ties, colorful strings of tobacco-filled pouches that we had constructed earlier, while (presumably) focusing on our innermost desires for the future, were strung between the wooden rafters, making a surprisingly festive display. Later, these thumb-sized cotton pouches would provide any visiting "spirits" with an attractive resting place.

Huddled in our bathing suits and towels on the cold earth, we welcomed the arrival of several large rocks which had been heating in a bonfire for the last six hours. Their temperatures elevated to a point where they emanated an amazing coral hue, these stones soon filled the lodge with a comfortable warmth. Herbs like cedar and sage were dropped on the rocks to emit the smoke which would cleanse the lodge and our physical beings of anything negative that we humans, traipsing in with our towels and problems, had carried with us, and soon our eyes and throats stung with the strangely comforting combination of smokes. As more and more stones were greeted in Lakota by our leader and placed in the central pit, the heat became increasingly oppressive. Finally, when the pit was full and the door was closed to seal us into the now-black womb of the lodge, the heat had reached a peak of intensity which I found to be alarmingly unbearable. Desperation overwhelmed me as I fought to bring my panicked brain to terms with temperatures I had previously assumed to be reserved for deep-frying and imploding novas.

As the sweat washed over my body in a steady stream, I became unavoidably aware of my own pounding heartbeat, and visions of impending cardiac arrest flashed vividly before me. As I struggled to control my hyperventilation, I suddenly became aware of a disembodied voice snaking quietly through the darkness. I focused on its plaintive, rhythmic song, and almost immediately I felt rising within myself a powerful sense of connection and recognition. To my astonishment, I heard my own voice rise to join our leader's chant.

All sense of time and physical discomfort fell away as I immersed myself in the overwhelming cadence of what seemed unquestionably to be the most unadulterated worship I had ever experienced. Even though I had no idea just what I was singing out, there was no question in my mind that these words and the sentiments behind them were the purest and most immediate form of prayer that I had ever offered. Looking inward, I realized that the formidable opponent I had been struggling with earlier had not been the heat, as I had assumed, but rather the weight of my own fear and self-doubt. "Look at what you're holding onto," our

Prayer-ties, colorful strings of tobacco-filled pouches, make a festive display in the sweat lodge (photo by Rudy Marchesi).

leader told us. "Give it back to the Earth." With a sense of relief, I silenced the last mutterings of my brain and let my final inhibitions slip from me into the forgiving red glow of the stone pit. I realized then that there was nothing which I was truly unable to cope with if I allowed myself to exist solely in the moment and maintained faith in my own power as an individual.

As I let myself absorb the magnitude of this lesson, I became suddenly aware of the cool comfort of the earth beneath me. Though it had been present since the beginning of the lodge, I had been too absorbed in my own fears to notice it. Gratefully, I smoothed handfuls of the cold mud over my scorching limbs and pressed my body to the welcome chill of the soft loam beneath me. All but naked, curled face down in the mud, I felt an overwhelming sense of gratitude for and affinity with the Earth, not only for the cool release which was so effortlessly offered to me now, but also for the other natural forces our leader spoke of, the White Buffalo Calf Woman, the west wind and the rising Sun, the azure expanse of sky, the splendor of the hawk, the earth beneath my feet and the multitude of creatures which dwelled with me upon her skin. I was overwhelmed with a sense of unity with all things, a sense of our common origin and essential sameness, and this revelation brought me an unexplainable sense of joy.

The lodge continued, and the door opened several times to give those who needed it a quick break in the outdoors and to bring more stones in to challenge the rest of us. The remainder of time which I spent in the lodge was certainly not effortless for me, but I was able to draw on the strength I had found in the Earth and in the other spirits whose healing presence I had become deeply aware of. As to how long we lay in the embrace of that sultry, inky darkness, I could say hours, moments, lifetimes. It was both infinite and startlingly finite, and when the time approached to re-emerge, we raised our voices once again in celebration, this time singing songs of joy and renewal. As we crouched in the darkness together, each person speaking in turn of his or her experience of the lodge, the feelings of love and compassion seemed almost electric, not just between the individuals speaking, but also encompassing the forces and spirits from whom we had drawn insight and support throughout our journey.

Before my experience in the sweat lodge, my religious encounters had been vague and relatively one-sided, straining earnestly on a pew to be enlightened by one man's interpretation of a religious text. The lodge was something totally different. It confronted me unavoidably with the realities of my own being, and, because of the very physical immediacy of the situation I was forced to look both to myself and to a higher power for insight into spiritual realities.

From the sweat lodge, I emerged with a sense of harmony with nature, a sense of love and respect for the Earth, and a feeling of awe for the overwhelming omnipotence of natural forces. Today, I still find myself conscious of the intrinsic unity and equality of mind, body, and spirit, and I live with the joyous realization of the harmony that exists between myself and all the living, dancing elements which compose the cosmos in which I live.

The beginning of a bonfire to heat the rocks that will be placed in the central pit of the lodge (photo by Rudy Marchesi).

A circular frame of wood with a fire pit in the center . . . no, we are not describing a sweat lodge now, we are describing the wood henge of Gary T. Niall and Kat Clark, priest and priestess of the Tuatha De Dannan. Here Gary tells us something of the construction of the henge as well as some of the more suspenseful moments of practicing the Old Religion outdoors in the suburbs of New Jersey.

The ritual circle is located in the center of the yard. When completed, it will consist of a ritual area with a central fire pit. The perimeter will be ringed with an earthen mound and two shallow ditches. There will be four wooden "henges" in the ring. The whole is basically inspired by Stonehenge. The earthen ring will serve as a sacred garden. Grapevines have been planted on the ring at each of the four cardinal points. The wooden dolmens (or henges) will support these vines. Herbs and vegetables will fill the spaces between the grapes, providing a living ring around the outer edge of the ritual area.

Pouring a libation or lighting a candle out of doors is not likely to draw too much unwanted attention. However, as we have already discovered, it is not as easy to go unnoticed when a full ritual is taking place . . .

We recently had the pleasure of using our outdoor circle for the first time. Not wanting to be too conspicuous we opted for street clothes rather than robes. The central fire was kept very small since the fire pit had not been built yet. Tiki torches lit the four watchtowers. A small slab of stone lying flat on the ground served as an altar. On it were an athame, a bowl of salt water, incense, a jug of apple cider and a pentacle-shaped basket holding a loaf of fresh bread. The only other tools present were five chalices scattered around the perimeter of the circle (each covener having brought their own).

The central fire burnt very well for a while, then suddenly went out. We tried to rekindle it but nothing worked, even the embers died. Moments later two police officers walked into the yard. It would seem that there is an ordinance against open fires in our town and one of the neighbors had called to report us. The officers looked around (to their credit they did not cross the boundary of the circle which had been marked by red bricks) and one noticed the athame on the altar and asked, "Is that a knife?" One of the coveners promptly spoke up saying, "No, that is not a knife, it is an athame!" Both officers seemed to accept this without a second thought then one asked if this was some sort of religious observation. We answered that it was, and he said, "Well those torches are obviously not going anywhere so we will be leaving now. Sorry to disturb you." They left and there were no more interruptions. We thank the elementals of Fire, and the Lady and Lord for putting the fire out for us just in time. It has been decided that there will be no more fires until the fire pit is actually built.

Unless there is total privacy, most rituals will need to be rewritten for outdoor use. There was not enough time to do a re-write before our first excursion into the domain of Nature. Because of this we did a lot of improvising during that ritual. We were pleasantly surprised with how well it all went. Keeping things simple helped. In fact, it is probably best to just "go with the moment," and not make any complicated plans. Following is the Samhain ritual written especially for outdoor use.

Gary Niall hammering in the wooden pegs of the "henge," inspired by Stonehenge.

Set the circle up ahead of time, if possible during daylight. Mark your circle boundaries with stones, bricks, branches, a line of sand, etc. Tiki torches are best for the watchtowers as they give off a great deal of light. However, hurricane lamps or candles inside of lanterns could also be used. (One custom which I started several years ago is to place a jack-o'-lantern at each watchtower. These jack-o'-lanterns are carved with an angry/ugly face pointing outward from the circle to scare off any evil, and a happy face looking into the circle symbolic of the friendly presence of the Guardians.) The altar can be just about anything that will serve the purpose: a flat stone, a tree stump, even the earth itself. On the altar there should be God and Goddess candles (or lanterns), a spare candle, an athame or wand, dishes of salt and water, incense, a jug of apple juice, cider or wine, a pentacle with fresh bread, a basket of apples and a bowl of nuts or acorns. In the center of the circle should be a cauldron or large, dark bowl filled with water, or a small fire (possibly inside a barbecue grill). If you are able to have a fire, wrap potatoes in aluminum foil and let them slowly cook next to it to be feasted on when the ritual is over. A cast iron kettle full of soup could be warmed there also. If there is no fire it may be desirable to have insulated containers of warm soup, herb tea or hot mulled cider. Serve a platter of apples, nuts, hard boiled eggs and salmon (these are the foods traditionally associated with Samhain). Any fruits or vegetables grown in your own garden are very appropriate for this feast also.

Keep Craft tools to a minimum. Each covener should bring their own cup (chalice, goblet or whatever). Only one athame (or wand if you prefer not to use a blade) is needed. It will be used by more than one person, so you may wish to get a new one and have each member help to charge it as a "group tool."

For Beltain and Samhain we cast the circle with everyone already inside and do not allow doors to be cut in the circle once cast. On these two nights we also prefer that everyone take part in the casting of the circle. On Samhain, the Goddess candle on the altar is lit before the circle is cast. The God candle will be lit later.

First, one of the Elders should take a staff and trace the outline of the circle in the soil saying:

I draw the boundaries of this, our circle.
May it be strong in the Lady and Lord.

A covener cuts the circle with the athame saying:

I cut this circle loose from the world of men.
May it be a time and place set apart.

The next covener blesses the container of water:

I exorcise thee, O' creature of water.
Be pure, even as the Lady and Lord.

The same covener blesses the salt:

Blessings be upon this salt.
Be firm, even as the Lady and Lord.

They add the salt to the water, stirring deosil three times with athame or wand, then aspurge the circle using a sprig of herbs or their fingers:

May this circle be pure as the waters of life.
May it be firm as the earth itself.

The next covener lights the incense saying:

I purify this circle with air.
May our thoughts be clear and invigorating.

Incense is then carried around perimeter of the circle. The next covener lights the spare candle saying:

I cleanse this circle with fire.
May all impurity be burnt way.

The candle is then carried around perimeter.

Now the entire group turns to each of the cardinal points to invite the elementals. (There is no need to move around the circle, simply turn in place to face the appropriate direction.)

Coveners, facing east:

We greet thee, Elders, Old Ones of the east.

We ask your presence in this, our circle.

This is repeated at each of the watchtowers, substituting the name of the appropriate direction for the word "east."

Next, all coveners join hands in a circle facing inwards, saying in unison:

We greet thee Old Ones, Lady and Lord.
Be with us here and attend this rite.

All close their eyes and visualize a circle of pure, vibrant white light, a bubble completely enclosing them. Visualize, or feel, the presence of the Lady and Lord. Finally, one of the coveners says:

On this night there is one more greeting which must be extended. For this is the time of opening the Gates of Life and Death. Tonight those who have died are able to return to us once more before they pass through the gates and begin the long journey which lies ahead of them. We welcome all the dead this evening, especially those who were dear to us.

Coveners may at this time extend personal greetings to loved ones who have passed away. When finished, the coveners face one Elder who stands before the altar and says:

This is the night of the Great Celtic New Year. A night of beginnings a night of endings. A time to put behind you that which you would free yourself of. A time for setting forth on new paths. It is the custom among the peoples of the world to make "resolutions" at the time of the mundane New Year. So too would it be appropriate to make such pledges during Samhain. But, be aware that we now stand in the presence of the Old Ones, what you pledge to yourself here, you pledge also to the Lady and Lord, the elementals and the Guardians of the watchtowers. Any pledge made here will become a sacred vow, a geis*. Do not make any resolutions lightly at this time . . . for to break a geis will bring severe consequences.

Time is allowed for those present to make any desired resolutions. These can be made silently to oneself or aloud.

The coveners now sit around the central fire or cauldron, eyes closed, relaxing in a meditative state. One female covener stands in front of the altar facing the center of the circle. She holds aloft the Goddess candle from the altar and speaks for the Lady saying:

I am the All Mother, the Great Creatrix.
I am the ever-changing sea and the timeless earth.

---

*A geis (pronounced "gaysh"—plural, geise pronounced "gaysha") is a sacred obligation or taboo. Geise were common in ancient Ireland. Sometimes the geis would be taken upon oneself, at other times the geis would be placed upon a person by someone else such as a Druid, the King or one of the Fairie folk. Geise could cover anything from not eating a certain type of food, to never wearing a certain color or always doing a particular act upon a particular day, etc. Most New Year's resolutions such as: "I will meditate more often this year," "I will stick to my diet this year" or "I will stop smoking this year," would therefore become geise if those vows are made within the confines of the sacred circle.

From my womb comes all life and nourishment.
In the evening I set the dew upon the grass.
Mine are the gentle mists which rain upon the fields.
Spring waters flow at my command,
and I lead the rivers on their dance to the sea.
Without my guidance, no wave would reach the shore.
I take each seed into my bosom to protect it from the cold.
Then gently break open its shell, allowing it to sprout.
Flowers burst into bloom as I pass.
Corn stretches high to greet me, and fruit ripens at my touch.

You are my children.
Each spring I come forth to renew all living things.
My cool waters provide relief from the scorching heat
of summer.
In autumn I bring forth the greatest bounty of all,
a feast to prepare you for winters famine.
But now the time has come for me to rest,
for my work is done and I grow weary.

At this time, a male covener quietly arises from his seat and approaches the altar. He picks up the God candle. The female covener/Goddess turns to the male covener/God and says:

It is your time, I take my leave.

She lights the God candle from the flame of the Goddess candle, then extinguishes the Goddess candle and places it back on the altar. After this, she quietly goes to the seat vacated by the male covener, sits, and closes her eyes. The male covener now takes the place she vacated in front of the altar. He holds aloft the God candle and speaks for the Lord saying:

I am the All Father, the Dread Lord of Shadows.
Ruler of the forest wild, and the open pasture land.
The vineyard is my sacred domain,
and the craggy mountain my home.
By my leave does the valley hide,
or the mountain boast its peak.
I am the Green Man, Lord of the woodland.
My refuge is granted to each beast, but only for a time.
I taught the farmer to plow, the hunter to kill,
and gave the blacksmith his magic art.
Mine is the shepherd guarding his flock,
and I lead the Wild Hunt.

You are my children.
I am your protector, and your wise counselor.
In times of sorrow I comfort you,
in times of loss I console you.

*During winter's cold, my blanket of snow
covers the sleeping seed.
Then my waxing light awakens the earth,
and ushers in the spring.
In summertime I reach my peak,
and the crops reflect my golden glow.
In autumn I drain all life away,
to prepare the world for its coming rest.
In me all things find their beginnings and their ends,
for I am the Giver of Life and the Bringer of Death.
Without me there would be no rest,
without rest, no new beginnings.
Know ye that death is but a time of rest, a time of learning.
It ends with the awakening of life.
And now the year begins, this is my sacred night.*

The Tuatha de Danann circle in winter.

He quietly places the God candle on the altar, still lit, and joins the others around the central fire/cauldron. At this time all coveners will do a "group scrying."

The most important thing to remember in scrying is that you must relax. The fire or water are focal points, there is no need to stare at them "unblinking" this will only strain your eyes. After gazing at the focal point for a while you may wish to close your eyes, this is fine and may actually help. To scry in the fire, first let it die down until there are only embers to see what will be revealed in the glow. If scrying in water, the surface must be dark and reflective. This may be achieved by stirring a handful of soil (or black ashes) into the water. With a cast iron cauldron (or very dark bowl) this will not be necessary. When done, the coveners will compare notes on what they saw or "sensed." All "visions" etc. should be written down, for only time will tell if they are accurate. Other forms of foreseeing may be used to replace the scrying. For instance, you may wish to read Tarot cards, toss rune stones or use a pendulum or wine glass on a board with the alphabet and numbers on it similar to a Ouija board. The reading of palms or tea leaves or any other form of divination would also be appropriate.

If the group wishes to add anything else to the ritual, now would be the time to do it. However, scrying on Samhain tends to be very draining. It is quite likely that by this time everyone will be cold and tired. If that is the case then it is time to feast! Instead of the usual cake and ale ceremony, place a plate of food and a cup of hot tea/cider near the edge of the circle. This should then be left there until morning for the "Fairy Folk." After setting out food and drink for the Fairy Folk, it is time to feed the humans.

Selena Fox, who described the Witch Tree Shrine in the previous chapter, is High Priestess of Circle Sanctuary in Mt. Horeb, Wisconsin, which will be described completely in Chapter Nine. She tells us here of one of the most important sites at Circle Sanctuary, the Stone Circle.

The Stone Circle is the most frequented and most well known of the ritual sites at Circle Sanctuary. It is located within a grove of oak and birch trees atop a hill known as Ritual Mound.

I first journeyed to the place that was later to be the site for the Stone Circle during the summer of 1983. I climbed the mound and discovered a naturally occurring grassy circle space that was ringed by two types of sacred trees. The place was strong with Earth energy. Immediately after coming upon this spot I knew it was to be the place for the Stone Circle.

The first Wiccan ritual done at the site took place on Halloween night in 1983 just prior to the signing of purchase papers for the land. Jim Alan and I did a Samhain rite there. It was during this rite that we discovered that this place was a gateway to the Spirit world. A radiant white ball of light appeared in the darkness and we strongly connected with the spirits of the land. Since that time, others have reported encountering physically perceptible spiritual manifestations on several occasions. Whitley Strieber includes an account of his experiences at the Stone Circle during June 1987 in his book *Transformation*.

Construction of the Stone Circle began at Yule 1984. Eight of us, including a child, carried rocks and trekked through snow and cold to the circle area. As part of our Yule rite, we placed a large altar stone in the center of the circle and smaller stones to form a fire ring. We lit a small fire and dedicated the place as a ritual site. We started placing stones to form cairns at each of the directions at Spring Equinox 1984 and we continued this during rituals that summer. At Fall Equinox, we began forming the stone ring that connects the quarter points. The Stone Circle was dedicated as a planetary healing place in a ritual just prior to Yule 1985.

The Stone Circle at Circle Sanctuary (photo by Selena Fox).

Numerous rituals have been held in the Stone Circle, including several weddings and child blessing ceremonies. My husband Dennis Carpenter and I were married there in June 1986. A few of the rituals have been covered by the media, including film, television, and press.

Over the years, the ring of stones has continued to grow. The Stone Circle is comprised of rocks, pebbles, boulders, and crystals from all over the world. Some of these have come from other sacred places. The circle also includes a variety of small objects, such as amulets, coins, shells, feathers, and beads. Stones are added to the Stone Circle at most group rituals done there. Individuals also make additions as part of individual meditations.

Contributions of stones and crystals for the Stone Circle are welcome. Stones can be any size. Mail stones to Circle or place them in the circle yourself during a visit (by appointment only). *(See resource page—Circle Sanctuary.)*

The standing stone marking Equinox sunrise point located to the east of the Stone Circle at Circle Sanctuary (photo by Selena Fox).

CHAPTER EIGHT

Outdoor Groves

"No one who has seen the calm water of the lake of Nemi, lapped in a green hollow of the Alban Hills, can ever forget it. Diana herself might still be lingering by this lovely shore, haunting these woodlands wild. In antiquity this sylvan landscape was the scene of a strange and recurring tragedy. On the northern shore of the lake stood the sacred grove of Diana Nemorensis—Diana of the Woodland Glade."

Anyone familiar with the literature that has helped to shape the Neopagan movement will recognize these words as the opening sentences of the great classic *The Golden Bough.* So important were sacred groves to ancient Pagans that Sir James Frazer chose to begin his master work with the description of one.

Ellen Evert Hopman, known in the Craft as Willow, is author of Tree Magick, Tree Medicine *(Phoenix, 1991). In Chapter Five she told us of her coven's Keltrian Druid altar. In this chapter she describes for us the beauty and magick of Crystal Springs Grove.*

Nestled in the hills of western Massachusetts, the Crystal Springs Grove is located next to a fifty square mile wildlife sanctuary. Our visitors include foxes, eagles, possum, raccoon, and white-tailed deer. We've even heard *something* out there that we figure was a bear or a large cat (bobcat? cougar?).

The forest is mostly composed of oak, birch, maple and white pine. The grove itself is a ring of four giant white pine which almost exactly define the four directions, with some young birch and one oak interspersed. There are tobacco ties on the large pines which were placed there by visiting Lakota friends when they came here to do a Full Moon ceremony.

The environment is basically natural except that every spring someone has to go out to clear away the fallen branches left after the ice storms and snows of our region. We did some vigorous pruning in the first year, of small trees that were coming up. Of course we had to dig the fire pit and bring in the large "Mother Stone." The altar is actually a collection of stuff we found at the site—some old cinder blocks topped by an old door. We cover it with a cloth for rituals.

The circle is about forty feet in diameter, wide enough for an energetic morris dance with spectators!

We perform about eight ceremonies a year in the grove, major sabbats as well as cross-quarter days. The grove has also been used for all night vigils, Full

Moon rituals, and initiation rites.

Except for ceremonies with a more "Native American" flavor, most of our rituals have tended to be Druidic in orientation. A typical rite will follow the Keltrian Druid model. We typically begin with a procession from the house to the grove where we sing, chant, play drums, rattles, chimes, etc. until we are in a slightly altered state. Someone generally meets us at the entrance to the grove with some lit sage or other scented smoke and we are ritually "smudged." Needless to say there is no side talking once the ritual begins.

We next call in the four directions plus the center in the Celtic manner (Earth in the east, Water in the south, Air in the west, Fire in the north). Someone announces the purpose of the ritual which is always a combination of the seasonal observation plus whatever magickal focus we have mutually agreed on. We have focused on the rain forests, stopping violence against women and children, protecting animals and wilderness areas, and sending energy to the new democracies in Eastern Europe and other causes.

Crystal Springs Grove in western Massachusetts, Beltane 1990 (photo by Mark Harubin).

We then do a tree meditation in order to attune more fully with the forest around us. Then we ask Mannanan Mac Lir, Son of the Sea, to part the veils that we might have vision into the Otherworld. We ask his assistance in bringing us to the attention of the Celtic deities of the occasion.

The company at Crystal Springs Grove, Beltane 1990. From left to right: Leaf Eriksen, Taig O'Mis-teil (not visible), Moon Dragon, Willow, Steinos (Henry Canby), Dorothy Moon Song, ElkLynn, Windwalker Bear (not visible), and Mathonwy Owens (photo by Mark Harubin).

The three small cauldrons on the Druid altar contain water, earth and smoke and represent the three worlds of Land (Nature), Sea (the Ancestors) and Sky (Deities). We use these to bless the congregation by means of a feather or a tree branch which is dipped in the cauldron and used to sprinkle the worshipers.

In order to keep everyone focused someone then explains the rite in detail and the patrons of the feast (Bridget, the Dagda, Angus Og, Boann, Bile, Danu, Lugh, the Morrigan, etc.) are petitioned to lend their efforts in the work at hand.

We "raise energy" by means of music, dance, singing, recitation of poetry or other creative acts which we dedicate to the Gods. Someone is chosen to send the energy to the agreed upon "target." Divination is then used to see if the offerings were accepted or if the Gods have a message to impart.

Two large chalices are on the altar, filled with water and tree sap or spirits. The chalices are consecrated and passed from person to person in a communion feast. Thanks are then offered to the presiding deities and to the spirits of the directions (if the seer has determined that the ritual has been accepted). Finally Mannanan Mac Lir is asked to close the portals and the tree meditation is reversed. We progress to the house where a potluck feast and good cheer awaits!

Willow with Cerridwen the cat at the forked stream, Beltane 1990 (photo by Mark Harubin).

Gem Caccetta of Gainesville, Florida has been a contributor to Circle Network News. *She and her husband also have created a beautifully haunting and evocative Pagan music album called* Cave Diver *which is available through Lady Slipper Inc. In the following pages Gem tells us not only of the beauty of her sub-tropical grove, but also of the magick of her own initiation.*

I moved to northern Florida from Maine in 1987. After settling in, I began to explore the woods surrounding my home, acquainting myself with my drastically new environment. I wanted to build a relationship with this landscape, feel at home with the palms and pines. I'm sure the grove was always there, but it wasn't until six months later, when I was swept up into the wonder of Wicca for the first time, that I saw the grove for what it was. On that day, when out for a walk, a great blue heron rose out of the stream beside the path. I stopped, taking in the sight of it fully, and then noticed a clearing off to the right. I walked into the middle of it, and at once felt as if I was someplace sacred, magickal, apart. Here, I thought, if I am worthy, I will retreat for my self-initiation. And so it was, a year later, on the afternoon before the Spring Equinox, that I returned to the grove.

The approach to the grove has changed over the past two years, due to humankind's strange drive to build more, more, more. I used to walk out my back door and head east, following a path through the woods, a stream bed crossed the path, and I would run quickly down and up it, turn north, and so on to the grove. Now, the initial path is a paved road. The stream bed has been piped and filled in where it crossed the path. But, when I head north, the path through tall pine trees still exists. The path is fairly clear until forty feet before the grove, where the tall grasses, ferns and shrubs begin to obstruct the path. Looking off to the right, the clearing appears.

Looking into the grove from the west, with a view of the altar in the north (photo by Gem Caccetta).

You enter the circle through the western gate. The clearing, from west to east, is approximately twenty feet wide. Two fallen pine logs, straight and narrow, dissect the space, like two sides of a triangle, making the actual working circle eight to nine feet in diameter. The floor is a carpet of pine needles. Facing the north is a natural Goddess altar, the remnants of a large tree trunk. It stands three feet high, and is covered with lichen, with swelling hips and a cavernous womb (the womb-hole in the trunk created by fire). A powerful symbol, created by Nature for the gate of the north.

Rising opposite Her in the south is a pole, eleven feet high. This tree trunk is narrower than that in the north, fully rounded, and stripped clean. No bark, no lichen—a tall, smooth gray pole, rising out of a spray of ferns. A fitting, phallic complement to the womb in the north. In the west, a small creek trickles (when the stream bed collects rain). A pine forest rises into the air in the east.

My self-initiation retreat began with a late afternoon ritual bath in a small pond/waterfall in my backyard. I offered salt, rose petals, and myrrh to the water. Gently, as I entered the water, I concentrated on cleansing, purifying, forgiving.

With each anointing of my body, I saw the worries washing away. I was made pure. As I walked to the grove, I chanted silently, in rhythm to my steps . . . grace, beauty, perfection.

The natural Goddess altar, with ritual objects, at the north gate of the grove (photo by Gem Caccetta).

My husband was waiting for me there, having put up a tent and placed some candles while I bathed. I approached the circle, and was challenged.

"Who comes to the gate?"
"It is I, Gem Seabird."
"What do you want here?"

I am challenged for my purpose and motives, and my ability to confront the Land of Shadow without fear. In the presence of the Old Ones, I have nothing to fear. In perfect love and perfect trust I entered the circle, and the Guardian of the Gate left me with the Goddess, God, and my shadow.

I placed my offerings at the altar . . . a candle at her womb, and an abalone shell filled with sage. A red cord draped her neck—to be cut to my measure the following morning. I breathed deeply, and settled in for an evening of meditation. At first, I was apprehensive when sounds of humanity filtered through. Was I secluded enough? Would I be left alone? I looked up at the tall pine trees that encircled me, my silent guardians, and felt calm, protected.

When the darkness came, I crawled into my tent, and focused my concentration on a request for a gift from the Moon in my dreams. Send me a flying dream, sweet Aradia.

I awakened, having had my request granted! In my dream, I'm on the ground trying to fly. I get in the air, but not very high, wondering how I can do better. I look up, and see a woman mountain climber, hanging by one hand to the very peak of a mountain. I fly up to her quickly, pulling her up to stand on the peak, and then joyously fly down, diving off the high peak, thrilling to how high I'm flying. I thanked the Moon for this wonderful "birthday" gift, crawled out of the tent, and began the ritual.

Skyclad, I cast a circle. Then, facing north, with arms upraised, I called out this invocation:

This the day, this is the hour,
Cry aloud the Word of Power—
ABRAHADABRA!

By blazing noon or black midnight,
It Is my will to seek the light—
ABRAHADABRA!

Be far hence, all things profane,
From the portals of this fane—
ABRAHADABRA!

Eleven-fold the right I claim,
By the virtue of this Name—
ABRAHADABRA!

Faring forth adventurous,
By the pathway perilous—
ABRAHADABRA!

Fend me from the fear of fear,
By the voice of the Chief Seer—
ABRAHADABRA!

Show within the darkness night
The Extension of the Light—
ABRAHADABRA!

Great Ones who have gone before,
Speak the blessing evermore—
ABRAHADABRA!

Here between two worlds am I,
Child of the earth and sky—
ABRAHADABRA!

Deeply do I dare assay
One step on the mystic way—
ABRAHADABRA!

Aid me from the realms above,
Powers of Life and Light and Love—
ABRAHADABRA! (1)

I passed a small vial of myrrh through the altar candle flame three times, then anointed my forehead, breast, and genitals with an X, saying "Let the mind be free, let the heart be free, let the body be free." Next, I took the cord from the altar, measured myself from head to toes, and cut the cord—"Let the body be free." I measured around my forehead, making a knot at the measure—"Let the mind be free"— and again around my chest— "Let the heart be free." The cord was consecrated and charged by holding it above each of the symbols of the four elements, imagining the power of each element flowing into it. It was raised to the sky, lowered to earth. I breathed my energy into it, kissed it, touched it to my heart, and tied it around my waist. Then, kneeling before the altar, I repeated the following invocation:

By night's dark shade, and by this ritual hour,
Most ancient of the Gods, on you I call.
Remembrance of past lives in me awaken,
That day's delusion no more shall enthrall.

I claim my life, my liberty, my light,
Part of all life that flows eternally.
I am the microcosm of the Whole,
Kindred of star and stone and greenwood tree.

Awake in me the power to do my will,
Kindle within me love's eternal flame.
Accept me as your own, a Pagan soul,
O Powers of Life, that did this Cosmos frame. (2)

I wrapped a blanket around me, and sat to meditate. At the end of this period of stillness, I rose, re-lit the sage and smudged the circle again, raising it high at the four directions. Returning to the altar, I repeated this affirmation:

I am unique. There is no one else exactly like me. And yet I am One with the whole of Nature.

I have the right to be what I am. My essential Self is divine and beautiful. I have the right also to be better than I am, that the outer manifestation may be more true to the inner reality.

Beloved Pan, and all the other Gods who haunt this place, grant me beauty in the inward soul, and may the outward and the inward life be at one. (3)

I began to whoop and holler, danced deosil around the circle, clapped and chanted the names of the Gods and Goddesses, rejoiced in being naked and free and a *Witch*. When out of breath, I collapsed, and enjoyed the beauty of the space. Eventually, I closed the circle, and began to pack up. Soon my Prince of the Sun appeared, with a libation (juice and seltzer!) He took his Dark Maiden out of the Land of Death, and reborn, we ritually made love in celebration of Eostar—offering our energy to all growing things, to a healed planet.

And so the grove remains, a place I can always go to for meditation or ritual. The beginning stages of this article took place within a circle cast in the grove, under the lightest sprinkling of rain. I love this spot, but know I must remain detached, as the developments creep closer and closer. It is a far different world we Pagans live in today than that of our ancestors. How many unknown sacred spots have been bulldozed? Let us seek them out while they remain, and raise our voices in joy and appreciation within them! Blessed be!

References

(1) Valiente, Doreen. *Witchcraft for Tomorrow*. Custer, Washington: Phoenix Publishing, 1978, pp. 160-161.

(2) Valiente, pp. 161-162.

(3) Valiente, p. 162

Brigid Hagan of upstate New York, who told us of her altars, both indoors and out, now shares with us her recollections of the grove of her childhood.

I spent the first 20 years of my life growing up on a farm in western New York State. At my birth in 1944, the farm was about 250 acres of working dairy herd, corn, wheat, oats, and pasture land. My first memories are of the earth and out-of-doors . . . being lifted high, high up to the big flat backs of the team of workhorses, Prince and Bill. We had chickens and pigs, and in the days prior to artificial insemination, a huge terrifying bull. I was always aware of the cycle of life, nature giving and taking away. Birth, life and death and rebirth were commonplace and very much taken for granted. Certain animals were raised as food for the family. Dairy cows were for milking and reproduction.

Later on, the Angus and Herefords were for slaughter. (My sister and I named one Harvey, and he turned into a pet. We've had a rule since that time, "Never make friends with your food." I've given up eating red meat, as an adult.)

All seasons were beautiful at the farm. There was a grove of trees, a "mini-woods," which was in a field used as pasture. It was about a half-mile from the house. It was a sylvan spot, with areas which filled up with water in the spring and served as birth places for tadpoles and various insects. It was the home of squirrels, chipmunks and all kinds of birds. Occasionally a family of red foxes would live there, although the local hunt club (fox hunters), kept the population moving in our area. There were huge boulders in a couple of places, and I used these as meditation and thinking spots. One of the boulders was slanted, and I was able to lie back and see the sky through the leaves of the overhead trees. There were all kinds of trees, too . . . wild cherry, maples, oaks, tall poplars and bushes and shrubbery. The area was round as if in a natural circle. There was a sandy path all around the perimeter and a few through the center of the grove. My sister and I would take our friends around and around the paths . . . making up stories of Indians who had lived there . . . and Faeries . . . any kind of nature story we could think of, we impressed upon our little friends!

I think that summer and fall were my favorite times in the grove. Walking up the lane on a hot afternoon in the summertime was magick! Buzzing of insects and the vibrations of the earth put me into a special mood, so that by the time I reached the "thinking rock," it was rather trance-like. The rock, now that I think about it, was like the home of an oracle. That was the spot I'd go to "receive messages," and to ask questions. I don't remember actual voices, but certainly there was a feeling which permeated that grove of trees and that rock that I was drawn to.

I especially was drawn to the corn fields, whether in late summer when the corn was high and green and smelling "corn-like," or later, in the fall . . . that dry, crackling, musky scent filled my nose and head with thoughts of Halloween and fall . . . the fields were a sacred space for me.

I remember taking my horse, Toss-Up, to the grove to ride around the perimeter. The wind was strong and it was very cold (probably late November). He was prancing around and shaking his head and mane . . . it was enervating, exciting! I couldn't put a name on it, but *magickal* comes to mind today. The grove was a place I *always* visited when I needed to cry or be alone.

Tairie and Jim of central Pennsylvania, whose 4-year-old son, Erin, has his own altar, share with us here their grove and the joys of their Beltain celebration.

We live on the edge of a large field and it gives the illusion that our yard is larger than it really is. We take advantage of this little used field for our outdoor rituals. It is a grove that is rarely traveled by other neighbors and the cows that winter in it provide company and fertilizer for our garden.

We have used the highest point in this grove for Moon rituals but choose a spot closer to our house to plant our Maypole. The readying for Beltain starts about a week before when we start to cleanse the area. As we prepare and cleanse the area with broom, water, salt, and incense, we look upon the space as a young woman, budding and sensual, readying her for her equally eager partner. The different birds that live on and around the field leave beautiful feathers when they preen in the spring. These are gathered at this time.

A few days before Beltain, we have a separate ceremony for the Maypole. Within a circle cast with candles, the pole is anointed with oil. We use linseed oil perhaps laced with patchouli. The wood is dry after the long winter and absorbs the oil quickly. It takes a few coats of oil and a lot of rubbing before it is fully saturated. Everyone involved then takes large pieces of beeswax and coats the pole by rubbing and chanting their wishes of fertility for the following year.

On the morning of Beltain, the first thing we do (including our cats) is run to the grove and bathe in the dew. Being in central Pennsylvania, this is usually a chilling and invigorating experience. After dressing, we then collect flowers from the field and surrounding wooded area, thanking the plants that we take them from. These are used to decorate the top of the Maypole, used to mark the edge of the circle, made into wreathes to be worn by ourselves and guests, and put into May baskets.

"The pure joy of May Day celebration," with Taerie, Jim, Erin and friends of central Pennsylvania.

We take the Maypole into the grove and with music and happiness we allow the earth to take in the pole. The ground is usually (except in the dry 1988) moist and yielding and the one foot deep hole is lined with 4 stones to steady the pole. After the earth is packed around the base, we send up a cheer along with a crown of flowers and colored ribbons to top the Maypole.

All attending bring their own ribbon, the color symbolizes something that person wishes to grow for themselves in the following year. Whether it be a new job or state of mind, if the dancers choose their own ribbons they then see their personal hope mesh and take form during the weaving dance.

There is much laughter, visiting, and merrymaking afterward between Pagan and Christian and atheist guests. We are as diverse as the foods we bring to share yet we all come together on this day to enjoy the start of the year's fertile season.

Many other circles are cast in this grove throughout the year but none are as colorful and full of love as our Beltain celebration.

A grove need not be a grouping of trees. Hex artist Nan Conner of Exton, Pennsylvania considers her herb garden and its adjacent dogwood tree, a grove where she has had some interesting contacts with the animal spirits.

Nan Conner's grove/garden from the front (photo by Anastasia Kean).

My herb garden has always been a sacred space for me. I began it over five years ago, digging the first beds while I was pregnant with my daughter. She was born in May, and I worked the garden through that summer while she slept, shaded by the dogwood tree. The main part of the garden is around 27 by 40 feet, which takes up the front of the house, with smaller patches making their way around to the back. Over the years I have built it, layer upon layer. It is my connection to the Earth Herself, and the turning of the seasons.

The thyme garden with Pooka (age 7). Part of Nan Conner's grove (photo by Anastasia Kean).

The south side is the "working" side. This is where I grow vegetables and annual herbs. I've experimented with small space gardening, as well as companion planting. Each year I try a little something different, but the herbs are my first love.

The bulk of the garden is dedicated to all sorts of perennial herbs. Each year I try to add new varieties, learning the myths and lore of the herbs as I've gotten to know the plants themselves. My only problem has been space requirements of each plant, and then planting the beds. What I had not counted on was the fact that each of the plants seemed to grow about twice the expected size. If the instructions were that the plant would need 18 inches of space, I've learned to give it a full three feet. It's hard for me to believe that one six-inch mugwort plant planted five years ago was the mother to a twenty-foot hedge. The garden is such a wild place, well-meaning friends have warned: "Better be careful. People will think you're a Witch!"

Under the dogwood tree of Nan Conner's grove/herb garden, with Tobie (age 15) (photo by Anastasia Kean).

I've tried to use the garden to teach my children about the changing seasons. In spring we watch the crocuses coming up. On Beltane, we go into the garden to find flowers to take into the house—this year violets and Johnny-jump-ups. On the Summer Solstice we marched out in a small procession to align the sundial, then held a vegetarian barbecue. Mostly, we do simple work—weeding, watching the plants grow and change, harvesting.

Each year something a little different happens within the garden. One year it was a rabbit who took up residence, digging her den in the middle of the culinary patch. The next, a bird built her nest in the young maple tree, and we watched her raise her young. This year, we've been watching the life cycle of the praying mantis unfold.

I first noticed the mantis last summer. It would have been hard not to notice an insect four to six inches in length. Every morning for months we were greeted by a mantis hanging on the living room window. He would be gone by noon, only to return the next morning. My daughter got into the habit of wishing "Good morning, Mr. Bug!"

Each day I would sit in the garden reading or writing, with the kids playing nearby, and each day the mantis would come to me.

Each time I entered the garden, they seemed to seek me out. Three at a time, seven at a time; one day I counted fourteen in one place. Since that summer was when I had also begun my shamanistic studies, I paid attention, and wondered about it.

One day, one of them managed to get trapped, getting caught in the window screen trying to get into the house. After freeing him, I walked him back to the garden, and laughingly asked, "Are you guys trying to tell me something?" and returned him to the bean patch. The next day, they were all gone. No more on the window sill, none sitting next to me in the garden. If I went looking, I found them still there, they just no longer sought me out.

When I mentioned this to a shaman I met, he told me he felt I was being "stalked" by the mantis power. When I spoke to them, I entered their world, so they stopped stalking. Another shaman told me they might be spirit helpers, but I'm not sure yet. I just feel at this point, they wished to convey a message, I accepted it, and things went back to normal.

Over the winter, I studied the lore of the mantis. The word mantis means "prophet," or "diviner." The insects are widely believed to have supernatural power. In England, one name for the mantis is "soothsayer." In some parts of rural United States, they are called "Devil's horse." Part of the mystic comes from the posture of the mantis, forearms reverently folded in an attitude of prayer as it stalks its prey. It also is capable of staying motionless, or taking up to an hour to cover twelve inches in distance. At other times, it advances, swaying rhythmically in an almost ritualistic dance.

In parts of Africa, the mantis is a figure of great power and legend. To some, it is regarded as creator of the world. The mantis is also a shape-shifter, able to take various forms, including a hartebeest (a type of antelope) or a human. Barbara Walker, author of *Woman's Dictionary of Symbols and Sacred Objects*, sees the mantis as a symbol of woman power, since the females grow larger then the male. She also equates them with the crone aspect of the Goddess, because like some spiders, the female will attempt to kill the male after mating.

Over the winter, I discovered seven mantis egg pods scattered throughout the garden. One was right by our front door. This is the one we watched in hatching, hundreds of small pale mantises coming into the world. Over the summer, we've been able to watch them grow, greeting them like old friends when we meet.

The magickal powers and symbolism of trees naturally become a part of the place where they grow. Professional horticulturist Degan, husband of Amethyst who creates circles of flowers, describes for us how he created a sacred grove on a suburban property.

It's time for Pagans to come out of the closet and into the yard. If you are weary of setting up sacred space staring at a painted sheet of dry wall, read on. Your sacred grove is as close as your own back door, you just have to figure out where it's all gonna grow.

Landscape design is a fairly straightforward process. Designing to accommodate the special needs of an individual's spiritual path while maintaining the elements of good landscaping is a little more complex. Fortunately the process of design sorted it all out for me, and it will for you too. Let's look at that process.

Designing is the simple task of defining needs and desires, and incorporating those elements back into a cohesive whole. If you hire a landscape architect to design your yard, that person will probably begin with an interview to determine those needs. It gets pretty personal, the landscape has to fit your lifestyle. Will the yard someday have to accommodate children? Do you have any allergies? Do you party naked, outdoors, with ten or twelve close friends every Full Moon? These things have to be addressed if the landscape is going to work for you.

This was a design nightmare, a nondescript ranch house placed on too small a lot (only 3500 square feet) positioned on a severe slope. The slope rises diagonally from the southwest (low point), over five feet to the northeast. The site determines one set of needs; due to the limited amount of space, plant material and slope, terracing was in order and the grade must be properly addressed to avoid drainage problems.

Ah, but these are mundane problems compared to the second criteria. The homeowner is a solitary in the Craft. His work relocates him every five or six years and the house will be on the market long before the landscape is mature. The client is very concerned with ecology and conservation, and the landscape must improve the energy efficiency of the home. These are our second criteria: the client does not worship with a group, so the required space for outdoor work is not as great (or he would never have bought such a dinky yard!), because the house will be for sale in a fairly short time the landscape must reflect modern good taste (a concrete pentagram in the front yard may turn off less broad minded prospective buyers), and as stated above, the landscape must reduce the energy consumption of the house (this should be a design criteria anyway).

The last concerns are the most obscure. What determines a sacred plant? Aren't they all? What direction should they be placed? Why should a water-loving tree be placed in the west where it will dry out the fastest? What plant materials not listed as traditional are useful in a sacred scape, and where there exists a discrepancy as to what goes in the north, for instance, do I consult my high priest/ess or my landscaper? I don't think there are any set answers to these questions. As a greenwitch and nurseryman, I offer you my thoughts on these problems.

If you are placing plant materials in your landscape to honor the Lord and Lady (a noble pursuit I believe; I've dedicated much of my life to it) every care should be taken that they are located where they thrive, and not suffer. I am aware of no traditions where knowingly torturing plants is acceptable. Likewise with selection of plant materials; if it doesn't grow here, don't plant it here. Plants can do wonders for inspiring a feeling or mood. In general, I place conifers and other "woodsy" (timber) trees north; airy (lacy or fern-like) plants east; plants with hot colors (red or orange foliage) south; and watery plants (if the site will allow it) in the west. The names of the plant varieties may influence placement also. (Could you put a flame amur maple anywhere but the south?)

So this is how I balanced all these concerns into one difficult-to-fit landscape. A windbreak of conifers was planted in the north on the upper trace. The fir trees placed there will aid in winter heating by blocking the cold north wind, and the trees will get good drainage (important to most needled evergreens) by being planted at the highest point of the landscape. Underplantings were made of "northern lights" rhododendron should the client forget that this is, in fact, north. The view from the back yard is directly at the terrace, earth thus rounding out the symbolism for that direction.

To the east I planted nothing. If you look in that direction you "see" . . . air. Planted in the northeast and southeast are airy plants—staghorn sumac (great name!) and skyline honey locust. This would be a great place to locate some tasteful wind chimes, too.

In this design, the south looks and sounds hot . . . but it isn't. Large shade trees placed in the south and southwest offer natural cooling in summer. After dropping their leaves in the fall the house will still be warm in the winter sun. Thoughtful placement of trees in the whole landscape has created a microclimate around the house that will greatly reduce utility bills (you'd be *amazed*), and makes the house more comfortable year round. Crimson King Norway maple retains red foliage from spring through fall, with this evocative name, it is planted due south. The barbecue was used in the south of the back yard.

West had unique problems. It is a narrow area, the house needed shade there, and plant materials need to be west correspondences. Tall shrub willows were planted as a hedge due west. The grade of the yard diverts additional water to them during rain and watering, and a solid privacy fence runs the length of the hedge, offering shade to the planting itself. A garden pool was placed west in the back yard.

The gate in the northwest leads to the alley, offering passage into the sacred space in keeping with the clients particular tradition. Front yards are public places. Only you, me, and the home-owner need know that the plantings were chosen with magickal correspondences. The plantings are tasteful (color-coordinated even!), and should improve the value of the property far more than the cost of the materials.

The back yard is private use area in a landscape. The client may do what he will there in seclusion thanks to the privacy fence and the plantings themselves which block visibility into the yard. The raised terrace in the north, wind chimes to the east, barbecue south, and the pool in the west complete the symbolism for this special place. Yet the comfortable design of this landscape might appeal to the most fierce fundamentalist should he ask to purchase the home when the current owner leaves it. Pretty neat, huh?

Landscape design is a combination of inspiration, intuition and common sense. Compromises must be made to make it all work, but if you define your goals beforehand, you should be able to address all your needs to some degree. If not, keep working on it. I laid out the blank plot plan by incorporating some of the most difficult components that I have encountered in ten years of doing this sort of work professionally. I wanted to illustrate just how much can be done with a problem yard, even in the middle of the city. The most tragic thing I encounter (and all too frequently) in my work is a poorly designed landscape that is beginning to mature. Hardy plants under stress from being badly placed, or perhaps worse, healthy plants getting too large for the space allotted for them are the wages of poor planting. We can do so much better!

Fall is statistically an excellent time to plant nursery stock. Survivability is very good. Nurseries in temperate parts of the country should begin running clearance sales on their trees and shrubs rather than invest the time and money it takes to over-winter the plants in their containers. Plan now for fall planting and you can rescue some good plants (and your budget) from a tough winter. Often the plants will be priced less than the nursery paid for them (look for 50% off sales). If the nursery offers a winter guarantee on the plants (a few still do), you are definitely money ahead on winter plantings.*

Here Degan is joined by Gary T. Niall in solving the problem of creating sacred space within the confines of a small suburban sub-division. In their backyard, with the wood henge circle (described in Chapter Seven) in the center, in the corner opposite the Lady Shrine (described in Chapter Six), Gary created the Solar Grove dedicated to the God in his aspect as a solar deity.

A cozy little cottage nestled among sacred trees, the front yard is a garden of earthly pleasures—roses, wisteria, iris, hyacinth, lilacs, daisies and much more. The back yard is a peaceful, private world for meditation and worship. This is the house my wife and I dreamed of. The reality which we moved into was a far cry away. The small ranch house was in a sad state of neglect. The front yard contained two small bushes (a yew and a juniper), nothing else. There was no privacy in the back yard, which was littered with rubbish and broken furniture.

At this time we have been in the house slightly more than a year, and there have been many changes. (The house itself needed a major overhaul, but I will not get into that here.) In the front yard we now have a clump of white birch trees, a poplar, and holly. There are also roses, azaleas, rhododendrons, barberry and pyracantha. A stone bench under the birch trees, and another of wood and cast iron near the front steps, both invite one to stop and rest for a moment. It is a friendly, happy area.

The back yard has seen even greater changes! Slowly but surely, our private sanctuary is becoming a reality. The first thing that I did was to let the borders grow wild. Weeds, grasses, overgrown bushes and trees have joined together to form a natural "screen," hiding this paradise-to-be from the outside world. Besides offering privacy, the lush growth also provides plenty of shelter and safety for birds and small animals. Eventually the entire back yard will become a miniature wildlife refuge. There will be an assortment of trees, shrubs, fruits, berries, herbs and flowers. many robins and other smaller birds have begun to feed here

*This article first appeared in *Sacred Hart.*

already. One of the neighborhood cats has claimed the evergreen grove as her favorite resting spot. Luckily, when she is here she tends to lie in the sun napping, and thus does not attack the many birds. This past winter a baby rabbit began frequenting the yard. When leaving for work in the morning, I would often find him asleep on the front steps.

Last year rabbits were not exactly at the top of my hit parade. They kept nibbling the rue plants right down to the ground. This year I edged the rue patch with landscape ties, and covered the ground with root mulch. Certainly this presents no real barrier to the rabbits; however, they have stopped nibbling the rue which is now over two feet high. Perhaps they got the message; there is plenty for them to eat, without taking the few plants which I grow for my own use.

There are now many "magickal" spots in our yard. From a six foot tall Goddess statue to a six inch long protective scarab, from gardens filled with numerous herbs to a lone, sacred rowan tree (my favorite), every corner holds another mystical delight, another treasure to behold. This sanctuary contains three sacred areas: the Gods' (or Solar) Grove, the Lady Shrine and the circle. I will describe the Solar Grove here.

In our hereditary Irish Tradition (Tuatha De Dannan), the arrangement of the elemental directions and their colors are different from those which most Pagans are accustomed to. We place the feminine elements of Water (blue) in the north and Earth (green) in the east, while the male elements are arranged with Fire (yellow) in the south and Air (red) in the west. This works very well for us. However, it would be best to stick with the directions and colors with which you are comfortable when designing any sacred areas for your own use.

In the southwest (male) corner is the grove—dedicated to the Father God in his aspects of Solar Deity and Lord of Forests and Nature. This is a wild spot, full of trees, evergreens, wild roses, overgrown bushes, brambles and dense weeds. An upright, wooden post, in the center of a small clearing, represents the male fertility concept. The trees currently in this grove came from several sources: two spruces were Yule trees of years past. (We prefer live trees for Yule. Each year's tree will be planted in the grove. When there is no more room, we will begin donating these live trees to other Pagans, families, parks, etc.) A hemlock and a spreading blue juniper were purchased, a small yew was already there. I salvaged thirteen wild cedars from land slated to be bulldozed for construction, and eight of them are in the grove (the rest are at the Lady Shrine). Two acorns which I gathered in the late winter were planted indoors in peat pots, sprouted, and later transplanted to the grove.

During the winter, the grove is a palette of cool greens and blues. The needles of the spruces, cedars and yews refuse to die, a reminder that the God is not dead, but resting. A mass of bright yellow forsythia blooms are the first sign of spring in the yard. Growing on the edge of the Solar Grove, they blossom into a mound of living sunshine, symbolic of His renewing strength.

During the summer months, the life giving flames of the Sun are represented by the reds, oranges and yellows of marigolds and day lilies, while the giant sunflower lifts its golden solar disk high into the air in honor of the God. As the Sun's energies wane with autumn, there will be mums the color of dying embers:

deep reds, bronzes and burnt oranges. Finally, the warmth of color will be drained away as the cold of winter falls over the grove once more. Now the world settles down to rest and renew its strength, the first step in preparing for next year's season of growth.

Since we have a circle area for rituals, the Solar Grove and Lady Shrine are used mainly for personal devotions and meditation. Periodic devotions could be performed daily, weekly, monthly, or whenever the time "feels right."

On the four great solar festivals, we honor the God by placing, in the grove, a lantern containing a lit yellow or gold candle. The lantern prevents the wind from blowing out the flame, while at the same time ensuring that the candle does not start a fire should it be tipped over. It is placed there at sunset on the day before the festival and allowed to continue burning until sunrise. This devotion could be performed more often by placing the lantern in this same spot every Saturday night, since this is actually the beginning of Sunday, sacred to the Solar God. (In the Irish tradition, we follow the ancient Celtic belief that darkness comes before light, therefore the day begins at sunset.)

Place the lantern upon the altar, a flat-topped stone or a patch of bare earth. Light the candle saying:

> *I light the sacred flame.*
> *The spark of life, a beacon of love.*
> *Its gentle glow a pale reflection*
> *Of the light of the Solar Disk.*
> *Let it be a reminder, through the dark of night,*
> *That His knowledge and love are with us always,*
> *Guiding, protecting, teaching.*
> *And with the dawning of the new day,*
> *May its warmth greet our God,*
> *Welcoming Him into our hearts and lives once more.*

Upon arising the next morning, go to the grove, lift the lantern towards the east, and greet the rising sun personally. For this a simple, but heart felt "Good morning Lord," or "Blessed Be" will do. If, however, you feel the need for something more elaborate, you may use the following or similar words:

> *Greetings to thee oh Lord.*
> *With joy are you welcomed to this grove.*
> *Spread the loving warmth of your rays*
> *Upon the flora and fauna of your shrine.*
> *Let your light sparkle in the morning dew,*
> *And dance among the leaves at noon.*
> *Create warm pools of light,*
> *To ebb and flow around the cool shadows as you pass.*
> *Caress all here with your life giving touch,*
> *Healing wounds and nurturing growth.*
> *And grant the light of your wisdom unto me,*
> *That I may follow in thy path.*

A vigil lantern in the Solar Grove. The stone mortar and pestle is used to hold incense. The wooden pole represents the male fertility principle (photo by Gary T. Niall).

May you be with me this day,
As guide and shepherd, protector and friend.

Leaving a lantern to stand "vigil," on days sacred to the Sun, is one way to honor the God. Following are suggestions for several other ways of paying homage.

One of the simplest, and perhaps oldest ways of honoring a deity is to pour a libation. Wine is the most traditional libation, yet there are many other drinks which would be equally fitting for such an offering. You may wish to use honey mead, ale or even the juice of citrus fruit. Nectars (such as pear or apricot), have always been sacred to the Male Divinity. In addition to pouring a libation, you may wish to drink a toast or leave a daily goblet of drink on an altar (very often when passing by, you will be greeted with the fruity scent of the wine, reminding you of the presence of the Old Ones).

It goes without saying, that the fruits, vegetables and grains of any harvests would be suitable items to place in the grove, or on the altar, as a token of your gratitude for the Sun's life giving rays. Flowers may also be left as offerings. Try to choose blossoms in colors appropriate to the God. For instance, in our tradition reds, oranges and yellows are sacred to the Solar Deity, while shades of forest green, earthy browns and sky blue would honor the Lord of Nature. Or, you might prefer to plant a tree in the God's name.

Of all the offerings possible, probably the best offering you could make is yourself. Spend a little time in your grove or before your altar, "being with" the deity. Meditate. Talk to Him. And best of all, *listen to Him!*

Glen and Geri from Spokane who told us of their portable altar describe for us here their reasons for visiting a natural grove, and share with us an ancient blessing.

My wife and I find rest and meditative energies abound at a "grove" of trees on property owned by her brother, near Priest Lake, Idaho. The property was an old homestead before being purchased by him just after the Korean War. Approximately 54 acres, much of it is seasonal marsh land. The places which are particularly energetic are used by the deer and other creatures as bedding spots. I would recommend any spot where the tall grasses have been bent down by the local animals as one where magick will occur. Any morning when we are up there, one can look out the window of the house and watch the animals early browsing and feel renewal. Getting in off the main road is difficult in the winter but we plan to spend more time there in 14 years or so after I retire. We perform a ritual of thanks there similar to Scott Cunningham's blessing for a garden.

Most of the areas I grew up with as a child are now overpopulated urban sprawl. Wall to wall houses, the sacred nature gone. It has become difficult to find the private places the soul needs to refresh itself. My wife and I have only emerged from the Wiccan "closet" in the last two years. Point of fact, we discovered a name for the religion we practiced after reading Cunningham's book *The Truth about Witchcraft*.

I will leave you with the version of "Blessed Be" I heard many years ago:

Blessings for thy feet,
they cause us to meet.
Blessings for thy knees,
they bend at the altar.
Blessings for thy hands,
they prepare the sacred anointment.
Blessings for thy lips,
they call the Holy Spirits.
Blessings for thy heart,
for the love shared with all.
Blessings for thy spirit,
may thee rejoice in total freedom.

A tree in the grove, hung with mosses, from Glen and Geri of Spokane, Washington.

Sometimes a single tree can have such great magick that it might be considered in the same way as a grove. Jan of Toronto, Ontario, Canada, tells us of her experiences as a solitary practitioner, and of the solitary oak tree that she came to regard as a sacred grove.

Although I have been "practicing" only a short time, I realize now that, deep down, I have always been Wiccan. I was always fascinated with stories of "Witches." At least once a year, in high school, I centered my history project on the "Burning Times." I have always been concerned with the welfare of animals and nature. People frequently comment that I have "a way" with animals. I am always happiest when I am at our cottage in the summer—surrounded by the magnificent old oaks, hawthorns, maples and pines. Birds of all species feed at the different feeders we have out and, just this past summer, tree swallows decided that the hollow bumper of our mobile home would make the best nesting place!

My mother was (and still is) very much involved in the Anglican (Episcopalian) Church. Although she is aware of my religion, she is not happy about it and says that she feels it is "not healthy." However, she allows me my Full Moon rites and sabbats.

The person who surprised me the most was my husband. He is Portuguese and was brought up in the Roman Catholic faith. Although he doesn't go to church, he still considers himself "Christian." He has been most supportive in my decision to become Wiccan. When my mother would ask why she could not disturb me (my husband still has to "run interference" for me during my rites), he said that the best way to explain it was that I was in my "church"!

Just after I confided to my husband my decision to practice Wicca, I came home from work to find a beautiful, hand carved and polished pentagram. The next day I came home to a solid oak chest, complete with protective runes and my craft name engraved in it. It has brass hinges with chains and a lock to which I have the only key. He has since forged the blade for my athame and taught me to engrave on wood so that I could make the handle. He has promised to make a proper altar for me for either my birthday (early December) or Yule.

He has been present during Full Moon rites and often asks me questions so as to better understand. If only everyone could be as open-mined as he is.

One thing that surprised me this past year was the fact that, prior to my self-initiation, plants refused to grow for me. Since reading *Wheel of the Year* (and others), and adopting (and adapting) some of the rites, my garden has gone *crazy*! From 3 tomato plants I receive over 60 pounds of tomatoes—in fact, they were still blooming in early November! Carrots and onions that had very little care, other than that of the elements, were over-sized and more than our family could eat (even after canning!). Everyone kept asking me how I did it. I told them that, other than weeding and watering, I left them to themselves. I didn't feel it wise (with most people) to tell them that as they had been planted, I had asked the Goddess to watch over and care for them when I was unable to.

My husband often asks me what made me decide to finally practice the Craft. I tell him that since I made the decision, I am more at peace within myself and it feels like I've "come home." The thing that I don't tell him is this:

Every day as I drive to work on the main freeway, there is an old oak (it must be at least 150 years old) on a merge median. As I pass it each day, I send it feelings of love, respect and warmth. One day, when I was particularly "stressed"—traffic was heavy, I was 15 minutes late and I was trying to figure out how to tell my Catholic husband that I wanted to be a Witch—I forgot to say "Hi" to the old tree. As I passed it, I glanced up and felt this great flood of warmth and love spread through

Jan from Toronto would say "Hi" to the old oak on her way to work.

me. I felt (and still do) that the tree was sending this back to me because I needed it. As I continued to enjoy the feelings that were still resonating throughout my body, I went back to the task at hand—telling my husband of my decision. This time, however, there was no stress associated with it. Only a feeling of calm surety that this was the right thing for me to do. I still pass by this tree everyday, although he sleeps now, and I look forward to spring when we can give each other the love and support we do.

To cowans, I know, this sounds a little strange. It might even sound strange to "would-be Wiccans." I remember when I was reading a book by a Wiccan who had said when you feel very stressed and wound up, to sit with your back against a tree and that, after a moment or so, you would feel the stress draining from you and being replaced by feelings of calm and peace. I remember thinking, "Oh sure. It's just your subconscious doing it. It can't really be the tree." So you can imagine my surprise when the old oak did this for me and we weren't even touching! It helped to teach me that things I wanted to believe are true, really are—if I let them (or even if I don't).

Since my self-initiation, I find myself more at peace—with myself and others. I know that there is still much for me to learn but I know that I will be the better for it.

The one thing that I long for, though, is my own home so that I can have a shrine that will not be disturbed (one indoors and one out) and a room that is set aside for rites only.

One day, hopefully, we will have children and I look forward to teaching them the Craft (along with Christianity) and the respect and love for Nature.

Four months later, Jan wrote to us again.

Unfortunately, I have some sad news. Last Monday, as I was driving to work, I noticed something wrong—my tree has been cut down! I couldn't believe it. Now I'm really glad I took the picture. I was going to stop on my way home from work that evening to get some branches but they had already been cleaned up.

Not all stories need to end this way. For every tree cut down, many more *must* be planted.

When Pauline and I moved to the old stone farmhouse in western New Jersey in 1976, our first order of business was to restore and reclaim the building and its surrounding grounds. The old homestead had seen much better days.

The original human inhabitants of the area, the Leni Lenape Indians had ancient hunting grounds on this property, they set up encampments along the ridge/hill facing south where they could be close to fresh water and game. The colonial pioneers of the mid-1700s cleared the lands of rich forest for their log homes and for farming. By the early 1800s our homestead saw the rise of the industrious peach business. By the turn of the century, the Peach Kingdom, as it was called, died due to disease, insects and Southern growers. Once again the farm adapted to change by becoming a dairy farm and turning the old orchards under with the plow. After the Great Depression, the farm and grounds were completely run down, depleted and in ruins. By the time we found the house, large maple trees were growing through the walls and foundations, and the grounds had become a forest of poison ivy.

While we were completing the restoration of the house, our gardening spirit never lapsed. We started a large vegetable garden, orchard, vineyard, herb gar-

The Grove of Faunus in winter at Flying Witch Farm (photo by Dan Campanelli).

den and wildflower/fern garden. By 1979 we had finished the house and gardens, leaving only a 1-acre tract unused. It was a prime location on an upper section of hill directly behind our home and orchards, facing south (the place that was once the old Indian camp site). Until now the neighboring farmer included it in his annual plowing and planting of over 300 acres, that had been subdivided from our property years ago.

At this time Pauline and I decided to use this last acre to grow trees to be used for firewood. After having the property plowed for the last time, I planted over 400 cuttings of fast growing hybrid poplar trees. All that first year I hand weeded, watered and nurtured the little one-foot plants. For the next few years I cultivated as we watched the trees become a small forest of young 10-foot saplings.

Each spring we counted new varieties of birds nesting in the trees and migrating through them in the fall. There was also constant evidence of wildlife taking up residence in the little wooded lot. By 1985, we knew that we could no longer see this area as a firewood forest, but would continue to nurture it as a wildlife sanctuary. We named it "New Forest" after the area in England famous for Witchcraft. It had become a refuge for hunted animals who had no place to hide in the open farm fields. Today among the 40+ foot poplars other varieties of native trees have taken hold, including maple, sycamore, wild cherry, an undergrowth of honeysuckle, wild roseberries and sumac with their bright clusters of red berries glistening after a snowstorm. A herd of white-tailed deer now reside there and in spring give birth to their fawns. Raccoon, red and gray squirrels, rabbits, opossum and even a red fox reside there. Ring-neck pheasants that are released by a local hunting club on the back farming fields in the autumn, take cover in New Forest, and in the spring the drumming of ruffed grouse can be heard. Nests of well over a dozen varieties of birds can be seen including orioles, eastern kingbirds, kinglets, mockingbirds, cardinals, doves and even a pair of red-tailed hawks and a great horned owl and ladder-back woodpeckers.

In the spring the morning air is filled with bird song, and speckled fawns browse in hazy summer afternoons. In autumn an antlered buck may be glimpsed, and in the dead of winter, the only time I allow myself to walk through New Forest, I can see the foot prints in the fresh snow of the multitude of forest residents. New Forest is alive with the magick of Nature throughout the living year.

We had decided to dedicate this grove of trees to the God Faunas, the Horned God of Wild Creatures and to the Spirits of the animals who dwell there now and who were hunted there in the past.

Pauline and I prepared a ritual, and on the day that the Moon was new in January, I went up to New Forest and performed this rite. We prepared for the ritual by placing large stones as markers on the center of each side of the square acre. On the southern side of the forest, facing north, nature had already provided a flat stone that protrudes from the slope of the hill.

Then, beginning at the southern point (which is the only practical way to enter New Forest), I defined the boundaries of the grove with the tip of my athame. When I had returned to the stone at the southern point we made an offering of Yule log ashes and addressed the Guardians of the South:

O Spirits of the South
Whose element is Fire,
We ask that you protect this grove
And those that dwell within it.
Let it be a sanctuary of safety
For the Wild Children of the Mighty Gods.

The "Sorcerer" on the southern stone marker of the Grove of Faunus at Flying Witch Farm (photo by Dan Campanelli).

At the stone in the west we made an offering of a vial of herb-scented water and repeated the enchantment, addressing the "Spirits of the west whose element is Water."

At the stone in the north we left an offering of a semi-precious stone, and I addressed the "Spirits of the north whose element is Earth."

At the stone marker in the east we made an offering of stick incense (which I only lit because there was an inch or two of snow on the ground) and spoke the same enchantment addressing the "Spirits of the east whose element is Air."

Two steps past the stone in the East, I found exactly what we had been looking for, a small menhir or standing stone about three feet in height. We had planned to find a stone of exactly those proportions to place just behind the flat stone in the south. So to complete the ritual, I carried the menhir back to the point in the south where I stood it in the spot that the Gods had given it to us for, and here we completed the enchantment of the grove with the words:

> *O Lord Faunus*
> *Horned God of the Hunted,*
> *We your servants*
> *Ask that you accept this grove*
> *That we dedicate to your honor.*
> *Let it be a sanctuary of safety*
> *For the Wild Creatures of your domain.*
> *So mote it be!*

As the Moon waxed to full, Pauline and I completed our plans for the Grove of Faunus. On the menhir/standing stone, Pauline painted a copy of the "Sorcerer," from the Cave of the Three Brothers in Ariage, France (Upper Paleolithic ca. 16,000-10,000 BCE), depicting a shaman covered in the skin and the antlers of a deer.

We placed the marker stone in the southern most point of the Grove of Faunus on the top of the hill, where it can be seen from all points of our property. This marker is now our statement of dedication to hold sacred this place, and protect the animals that dwell there.

Sometimes on summer nights when the Moon is dark and all is quiet, when we gaze up at the Grove of Faunus from our back porch, we can see the glow of campfires on the ridge of the hill, and silhouetted against the fire glow, we can almost see the Leni Lenape as they go about their chores. And we can smile knowing that within the protection of the Grove of Faunus, these hunters and the hunted can dwell together in peace.

CHAPTER NINE

Outdoor Sanctuaries

Magickal runes and ancient glyphs are still discernible beneath the growth of moss and lichen on an old stone wall and strips of colored cloth fly from the thorns of a hawthorn tree. The Goddess stares through the eyeholes of a mask that hangs in a tiny shrine to her honor, and Nature Spirits dance in the shade of a rowan tree.

For the purposes of this chapter we shall define an outdoor sanctuary as an area that contains more than one grove, shrine, altar, circle, or other magickal space. By this definition, Flying Witch Farm is a sanctuary, so let us take you on a tour of the many magickal places that surround our home.

Like many an 18th century house, ours is built very close to the road. Originally a wagon track that once bisected the old farmstead, the road is now our property line. The old farm has been subdivided and the meadow across the road, where in the winter of 1778-79 "sixty cavalry horses belonging to George Washington's troops were wintered and returned in the spring in excellent condition," now belongs to someone else, but horses still graze there.

As you approach our house from the road and step up onto the porch you will be facing a shrine of sorts. Here, between the two front doors (a peculiarity of the local "Country Georgian" architecture), an annual ritual takes place. On the night of Imbolc an offering of buttered bread is placed on the old red butter churn there, and before sunrise the following morning the spray of evergreens that adorned the front of the house since the beginning of Yuletide are removed to be replaced by three ears of corn—one white, one red and one black—to symbolize the return of the Goddess from her winter's sleep.

Just inside the doors a Pilgrim century table stands before the parlor fireplace, its polished oak surface, now covered by a small Persian rug, is the altar for all of our indoor rituals. In the keeping room magickal herbs hang drying from the smoky beams above the kitchen hearth and above that is the studio sanctuary where herbs and feathers, candles, books and tools are stored, spells are cast, and magick is made.

But this is a tour of the magickal places outside of our house, and:

I am a Witch, and to me this is the law.
From where I enter in, from there must I withdraw.

So let us step back out of the front door and to a small garden in the corner

---

of a fence just to the right of the front porch. Here is a small shrine to the God in his aspect as a God of Fertility and Rebirth. Here, embraced by the branches of a weeping hemlock and shaded by the bronze-colored leaves of a star maple, stands a small menhir we call the King Stone. The King Stone came to us a few years ago in a magickal way that is in keeping with its symbolism as the God of Resurrection.

Several years ago, Dan began building for me a small building to house my large collection of seashells, minerals, fossils, etc. Our plan was to build it of board and batten over field stone to match the other out buildings on the farm, The first stage was to dig a trench for the footing and foundation of my mini-museum. All the while he dug Dan kept asking, "Where will I ever find enough stones to do all this?" Neighboring farmers granted us permission to take the stones pulled from cultivated fields and thrown into hedgerows, but each trip only brought back two or three stones, and at that rate the foundation would never be finished. Then, as Dan dug the foundation trench, he suddenly encountered stones—cut stones like our house is built of—and some of them still mortared together. Apparently, Dan had dug down to the foundation of an old farm building that had long ago been burned and forgotten. There were all the stones we'd ever need to build a foundation up to thirty inches above ground—and they wouldn't even need to be carried any distance! But among these stones were two unlike the others, too oddly shaped to be of any use in building. One was a large flat slab with a natural hole in it, the other, the tall phallic King Stone. Once resurrected from its tomb four feet underground, we erected the King Stone as the center piece of the small corner garden, with one foot of its three and a half feet of length still in the underground, and surrounded it with plantings that symbolize rebirth. There are snow drops at Imbolc, crocus and tulips at Eostre, and at Beltane the King Stone is surrounded by dwarf and standard jonquils. All offerings to the God, libations of wine and some of the Lammas loaf, are made at this menhir, and on Beltane morning a special ritual is performed.

On May Day morning we walk out across the dew soaked grass to the King Stone, carrying with us some cakes and wine from the previous night's ritual and the wreaths of flowers and laurel that were the focus of the ritual. These we place one at a time over the King Stone, first the wreath of laurel leaves (in this case, cherry laurel), saying words like:

> *Lord of the Forest green is your crown*
> *Many be your children.*

Then placing the wreath of wild flowers and fruit blossoms over the King Stone so that they encircle its base we say words like:

> *Now enter the Circle of the Lady*
> *So life may be renewed.*

Continuing around to the back of the house we next come to the herb garden. An old rede tells us, "Cast your circle at a crossroads," and this solar or Celtic cross is the basis of the layout of the Magickal Herb Garden. Here where the two brick paths would intersect, a circular path of bricks surrounds a ring of chives and at the very center of this circle is a beehive, another symbol of the Goddess. It is within this magick circle of herbs at the base of the beehive that offerings are made to the spirits that inhabit this garden, and where the herbal portions of many a charm and spell is buried. In this garden culinary herbs like sage and thyme, basil and lovage grow among medicinals; southernwood, feverfew and agrimony. The ingredients of Witches Flying Ointment, hellebore, foxglove and aconite mingle with herbs that give color to the fabric of life, indigo and woad for

A chaplet of flowers surrounds the King Stone at Flying Witch Farm (photo by Dan Campanelli).

blues, madder and coreopsis for reds, coltsfoot for green, and almost anything for yellow. And throughout the garden grow the herbs of magickal power, wormwood with the power to banish evil, mugwort with the power to enhance psychic ability and bring prophetic dreams, rue with the power of protection, periwinkle with the power to enhance far memory, and many, many more.

The powers of all herbs wax and wane with the seasons and the Moon. By Lammas the majority of herbs are reaching their peak and are beginning to flower. This is the time of the Wort Moon, and as the Moon waxes to full so do the magickal properties of the herbs. On the day that the Wort Moon is full we will do a ritual harvesting. Using a knife that has been consecrated for this purpose, a circle is inscribed in the earth around the base of the plant to be harvested. Then pointing the knife directly at the center of the plant we say words like:

Spirit of (rue) grant me your power of protection
To aid me in my magickal work.

Then, with as swift and painless a cut as possible, the necessary portions of the plant are severed. Finally, when the harvesting is complete, offerings of water, fertilizer and incense are made.

The Stone Altar in the Faerie Garden at Flying Witch Farm (photo by Dan Campanelli).

The herb garden lies neatly tucked into the L, formed where the large stone portion of our house joins the older wooden portion. This wooden section, originally a log cabin, became the summer kitchen. Here in its huge hearth summer meals were prepared and in its ancient bread oven the weekly loaves were baked. For this reason this room is often chosen as the site of our Lammas rites and the

Corn Mother and Her son, the sacrificial God of the Grain, symbolized by the Corn Sun Wheel, are carried into this room in procession at the time of the sabbat.

From the back door of the summer kitchen a path of moss covered stepping stones leads to the vegetable garden. This path also bisects a small garden filled with native wild flowers, ferns and Nature Spirits.

When we first purchased the old farmhouse in 1976, this spot on the shady north side of the house looked more like a tropical swamp than anything else. Enormous ostrich ferns, planted perhaps a hundred years ago, grew five feet tall in the always damp soil. The then dilapidated summer kitchen, a crumbling stone wall, and the stone house itself all coming together at right angles to one another form the alcove that delineate this Wildflower-Faerie Garden.

As the stone house was restored and the summer kitchen walls rebuilt and painted, native wildflowers were collected and planted in this small shaded garden whose environment suited their needs so perfectly. Dutchman's-breeches that carpet the forest floor for miles along the Delaware in Bucks Co., bloodroot from the wooded hill up the road, jack-in-the-pulpit from near the old log cabin of a Pennsylvania German powwow doctor. Many of the giant ostrich ferns were shared with friends to make room for new plantings, a red trillium from a friend in Vermont or the endangered pink lady's-slipper bought from a professional grower.

Ancient magick symbols adorn the stone wall at the back of the Faerie Garden at Flying Witch Farm (photo by Dan Campanelli).

I used to see Nature Spirits as a child. I no longer can, but now we both sense their presence here. To acknowledge this we began painting ancient symbols on the stone wall at the back of the garden. These signs and symbols, some as simple as a Solar Cross or spiral, some from traditional pysanky, the decorated eggs of Pagan Eastern Europe, some runes and some designs more primitive still, were painted on the surface of the stones in purest white or life-giving blood red oxide. Now as weather washes away these signs, and mosses and lichens add their own designs to the ancient symbols, we have made it a part of our annual spring rites to renew these powerful magickal markings, and add a new one or two if so inspired, to celebrate the ever returning season of spring.

Offerings of apple blossoms for Mother's Day at the shrine to the Goddess at Flying Witch Farm (photo by Dan Campanelli).

Flying Witch Farm at the Winter Solstice (photo by Dan Campanelli).

The year wheel turned once, then perhaps once again, and Dan and I decided to plant a rowan tree at the edge of the woodland wildflower garden to add its dappled shade to the area and its protective magick to our home. Its bare branches in winter, white blossoms in spring, green leaves of thirteen leaflets in summer and red berries in autumn seemed to symbolize the turning of the wheel of the year, and so this tree in the wildflower garden became incorporated into another of our traditions. Each year at the time of the Summer Solstice we construct a Sun Wheel, or solar disc, of grape vine or some other similar material, and adorn it with naturally dyed gold streamers, rooster feathers, bright yellow flowers or other symbols of the Sun. This we hang high above our Midsummer altar as a reminder that at this sabbat we are honoring the God in His aspect as the Sun God at his height of power. During this ritual we burn the old Sun Wheel on the Midsummer fire, and afterward we hang the new one high in the rowan tree.

At the base of the rowan tree, beneath the nodding heads of Solomon's seal, with a back drop of Virginia bluebells, we arranged a small altar, a dolmen of a slab of stone placed on top of three small elongated boulders. The slab of stone that forms the top of the altar is the one with the naturally formed hole in it that Dan found along with the King Stone. Here offerings of colored eggs are made at the Vernal Equinox, rose petals at Midsummer, bread and ale at Lammas, and cookies and soda any time. These offerings are all made to the Spirits of Nature. We took it as a very special sign of favor from the Gods when, during our Beltane rites one year, a small fledgling robin, symbol of the God of the waxing Sun, still speckled-breasted, fluttered on to the stone altar, and after a few minutes flew for the first time, and perched on the Sun Wheel in the rowan tree.

In a small alcove formed by the house itself joining the summer kitchen, safe from the eyes of strangers, hangs a mask of an "Aegean Goddess." Below, a small classical bracket shelf serves as an altar. Here offerings are made to the Goddess Herself—wine, flowers, and the fruits of the season. From Her vantage point above the altar the Goddess in Her various aspects gazes out through the eyeholes of the mask at the strange symbols painted on the stone wall, at the woodland wild flowers as they bud and blossom and fade each in their own time, and at the small stone altar in the shade of the rowan tree where flower-faeries dance and play.

Eventually we decided to dedicate the garden as a sanctuary to the Spirits of the woodlands. On the day of the New Moon following the Vernal Equinox, just as the new spring growth was beginning to emerge, we lit joss sticks of sweet incense. With the athame, the boundaries of the garden were defined in the same way as a circle is cast. Then the garden was asperged with a pine branch dipped in spring water to purify it and banish any negative presences. The guardians of the four directions were invited and asked to guard this wildflower garden. Then the awakening spirits of the woodland ferns and flowers and other creatures were told that they were welcome here and safe in this garden dedicated to them. As we asperged the place where each species grew we visualized it in full leaf or bloom saying words like:

> Spirits of the Maiden Hair Fern
> Welcome to this garden.
> It shall be a sanctuary for you.
> So mote it be!

Round and round we went welcoming trilliums and tradescantia, spleenworts and lady's-slippers, toads and dragonflies.

When we had finally finished we declared the garden dedicated to the Spirits of Nature and the Faerie Folk. We left an offering of cookies and white wine on the stone altar, and left the joss sticks to burn sweetly away in the cool damp earth.

The following day a dogtooth violet, that we had planted almost ten years earlier, bloomed for the first time.

As we leave the woodland garden to the Faerie Folk we walk up the slope past the vineyard and through the gate that leads to the orchard and sheep pasture. Poised above the cedar shakes of the old smokehouse, Hecate, our flying Witch weather vane, protectress and mascot, squeaks rustily in her socket as she points her broomstick into the shifting breezes.

Adjacent to the smokehouse, no longer used for the smoking of meats, but only for the storage of gardening tools and animal feed, are the sheep shelter and the chicken coop. While we call our home Flying Witch Farm, it is not a farm in the sense of a place where animals are raised to be butchered for food, let alone sacrificed. "An it harm none," is the law that is practiced here. It is a farm in the sense that, as our ancestors did, we live in harmony with the Earth and Her seasons, and in turn the Earth supplies us with all of the fruits and vegetables we need to preserve and store for winter, the grapes for wine and the herbs to give flavor and magick to our lives. The animals also contribute.

Dan and Pauline, with Samantha kissing Willow (photo by Kevin M. Guyette).

The sheep give us fleece to be spun into yarn for magickal cords or warm woolen sweaters, and the chickens provide a steady supply of eggs. The hens, all named Morgana, and the roosters, both named Merlin, as well as the "chicklets" and the sheep, also provide another by-product which helps to produce the hugest tomatoes and the most enormous pears.

Beyond the smokehouse and animal pens rises the grassy slope where the sheep, fat and friendly Rowena, wild Rowan Bucket-Head, and sweet little Willow graze contentedly in morning mists and lengthening shadows. At the crest of the hill stands a menhir upon which a copy of "The Sorcerer" from the Cave of the Three Brothers in Ariage, France has been painted. This menhir marks the entrance to the Grove of Faunus, the one-acre wood lot set aside as a sanctuary for wildlife, and consecrated to the Horned God of the hunted, as described in the previous chapter.

Walking back down the eastern side of the slope, through the orchard, where in spring the trees all blossom pink and white, we now pass trees laden with fruit. At the center of the orchard is one tree, a stamen-Winesap, which is becoming gnarled with age, and which has abundantly produced the sweetest apples, in good years and in bad. This is the tree, this tree of Avalon, that we will wassail at Samhaintide.

At the foot of the orchard is a corn crib originally built at about the same time as our smokehouse, in the early 1800s. This corn crib however, was not originally built on this property. How it came to be here is typical of a life ruled by magick. One beautiful spring day, a few years ago, while driving through the magnificent Buck County countryside, Dan and I began to notice the old corn cribs and thought one would look great at Flying Witch Farm. So we went from farm to farm inquiring if any of the corn cribs, obviously no longer in use, would be for sale, and wondering how we would ever get one home in our tiny jeep if it was. Corn crib hunting became a summer preoccupation, but no Bucks County farmer would part with his slatted structure.

Then one afternoon antique dealer friends came to visit and Dan suggested going to a neighbor's barn sale. There, in our next door neighbors barn, Dan discovered a disassembled corn crib. And it was for sale! Dan and our neighbor agreed to a barter and the corn crib was at Flying Witch Farm that very evening!

Dan spent the next months reassembling the old hand hewn beams whose mortise and tenon joints fell perfectly into place, and finally attaching the slatted sides. This building has become for us a symbol of the way the Gods grant our wishes—no monkey's paw, no contracts—just simple requests granted simply. And so for this reason, and because of the close association between the corn crib and the Corn Mother, we plan to someday make this a shrine to the Goddess in Her aspect as the Earth Mother or Demeter, but just how, we haven't decided yet. Perhaps soon She will tell us.

Just below the corn crib is the vineyard, an area sacred to Dionysus. Here in winter the trunks of the vines, gray and twisted with age and pruned to a minimum, seem to symbolize death itself and in spring the rapid growth of the spiraling vines are the promise of rebirth. In autumn the vines will be hung with bunches of grapes, black and juicy, which will undergo a transformation and become a fluid fit to fill the sacred cup.

Like the corn crib, the vineyard is a sacred place, but one that has not yet been ritually consecrated.

Following the hedgerow down past the vineyard we come to a huge and ancient hackberry tree. Hackberry trees are a species of tree that is very likely to produce a peculiar growth called a Witch Broom, and trees with Witch Brooms are traditionally favored by the Faerie folk. This great old tree shows no signs of producing Witch Brooms, but if it ever does, the Faeries won't have to come from very far away.

At the end of the hedgerow, where it meets the main road, stands a hawthorn tree, a wishing tree that is a home to Faeries. This magickal tree, laden with white blossoms at Beltane and plump red berries in autumn, is adorned with brightly colored streamers placed there for wishes made, all the year around. Each strip of colored cloth was placed on a long black thorn one at a time while a magickal charm was spoken. There are red streamers for health and vitality, light green for growth and fertility, purple for mystical knowledge and blue for peace and protection.

As we leave the magickal hawthorn tree and follow the fence along the road back to the front porch, where we began this tour of Flying Witch Farm, we have tread a circle deosil, and it is now complete. Here where they once were hunted, butchered and their flesh hung to cure in hickory smoke, animals now graze and give birth in safety. Where colonial ladies once baked their weekly loaves of bread, we now make offerings of the Lammas loaf, and where walls built by men in days gone by once crumbled and decayed, now Faeries dance and wildflowers bloom.

After living in New York City for a while, Micha de Luida and William Oleson have returned to the New England countryside where they are creating a Pagan sanctuary.

When I met my husband he was living in an "Iron-Age" hay house. It cost $200 to build. The animals lived in one side and helped to heat it. Sod roof with flowers, dirt floor, mud walls, ferns growing out of the living room floor. Far out! That was in New Hampshire. He was a hermit in a swamp. Many Devas, Nature Spirits, were there on that land.

Vermont is a rich, fertile, green, mountainous place. I have been dreaming of starting a "Pagan-New Age" center for years. A place where (for free) people could meet, exchange ideas and worship freely Mother Nature and Her Consort. Our place is called Great Mother's Love Nature Center*. It is located in the northwest corner of Vermont. We chose this land for its beauty, openness, and wonderful springs. These springs are all in ley lines running southwest to northwest.

Last year my husband started building a reflecting pool on our small spring-fed brook. The pool is located under an old apple tree. It is cool and shady on hot summer days.

Our shrine will be for the "Lady of the Waters." We will spend years planting flowers, clearing brush, feeding birds and rejoicing at Her side. Deer, bear, and small forest animals may drink from the pool.

This year I am reclaiming the "Virgin Mary," as the Goddess again. She will be known as Mari (pronounced Ma-ree). I am taking a statue of "Virgin Mary" and painting her skin blue, clothes fire red and giving her a mate consort.

The "Lady of the Waters" will have passion and drinkable lusty waters from mountainside springs.

We are building a traditional Pagan/Baltic/Norway style Polish-"Eastern European" log house with bow roof. We will also be building a few yurts, stone huts, and "Iron-Age" buildings.

We dedicate our lives to the Spirits of the land, water, sky, Sun and Moon. We dedicate our blood, sweat and tears to make our life work with Nature, to protect Her as our birth Mother, as a child, as a very dear heart beating in the universe.

We put our wholesome energies into making Great Mother's Love Nature Center a meeting, gathering, loving place where folks of all kinds may worship the Goddesses and Gods in a beautiful, graceful and peaceful environment. We dedicate the future to our children and all the others of the world.

Uttermost is 19.3 acres located on the top ridge of the very first foothills of the Appalachian Mountains in southern Ohio. The property is a very large hill surrounded by cliffs and valleys with no frontage on any road, having a half mile of private drive to the house. The owner, Dr. Dan, due to his incredibly high IQ, has been invited to be a member of "The International Society for Philosophical Enquiry" and is presently the only U.S. member of "The Dark Lily Society" from London.

My father bought Uttermost for $5,500. in 1960. Land was so inexpensive in that area then that the farmer/owner threw in an old tractor and disks and a very old house, "for storing tools." Nobody was interested in helping father clean up the year's worth of garbage or helping him cut wood and mow, except me. Then when my mother refused to "live way out in the country," I decided to move into the old house. I wanted to live with natural systems so I didn't put in all the modern "conveniences." I rebuilt the stone root cellar for food, I put the old potbelly stoves back in order and fixed the chimneys. I enlarged the reservoir in the spring house and laid pipe to the stone root cellar for a shower and clothes washer, and piped it upstairs for a sink to wash dishes. Then I rebuilt the old outhouse. I was determined to use as little power as possible and to live close to the land so that it could communicate with me. Later I built a 70 x 40 foot pond next to the house to catch the water from the fine artesian springs that come from the hill there.

The pond is our sacred pool. During meditation I have had it visualized as going to the center of the Earth. It absorbs and carries away negative energy and one cannot go into it without a marked improvement in attitude. Even during an argument, if the people arguing will just get into the water, they suddenly wonder what they were angry about.

The tree next to the house has appeared to me in meditation as a great serpent or dragon. It is, to me, a strong guardian Earth Spirit. It has a short thick trunk which grows in a "corkscrew," and all the limbs are very long and wrap around the tree in the same direction that the trunk turns. It's quite a spectacular tree, and I'm quite thankful for its spirit choosing to live with me.

All in all, the entire area around the pool is developing into a Zen garden. A Zen garden is not important so much for its finished self but for the enlightenment and insight one gains in its construction and care.

Over the years we have always had a large solstice fire on top of the hill. Since we are so remote, we are usually skyclad. We have fires in the same place for other holidays and if the weather doesn't cooperate, we have a fire in the fireplace in the kitchen.

Summer Solstice fire at Uttermost.

I acquired a state minister's license for the convenience of people that wanted to get legally married but who didn't want to put up with hiring someone that didn't believe the way they did. Weddings were always large parties.

A few years ago I started a music festival there. The large upper field on the hill was used for camping and parking and I built a stage in the woods near the cliffs at the north end of the property. I built the stage with huge old sandstone blocks and hand-hewn timbers from old barns. Seating for the stage was on old farming terraces and I bought and moved a railroad crew building built in the 1850s to be used to sell food. I featured bluegrass music as it was the purest folk form I could find. But too many of the patrons drank a lot, so the program was allowed to stop.

All of Uttermost seems to be a rather powerful place. Once a friend brought someone with him when he came to visit me. The guy sat in the living room for about ten minutes and then got up and left saying "I don't know why but I can't stay here!" Another time another friend was flying over in a small plane and later came to see me. He said that neither he nor his passenger could look at the place from the air. He said it was as if the land itself was saying, "Don't look here, look away! Go elsewhere!" Many people have commented on the feeling of power there, some have said ley lines intersect there.

For the future, Dr. Dan plans new festivals oriented toward alternative religions, holistic medicine, and maybe some Native American music.

Lady Miw holding scourge and wand, seated on an altar as in days of old (photo by Tina E. Verras).

Far from the fields and forests of the countryside, hidden away behind the brick and cement facade of New York City's Greenwich Village is the secret Sanctuary of Lady Miw's New York Coven of Wicca*. Here behind the little shop called Enchantments, Inc. is the Enchanted Garden of the East Village Witches (not to be confused with The Witches of Eastwick). *Lady Miw tells us:*

We are Wiccan, plain and simple, although I was brought up in the Gardnerian/Welsh/Minoan Traditions. I was given third degree and made High Priestess in 1975 (New York Coven of Wicca). The shop employees are members of my coven. We meet at sabbats, all Full Moons (esbats) and some New Moons, when necessary. Weather permitting, we circle in the garden behind the shop. Most of the coven are women (3 males). It just worked out that way, for now. Some of our circles are only the women to allow us to work our mysteries. Our men are wonderful. They respect that. Sabbats, of course, we're all present, men and women in balance of both God and Goddess. We network a lot to many

Witches in many states to create our web of one family, with one goal—to save the Mother Earth—to redeem the Goddess. When you're in the garden at Enchantments, you can't believe you're in New York City. It's genuinely someplace else. The main reason I chose this site for the shop was because of the garden. The garden is larger than the store and I knew it would be a perfect sanctuary for the Gods.

Pele (volcano Fire Mother) is on Her way to the south quarter. She hasn't arrived yet. Aphrodite (Ocean Mother—Water) is in the west quarter. Demeter/Hecate (Earth Mother—Wisdom), with her sickle, is in our north quarter and Zeus, represented by the eagle, is in our east (Air) quarter.

Garden altar at Enchantments (photo by Tina E. Verras).

My dearest Mark, one of my coveners, had been carving Cernunnos from one huge log—exactly a year and a day in the sculpting process. Mark delivered Him to our "Garden of Enchantments" on Beltane—May 1, 1990. With a crack of thunder, the Lords of the outer spaces welcomed their effigy. After the welcome, the skies cleared up and we had a lovely, sunny Beltane! Cernunnos now resides in the north beside Demeter.

Offerings are many: Autumn Equinox sabbat, I spewed 40 pounds of wheat grass about the garden (we now have the greenest grass out there), 5 pomegranates, 5 ears of corn, Aphrodite got Her 7 red roses, wine, apples and mead, pine cones and acorns. Of course, the offerings vary per sabbat. Lammas—sea water, etc. Spring Equinox—spring flowers and wreaths. The Gods and Goddesses in our sanctuary are adored always, every day, but we pay extra special attention to

Cernunnos carved from one huge log by Mark and delivered to the garden of Enchantments on Beltane (photo by Tina E. Verras).

each seasonally. For example, at Lammas (August 1st), Aphrodite gets fresh ocean water filled in Her shell and a special ocean and herb bath. At Autumn Equinox, Demeter/Hecate gets special attention, and at Samhain, also the Crone season. At Yule, Zeus, the Sky Father, the Sun God, gets special attention on His return—His rebirth, and so on. Of course, the God and Goddess have a million names, and all are revered. But, we couldn't have a million statues to represent them all now, could we? They are all worshiped, all the time. Yes, the circle is cast each time we meet for worship, magick, etc. It is standard—consecrated with the four elements around the circle, cast with the coven magick sword and the Watchtowers are invoked. All of us within the circle are purified and then we chant and sing, dance and laugh, draw down the Moon, praise the Gods, work our magick for the world, bless our food and drink, offer some to the Gods and feast and close:

Witches all, our rites having ended,
Let us give thanks to the Glorious Ones
Who have graced us with their presence
And, I charge Ye as the cock doth crow,
To lock away all our mysteries within our hearts,
And, may the Gods preserve the Craft.
So mote it be!

Aphrodite in the west quarter of the garden at Enchantments (photo by Tina E. Verras).

Demeter/Hecate in the sanctuary garden at Enchantments (photo by Tina E. Verras).

There is always a mystery revealed to us in every circle. Always more wisdom revealed—always a lesson. I've enclosed as much typed information as possible of our work. Take and use what you need—whatever it will take to clear and clean up the word *Witch* and redeem the Lady and the Lord. Witches Heal! Witches are good folk that are the most compassionate of peoples I've ever had the pleasure to meet, know, and love.

Here is the kind of magick Lady Miw and her coven do!

Blessed Be! We're the Witches of East Village, at Enchantments, Inc. in New York City. We'd like to share our magick with you ... what we've been doing. We know that you are all aware of what's going on in this land, and we know that you've all been doing magick with the Gods to correct all the mess and fix all the mistakes. However, this is Armageddon *now! This does not mean "I'ma get-tin' out a-here now!" We, you and I, are the caretakers of the Green Earth—or, should I say, the not-so-green Earth. The garbage is really piling up ... even in our forests; our 800-year-old redwood trees are being cut down; our ozone layer is gone; our innocent animals are being trapped for expensive furs, killed for sport ... for the fun of it, and our cats, dogs, rabbits, chimps, etc. are being painfully tortured in experimental laboratories* all over this country; *our waters are filled with disease and filth; our air is semi-breathable; not to mention the "File 18" problem. There is bigotry, ignorance, and hatred ... because they all* forgot the Mother. *Naturally,* Mother Earth is dying ... *and all living creatures with Her. These are serious times. What can we do? Do more magick to heal the Earth,* our home. We must wash Her hair clean. *It's all tangled and dirty and She's disgusted. She does not want Her green children to walk upon filth; nor breathe it; nor feel the Sun's anger through the ozone; nor drink foul waters, and restrict our spirits. We're suffering ...* all *the elements ... Earth, Air, Fire, Water, and Spirit.* Tend the Earth, please, tend the Mother ... our Mother Divine and our Father of the Trees and Skies. *Get more involved. We're not going to stand for this any longer. Give back some energy to the Gods at New Moons and, especially, at Full Moons. Do this for Her, for yourselves, for our children of tomorrow. Let the Earth grow* green. Your magick, all of us together ... *We can do it. We can heal Her. Envision clean, green growth. Magick the environmental protection people to get to work and do their job. Give White Light energy to the animal rights people. Please, this needs all our ener-gies,* all of us together. *In unity, there is strength and, believe me, the Gods will give us added strength threefold. The cowans must find the love and the light within their own hearts and minds. Heal them and enlighten them. It's their Earth too. Pick up the Sword of Wisdom. This way, we* will *have the balance back of God and Goddess ...* all *that* is *and we will have a green, healthy, clean Earth. Do* your *will ... do* your *magick. See Her green and growing. Clean and repair* all *Her elements, all* our *elements, for us, for Her, for* She is *inside all of us. This is* our *plight, this is* our *purpose. Walk always in Her Light, al-ways in Her right, in Her name.*

Cindy Testerman who described for us her indoor sanctuary, and who has a mail order business called Visualization/Reality, now tells us about her sanctuary outdoors.

My herb garden is also my God/dess shrine and a sanctuary to spend quiet time or meditation. I spent about a year in planning and began my work in the fall. First I marked it off and then spread cow and horse manure and compost on the grass that was there. Next I added about one foot of mulch from pine, oak, maple, birch and willow trees. The mulch was given to me by a local company that took them down. (A lot of these small companies gladly give away the mulched up trees they take down but check for diseased trees first, no unwanted troubles need to be added to a fresh new birth of a garden!) I let the mulch lay until Spring Equinox, then rake it off and till the ground about 18 inches deep, mixing the soil well. Next, the mulch is raked back onto the tilled bed and let stay until Beltane.

On the Full Moon of July, Cindy Testerman buried stones, crystals and runes in her sanctuary/garden.

Cindy Testerman's sacred circle in her sanctuary/yard.

Statues of Gods as well as gargoyles add protection to Cindy Testerman's herb garden/sanctuary.

On Beltane we lit candles and incense and planted our first plants of the spring in their new home.

At Midsummer we added some more herbs, wildflowers, annuals and perennials. These plants were a bit more fragile or younger than the early plants. We even saved a spot for "love apples" (tomatoes).

Also at Midsummer we added our deity statues of Pan, Bast, Aphrodite, Moon Goddess and a few gargoyles for protection. What a happy, energetic landscape we have!

On the Full Moon of July, I took out a bowl full of stones, crystals, and runes made of wood and buried them after a blessing under Luna's Light.

The season has brought forth a wonderful garden. Ample tomatoes, magickal herbs, medicinal herbs and culinary herbs, and flowers for the table. We lost a few plants with the dry season but for our first year it is thriving beautifully.

To keep the area special I like to work in it at sunset and spend my time there at night. Each time I go out I burn incense and candles and try to speak as many blessings as I can recount in my life and give thanks for. Of course the neighbors aren't quite sure if I'm talking to myself or to the plants. I do believe they think me "touched." I just hope it brings them mirth too!

I don't use this area for any certain rituals as much as for meditation, relaxation, celebration of the Wheel of the Year, and my many blessings from my deities.

I painted the statues for the garden, they are plaster and will withstand the elements outside if not too wet.

The herbs and flowers we planted were comfrey, lavender, thyme, sage, rosemary, yarrow, verbena, tarragon, monkshood, belladonna, parsley, lemon balm, pineapple sage, catnip, chamomile, mugwort, wormwood, southernwood, passion flower, foxglove, aconite, luffa, day lily, iris, begonia, coreopsis, sunflower, silver thyme, oregano, basil, coriander, impatients, black-eyed Susans, daffodils, tulips and peonies.

Later some giant cannas and a leyland cyprus evergreen was added along with roses to give us privacy from the roadway.

My circle is a permanent outdoor circle. It has a diameter of nine feet. The perimeter is marked off with 13 stones. A larger stone or a flat stone marks each quarter. The ground here was prepared by tilling and raking out, then compost was added in, grasses planted and ferns off to the sides.

Under each rock was planted several stones and crystals as well as dried herbs, all to help amplify the power within. There is a variety of large crystals planted in the center which is also marked by a rock. Moving in a clockwise motion the ground was then purified by covering the ground first with sulfur, then sea salt, frankincense powder, frankincense granules, benzoin powder, and myrrh powder. Then each day I made an additional offering of 1/2 pound of herbs. Each herb offered was for a specific purpose: meditation, psychic powers, love, peace, spirituality, wisdom, invisibility, courage, beauty, divination, healing, magickal powers, purification, protection and astral projection. These are some of the goals I would be working on for myself and others as a solitary Wiccan.

I then burned incense for 5 days in the circle with herbs for purification and increased power. Then I anointed the circle with mugwort and mugwort oil. Then came the Full Moon—and the magick began!

I used a spontaneous heartfelt simple ceremony to do a final consecration and blessing, using Earth, Air, Water and Fire. I called to the God and Goddess and simply asked for their blessings on my work within the circle. I then called the quarters and presented the same blessings to them. Then I began my first circle in its new permanent home.

Behind the circle, in the background is my day-care equipment as I have a day care in my home during the day. And, yes, the parents all know that I am a Witch, and although they are all Christians, are very accepting and mellow about my religious choices and practices. They do realize, too, our creed: "An harm none, then be it done." They also are in favor of the children learning meditation, relaxation and creative visualization.

Circle Sanctuary Nature Preserve is located in the rolling hills of southwestern Wisconsin, about an hour's drive west of central Madison. A 200-acre spiritual Nature preserve, it includes forests, meadows, a remnant of pioneer prairie, streams, springs, ancient sandstone rock outcroppings, Nature trails, and an abundance of ritual sites and meditation places, including a stone circle, outdoor shrines, and an indoor temple room.

Circle Sanctuary Nature Preserve is owned and operated by Circle, a non-profit international Nature Spirituality resource center and legally recognized Shamanic Wiccan Church. Founded in 1974, Circle helps people from many spiritual paths around the world connect with each other as well as with the spiritual dimensions of Nature and consciousness. Wiccan and other Nature religions (Pagan) contacts are provided for practitioners worldwide through Circle Network News, *the* Circle Guide to Pagan Groups, *and other Circle periodicals. Circle is headed by Selena Fox and Dennis Carpenter, who work together with staff and volunteers to caretake the preserve and manifest the center's many activities and services. More information about this is available from Circle upon request.*

Circle began purchasing its land in 1983. In 1988, after a protracted legal battle, the entire 200-acre site was zoned as a church and Circle's rights to use the land for religious activities were upheld.

A variety of festivals, group and solitary rituals, weddings and other rites of passage, workshops, training programs, healing circles, meditations, vision quests, and other events take place at Circle Sanctuary throughout the year. Visitors come from throughout the United States, Canada, and other countries to take part in events.

Donations are needed to help cover the costs of land payments, facilities upkeep and development, Nature preservation endeavors, and the wide range of educational, counseling, and networking services Circle provides. All donations are greatly appreciated and are tax deductible in the United States.

The Stone Circle at Circle Sanctuary has already been described in a previous chapter. Here are some of the other important magickal sites at Circle Sanctuary described for us by Selena Fox, High Priestess and founder.

Another popular ritual site at the Sanctuary is Spirit Rock. It is one of the highest points on Circle Sanctuary land. Rising more than 1100 feet above sea level, Spirit Rock gives a spectacular view of most of the Sanctuary's 200 acres of fields and forests. It faces west and is a wonderful spot for enjoying sunsets.

Selena Fox at Spirit Rock (photo by Lynnie Johnston, courtesy of Studio D of the National Film Board of Canada).

From the very first time I visited Spirit Rock, I sensed it was used as a place of power by Native Americans. The name, "Spirit Rock," came to me on that first visit. Today, Spirit Rock also is used for small group and solitary Nature meditations by practitioners of many paths of Nature Spirituality. Spirit Rock also is used as a vision quest place.

Circle Sanctuary fields, hills and forests, with a rainbow in the sky and a festival participant walking the path from Ritual Mound, Lughnassad 1990 (photo by Selena Fox).

Magick Circle Garden is in the center of the main garden at Circle Sanctuary. Mugwort surrounds a central Maypole (photo by Selena Fox).

A Maypole dance ritual in the center of the Magick Circle Garden at Circle Sanctuary, Beltane festival 1990 (photo courtesy of Circle archives).

In the center of our main garden area is a magick circle formed by mugwort, a magickal herb connected with healing and intuitive development. In the center of the magick circle garden is our Maypole. At the beginning of each May, we weave colored ribbons around the pole in a traditional dance that is the heart of our Beltane festival fertility ritual. Each summer, we harvest some of the mugwort as part of our Lughnassad celebration. A crescent-shaped garden filled with other herbs is a short walk from the mugwort circle and borders our bonfire celebration circle, where we do rituals, drumming, dancing, singing, and merrymaking during the warmer months. Our gardens and bonfire circle comprise an area that once was an ancient Native American camp. This area is registered as a prehistorical site by the State Historical Society of Wisconsin.

A short walk from the north cairn of the Stone Circle is a shrine dedicated to the Earth Goddess in Her many forms. It is a small shrine, located in a sandstone rock outcropping. It contains clay and stone replicas of ancient Goddess images, including the Earth Mother of Willendorf and of Laussel. These images were created by contemporary Pagan artists and donated to Circle Sanctuary. Visitors to this shrine often leave offerings of flowers, crystals, coins and herbs.

Next to the Earth Goddess Shrine is the Gnome Home. It honors the Nature Spirits of the element Earth and venerates Scandinavian Pagan traditions. The focal point of this meditation place is a thirty pound, two foot high, European made gnome sculpture which Dennis and I acquired during one of our travels.

The Gnome Home was dedicated as a sacred site as part of the New Moon gathering held in October 1989. During the dedication ritual, participants did an Earth elemental meditation and then placed small amethysts and clear quartz crystals in the gnome's sack and on the ground nearby, representing the riches of the Earth, which according to ancient Scandinavian lore, are guarded by gnomes. True to its underground nature, our gnome's home is in the Earth under a sandstone rock outcropping.

The Bast Cat Shrine at Circle Sanctuary (photo by Selena Fox).

Our Bast Cat Shrine is located in a rock outcropping on the south-facing side of Ritual Mound. Its central image is a statue of Bast as a regal black cat with a gold earring. This statue is a museum replica of a statue used in connection with Bast worship in ancient Egypt. Around the statue are other small statues of cats representing a variety of cat types on this planet—domesticated cat, lion, jaguar, bobcat, tiger, and mountain lion. Cat-lovers who visit the Sanctuary often leave catnip and other offerings at this shrine. A variety of cat honoring and healing rituals have been done here.

The Healing Goddess Shrine at Circle Sanctuary (photo by Selena Fox).

The meditative focal point of the Healing Goddess Shrine is a bronze sculpture created by Tree, an multifaceted artist who specializes in Goddess-centered art, music, and theatre. He donated this sculpture and helped fashion the shrine as a thanksgiving for healings he had received. The sculpture portrays the Great Goddess as the primeval Mother of the World. She has the wings of Isis and holds an amethyst healing crystal in Her hands, pouring Her Love out to all. Her power to heal also is depicted by the dragon power image flowing up Her spine. She is shown rising out of planet Earth, which is encircled by the Ouroboros, an ancient symbol of the never-ending Circle of Life. The shrine was dedicated in October 1987. It is located under a birch tree on Ritual Mound.

Samhain offerings on the central altar of Stone Circle at Circle Sanctuary, Samhain festival 1990 (photo by Selena Fox).

There are a variety of other ritual sites at the Sanctuary as well. The Ancestors Crystal consists of a large smoky quartz crystal and is a multicultural place for honoring the ancestral realm. Along the stream that flows through the Sanctuary is a spring dedicated to Brigid, Celtic Goddess of Healing and Inspiration. On the side of one of the ridges in the forest is Cave of the Ancients, an ancient Native American rock shelter, which is an excellent site for vision quests and shamanic journeys. Full Moon rituals and meditations sometimes take place in the Meadow

Circle in the grassy meadow near Ritual Mound. A temple room for indoor ritual work is located in the Sanctuary's main building, a seventy-year-old remodeled barn.

In addition to connecting with ritually dedicated and named sites, many visitors find their own special places in Nature for personal spiritual work at the Sanctuary. Some experience healing and spiritual insight while walking Nature trails. There is time for personal Nature walks and meditations at most events held at the Sanctuary.

If you would like to visit Circle Sanctuary, you *must* make arrangements with the Circle staff in advance since drop-in visitation is not permitted. The best times to visit are in connection with the seasonal festivals and other events held throughout the year. Dates of seasonal festivals are included in *Circle Network News*, Circle's quarterly newspaper. Details about festivals and other events are published eight times a year in Circle's events newsletter, *Sanctuary Circles*. Free sample copies of these publications are available upon request from Circle.

Scholars, public media journalists, writers, and other reporters wishing to visit must make arrangements at least a month in advance. While the training programs and most seasonal festivals are usually closed to the media, Circle sometimes permits media coverage at other times.

All visitors must comply with Circle's rules for visitors. A brochure listing these is available upon request. To arrange a visit, write to Circle Sanctuary*.

In West Cork on the coast of Ireland, the "misty island in the sea," there is a ten-acre tract of land that is a sanctuary of the Old Pagan Gods, and the spirits of Nature that dwell there. In the near future, it will also become the home of Count Woland who presently resides in a major Irish city, and who visits the sanctuary only when time permits. This private sanctuary contains a number of shrines dedicated to various deities and the location of these shrines, and the deities to whom they are dedicated, were made known to the Count through signs, omens and dreams. Here the land is being lovingly planted and tended by Count Woland and his family (his wife and his dog), and here the Old Ones still hold sway, and still re-enact their cycle plays in an on-going process that, like the sanctuary itself, is still evolving.

The wind screams through the headlands in winter. Foam flies and sea horses ride the crests of waves, mounted by spirits of past and present. The land is usually bleak, grass dying back, what trees there were bent by the fierceness of the blowing gales and storms.

One headland sits astride the wildness, sentinel to the sea, protector of the land. The forests that covered her destroyed eons ago by man and beast together, or individually. Either scene, however, is the same, flowing rocky and hilly areas of grass and low bush. Few trees.

The land consists of over ten acres and sits partly flat and partly hilly. From here one can see at least thirty miles in any direction. At least you can see this from the top part of the land on a clear day. From the road it slowly winds its grass upwards to a fairly level area, again, near the top of the hill. The highest part of the headland lies still further south, over yet another small ridge. Once the high point is reached then open ocean stretches southward to the Antarctic. To the east can be seen Fastnet Rock crowned with its lighthouse. To the west the mountains of Kerry can be seen. Northward the low Cork Mountains lie. The bay below the property flows into sandy beaches. Looking eastwards again along the coast, small fishing towns and islands off the coast of West Cork, each claiming their own plot as a re-casting of the past.

Entrance to the sanctuary at West Cork, Ireland (photo by Count Woland).

Sanctuary, grove or shrine? This area is all of those things. The premise is simple. It is an area dedicated to the Triple Mother Goddess, as is the headlands, but the planting of trees is a dedication to the Spirits, Gods, Goddesses, fauns, demi-gods and the life of belief of whatever deity wishes to rest there. It is established in the belief that there is no overriding lower by any deity, even the Great Mother Herself, and that chaos exists, thus does life exist. Each tree planted is given as a place for whatever spirit of deity wishes it, and areas within the property are dedicated to each deity of spirit as it can and as it happens. As it is self-financing no offering is asked for from outside. If a person wishes a prayer made to a particular deity, then a note with a short prayer is sent, and as soon as practical a dedication is made. Whether it will be a shrine to a tree or to an area depends upon what signs occur. If a particular tree is wished for the dedication then it waits until the tree is available or choice is made to a near-relative.

Individual shrines are found by stumbling across them, placed where the shrine itself deemed it appropriate. The shrine itself usually has flower seed and such planted around it. If no tree is available then seed is placed and left to grow when it chooses to, but the area is marked in some way. There is no area deemed to be altar, grove or circle. The entire is a sanctuary and wherever you wish will a ceremony take place.

Shrines set up and dedicated at the moment are but four. One to the Great Triple Mother Goddess. She, as is fitting, sits at the highest point of the headland, a shrine of stone upon stone to a point, surrounded on three sides by the great sea. No planting has taken place there as of this writing but that may change within a year. Enough to say that the shrine is dedicated to her and that an offering of prayer made at her shrine.

Alecto sits on a ridge facing northward, the stone itself above a hollowed place of earth which must be dug. Clover and grass surround her of entrance to her worshipers at some future date. One of three outstanding hewed-like extensions of rock, she awaits her sisters, but it is not time for them to arrive, not yet. When others are here to soften their actions, to make them blend in and act as arbitrators, then Alecto's sisters will arrive, not till then.

All-illate flew from the far south looking for rest and sanctuary. A place where she could rest and gain strength away from the lands dominated by Allah. A place where her believers can again recover. Her shrine looks down on sandy beaches and draining ocean to remind her of her place to the far south which she will someday return. But she now rests. Flowers are planted around her outcrop and she will be happy for her shrine.

Astarte arrived on a wind and settled on top of a wind-driven ridge. The area of shrine, to be built, for she needs a shrine built for her, sits on all but barren rock. Little soil is there and must be brought up, which will be done. Her thought is that she is there for a while, and as the others, the dedication was done assuring the shrine to continue. The coming year will have the shrine built in some manner.

To be dedicated yet? Bast will have an area, as will Diana. But each that will wish will have a place or area to be in. The tree planting has started, and in one area in one field one could all but see the wish for a shrine to the cattle gods, but a dedication to them awaits a favorable moment. The Horned God awaits his entrance but awaits merely a name to complete his introduction. A glimpse of an eastern goddess is all but confirmed, but what name is she to be dedicated? The fauns and spirits are awaiting more cover, but if you but glance at the small strand of cover you can see a flicker of movement. It is being watched and hopefully being given what protection they can give until they can begin to be comfortable.

Seeds of many different types of flowers have gone into the land. A year or two before progress is seen. Seeds of various types of trees also have been planted, again we wait years for progress. Alders, hazel, sycamore, sequoia, seedlings and a small cherry have been planted. This year more sycamore, alder, cherry and red oak will be planted as will other seeds including honey locust. The following year will see the start of the serious planting, bushes and trees and plants of all types going down, surrounding the old ruins and in one instance the double round circle of an old burial or house. That the plantings will be difficult is affirmed. That it will be done is confirmed. That it will be successful for the deities and the helpers is accepted.

Looking down on the lower fields, and the sea beyond (photo by Count Woland).

Is it a shrine or a sanctuary that is being formed? Rather that in future it be said that here all worship will be acceptable here to whatever a man or woman wishes to worship, because here will be a free area where all will be accepted, whether man or deity . . . or even a player with a flute.

Several months later Dan and I received the following from the Count:

It was the whitish wild cat with the fox that finally forced me to do the shrine. That and the multicolored tom I saw stalking across the fields next to the house we rented in May 1990. The dreams of felines over the preceding weeks and seeing a fox and a cat together at 1000 hours, was the last item. That I had decided to make a small shrine to Bast already was of no account. Rarely had I seen cats so open, and never so noticeable.

The shrine itself is near the road, not on it and hidden from it, but next to an opening which leads to the road. From the shrine the view is the distant sea and the field it is in, a house in the background being completed and parts of the other fields. It even overlooks the road. Around it I planted catnip and the stone itself is capped with small crystals grayish and bluish in colored streaks. When I had finished it and dedicated it, the stone stroked felt almost as it was beginning to awaken. And still I don't like cats, but Bast has her shrine completed.

The wild day in May saw two other dedications. One was meant to be to Diana, but strangely when the dedication was begun and the naming reached the Goddess Athena interfered and took her seat, thus Athena now sits with a crown of green glistening stone on the upper land. She sits surrounded by standing stones which can only be handmaidens, but presently not named.

The other dedication that day was in the round double circle shaped like an 8. An old tomb with its center stone still thrusting itself towards the sky. It is not yet marked on any map and I found it by chance. Always within it, it seemed the wind died and was held by . . . whatever. Images of sound and movement always occurred here, sometime of swishing of cloth or clank of metal and always of magicians rather than men. That day I dedicated it to the Goddesses and Gods of the Tuatha De Danann. Not to any individual, but as a place for them all. The stones within and without still await naming but within all were there. I could sense two ancient warriors with spear and shield, cape over one shoulder, standing guard, and an old man sitting on a stone seat/throne/chair, bearded and strong watching. Sounds of drum and flute with swish of garments worn by ladies. Muted but with strength of manner these magicians are proud and unbowed. Thus another shrine exists.

A fire had occurred on the headland before I had arrived this May. The land was black and green. The green being what grass started growing after the burn. Little but black covered other areas. The fire had swept across the hilly patch between the lower and upper land and through part of the upper land. Clover seed I bought and decided to sow before I left, and when I started up the mountain the wind sprung up from the east. As I walked I took a handful of seed from the bag I carried and I held my hand out slowly letting the seed be plucked from my hand by the wind. The wind was neither too strong or too weak. It was enough to ensure a dispersal of the seed on the blackened earth evenly. It was as if a helper was here. I completed the seeding on the upper land covering areas of death with seeds of hope. I walked to the boundary stone wall which looked downwards towards the lower fields and road, stopping at a small cluster of rocks and began to pick up other rocks and made a mound, caped and toped; made secure. I looked and felt the wind strengthening, the gray clouds and sky running, the sea of whitecaps singing and springing in the bay. The Sea God wanted a shrine so a dedication was made and Poseidon had his shrine.

As I walked down the hill the breeze slackened and the Sun came out and I turned to see where he sits, and the Sun lit the stone just for an instant before being blown away by clouds again.

When a tree or a site is dedicated all that is required is a short prayer written on a small piece of paper. The dedication is simple, the Count and his family read the prayer and then bury it at the site. The form ends with:

> *Do not stand at a grave and weep,*
> *I am not there, I do not sleep.*
> *Do not stand at a grave and cry,*
> *I am not there, I do not die.*

Dan and I hope that when Count Woland finally deems his sanctuary complete, he will write a book of his own, using his beautiful words to describe the entire process.

Conclusion

From the Batman canteen that represented the element of Water on the altar of a four year old, to the spiritual sanctuary of Grandfather, from a second century stone altar on a wooded hillside in Germany to a circle cast by computer, from a ring of sacred trees in England to a circle in the sands of Desert Storm, from an inconspicuous altar in the corner of an apartment kitchen to a 200-acre wildlife sanctuary, we have had the privilege of being given a tour of sacred spaces from the most personal and private to that which is open and public. We have visited magickal places in countries around the world and in most of the United States, places that were dedicated in ages past and those that will be consecrated in the future. It is our hope that the sacred spaces shared with us by Pagans and Wiccans from many backgrounds and traditions will serve as inspiration for others already on the path and those with leanings and longings for the path, to continue to create a network of sacred space that will one day en *circle* the Earth.

Resources

Circle Sanctuary/
Circle Network News
Selena Fox—Priestess
Box 219
Mt. Horeb, WI 53572
(608) 924-2216 (weekdays 1-4
Central Time)
(not open on drop-in basis)

Coven of the Spiral Castle
P.O. Box 531373
Miami Shores, FL 33153-1373

Crystal Springs Grove
P.O. Box 219
Amherst, MA 01004

Weland Ergwald
P.O. Box 396
Whitehall, MI 49461

Golden Isis Magazine
Gerina Dunwich—Editor
232333-105 Saticoy Street (Suite 137)
West Hills, CA 91304
(Please include S.A.S.E.)

Great Mother's Love Nature Center
P.O. Box 42
Fairfield, VT 05455

Green Egg Magazine
Church of All Worlds
P.O. Box 1542
Ukiah, CA 95482

Kansa Holt Circle
Kyle and Penny Peterson
1016 Pierre
Manhattan, KS 66502

Kati-ma Koppance
Iseum of Mielikki and Tapio
P.O. Box 452
00101 Helsinki
Finland

Mother Spirit
Nan Conner—Coordinator
P.O. Box 1360
Exton, PA 19341

New York Coven of Wicca/Lady Miw
Enchantments, Inc.
341 East 9th Street
New York, NY 10003
(212) 228-4394

Bob Place
P.O. Box 541
Saugerties, NY 12477

Sacred Hart Magazine
Bried Foxsong—Editor
Wyrdd Enterprises
P.O. Box 72
Kenmore, NY 14217

Silver Chalice Magazine
Steven R. Smith—Editor
P.O. Box 196
Thorofare, NJ 08086

Silver Elves
Zardoa Silver Star and Silver Flame
P.O. Box 2035
Guernerville, CA 95446

TechnoPagans
Mark Peters can be reached
electronically:
Q (Quantum)—Link by sending
E-Mail to Wiccan 3.
For E-Mail and on-line conversation
use Portal (his "handle" is Wiccan 3).

Tuatha De Danann
Katharine Clark
P.O. Box 178
Franklin Park, NJ 08823-0178

Gary T. Niall
P.O. Box 10641
New Brunswick, NJ 08906-0641

Visualization/Reality
Cindy Testerman
3134 Acton Rd.
Baltimore, MD 21234

Wicca International Witchcraft
6 Rue Danton
94270 Kremlin-Bicetre
France

Wiccan/Pagan Press Alliance
Silver Ravenwolf—Editor
P.O. Box 1392
Mechanicsburg, PA 17055

Witches Almanac
P.O. Box 348
Cambridge, MA 02238

STAY IN TOUCH

On the following pages you will find listed, with their current prices, some of the books now available on related subjects. Your book dealer stocks most of these, and will stock new titles in the Llewellyn series as they become available. We urge your patronage.

To obtain our full catalog, to keep informed of new titles as they are released and to benefit from informative articles and helpful news, you are invited to write for our bi-monthly news magazine/catalog, *Llewellyn's New Worlds of Mind and Spirit*. A sample copy is free, and it will continue coming to you at no cost as long as you are an active mail customer. Or you may suscribe for just $7.00 in the U.S.A. and Canada ($20.00 overseas, first class mail). Many bookstores also have *New Worlds* available to their customers. Ask for it.

Stay in touch! In *New Worlds'* pages you will find news and features about new books, tapes and services, announcements of meetings and seminars, articles helpful to our readers, news of authors, products and services, special money-making opportunities, and much more.

Llewellyn's New Worlds of Mind and Spirit
P.O. Box 64383-Dept. 108, St. Paul, MN 55164-0383, U.S.A.
• • •
TO ORDER BOOKS AND TAPES

If your book dealer does not have the books described on the following pages readily available, you may order them directly from the publisher by sending full price in U.S. funds, plus $3.00 for postage and handling for orders *under* $10.00; $4.00 for orders *over* $10.00. There are no postage and handling charges for orders over $50.00. Postage and handling rates are subject to change. UPS Delivery: We ship UPS whenever possible. Delivery guaranteed. Provide your street address as UPS does not deliver to P.O. Boxes. UPS to Canada requires a $50.00 minimum order. Allow 4-6 weeks for delivery. Orders outside the U.S.A. and Canada: Airmail—add retail price of book; add $5.00 for each non-book item (tapes, etc.); add $1.00 per item for surface mail.

FOR GROUP STUDY AND PURCHASE

Because there is a great deal of interest in group discussion and study of the subject matter of this book, we feel that we should encourage the adoption and use of this particular book by such groups by offering a special quantity price to group leaders or agents.

Our special quantity price for a minimum order of five copies of *Circles, Groves & Sanctuaries* is $38.85 cash-with-order. This price includes postage and handling within the United States. Minnesota residents must add 6.5% sales tax. For additional quantities, please order in multiples of five. For Canadian and foreign orders, add postage and handling charges as above. Credit card (VISA, MasterCard, American Express) orders are accepted. Charge card orders only ($15.00 minimum order) may be phoned in free within the the U.S.A. or Canada by dialing 1-800-THE-MOON. For customer service, call 1-612-291-1970. Mail orders to:

LLEWELLYN PUBLICATIONS
P.O. Box 64383-Dept. 108, St. Paul, MN 55164-0383, U.S.A.

Prices subject to change without notice.

ANCIENT WAYS: Reclaiming the Pagan Tradition
by Pauline Campanelli
Illustrated by Dan Campanelli

Ancient Ways is filled with magick and ritual that you can perform everyday to capture the spirit of the seasons. It focuses on the celebration of the sabbats of the Old Religion by giving you practical things to do while anticipating the sabbat rites, and helping you harness the magickal energy for weeks afterward. The wealth of seasonal rituals and charms are drawn from ancient sources but are easily performed with materials readily available.

Learn how to look into your previous lives at Yule . . . at Beltane, discover the places where you are most likely to see Faeries . . . make special jewelry to wear for your Lammas celebrations . . . for the special animals in your life, paint a charm of protection at Midsummer.

Most Pagans and Wiccans feel that the sabbat rituals are all to brief and wish for the magick to linger on. *Ancient Ways* can help you reclaim your own traditions and heighten the feeling of magick.

0-87542-090-7, 192 pgs., 7 x 10, illustrated $12.95

WHEEL OF THE YEAR: Living the Magickal Life
by Pauline Campanelli

If like most Pagans you feel elated from the celebrations of the Sabbats and hunger for that feeling during the long weeks between sabbats, then *Wheel of the Year* can help you to put the joy of celebration and the fulfillment of magic into your everyday life.

The wealth of seasonal rituals and charms contained in *Wheel of the Year* are all easily performed with materials readily available, and are simple and concise enough that the practitioner can easily adapt them to work within the framework of his or her Pagan tradition. Learn how to perform fire magic in November, the best time to make magic wand and why, the ancient magical secrets of objects found on a beach, and the secret Pagan symbolism of Christmas tree ornaments.

Whether you are a newcomer to the Craft or found your way back many years ago, *Wheel of the Year* will be an invaluable reference book in your practical magical library. It is filled with magic and ritual for everyday life and will enhance any system of Pagan Ritual.

0-87542-091-5, 192 pgs., 7 x 10, illustrated $9.95

THE FAMILY WICCA BOOK
by Ashleen O'Gaea

The number of Witches raising children in the Craft is growing. The need for mutual support is rising—yet until now, there have been no books that speak to a Wiccan family's needs and experience. Finally, here is *The Family Wicca Book*, full to the brim with rituals, projects, encouragement and practical discussion of real-life challenges. You'll find lots of ideas to use right away.

Is magic safe for children? Why do some people think Wiccans are Satanists? How do you make friends with spirits and little people in the local woods? Find out how one Wiccan family gives clear and honest answers to questions that intrigue Pagans all over the world.

When you want to ground your family in Wicca without ugly "bashing;" explain life, sex, and death without embarrassment; and add to your Sabbats without much trouble or expense, *The Family Wicca Book* is required reading. You'll refer to it again and again as your traditions grow with your family.

0-87542-591-7, 240 pgs., 5-1/4 x 8, illustrated $9.95

WICCA: A Guide for the Solitary Practitioner
by Scott Cunningham

Wicca is a book of life, and how to live magically, spiritually, and wholly attuned with Nature. It is a book of sense and common sense, not only about Magick, but about religion and one of the most critical issues of today: how to achieve the much needed and wholesome relationship with out Earth. Cunningham presents Wicca as it is today—a gentle, Earth-oriented religion dedicated to the Goddess and God. This book fulfills a need for a practical guide to solitary Wicca—a need which no previous book has fulfilled.

Here is a positive, practical introduction to the religion of Wicca, designed so that any interested person can learn to practice the religion alone, anywhere in the world. It presents Wicca honestly and clearly, without the pseudo-history that permeates other books. It shows that Wicca is a vital, satisfying part of twentieth century life.

This book presents the theory and practice of Wicca from an individual's perspective. The section on the Standing Stones Book of Shadows contains solitary rituals for the Esbats and Sabbats. This book, based on the author's nearly two decades of Wiccan practice, presents an eclectic picture of various aspects of this religion. Exercises designed to develop magical proficiency, a self-dedication ritual, herb, crystal and rune magic, recipes for Sabbat feasts, are included.

0-87542-118-0, 240 pgs., 6 x 9, illustrated $9.95

CUNNINGHAM'S ENCYCLOPEDIA OF MAGICAL HERBS
by Scott Cunningham

This is an expansion on the material presented in his first Llewellyn book, Magical Herbalism. This is not just another herbal for medicinal uses of herbs—this is the most comprehensive source of herbal data for magical uses ever printed! Almost every one of the over 400 herbs are illustrated, making this a great source for herb identification. For each herb you will also find: magical properties, planetary rulerships, genders, associated deities, folk and Latin names and much more. to make this book even easier to use you will also find a folk name cross reference, and all of the herbs are fully indexed. There is also a large annotated bibliography, and a list of mail order suppliers so you can find the books and herbs you need.

Like all of Scott's books, this one does not require you to use complicated rituals or expensive magical paraphernalia. Instead, it shares with you the intrinsic powers of the herbs. Thus, you will be able to discover which herbs, by their very nature, can be used for luck, love, success, money, divination, astral projection, safety, psychic self–defense and much more. Besides being interesting and educational it is also fun, and fully illustrated with unusual woodcuts from old herbals. This book has rapidly become the classic in its field. It enhances books such as 777 and is a must for all Wiccans.

0-87542-122-9, 352 pgs., 6 x 9, illustrated $12.95

THE MAGICAL HOUSEHOLD
by Scott Cunningham and David Harrington

Whether your home is a small apartment or a palatial mansion, you want it to be something special. Now it can be with *The Magical Household*. Learn how to make your home more than just a place to live. Turn it into a place of security, life, fun and magic. Here you will not find the complex magic of the ceremonial magician. Rather, you will learn simple, quick and effective magical spells 'that use nothing more than common items in your house: furniture, windows, doors, carpet, pets, etc. You will learn to take advantage of the intrinsic power and energy that is already in your home, waiting to be tapped. You will learn to make magic a part of your life. The result is a home that is safeguarded from harm and a place which will bring you happiness, health and more.

0-87542-124-5, 208 pgs., 5-1/4 x 8, illustrated $8.95

BUCKLAND'S COMPLETE BOOK OF WITCHCRAFT
by Raymond Buckland, Ph.D.

Here is the most complete resource to the study and practice of modern, non-denominational Wicca. This is a lavishly illustrated, self-study course for the solitary or group. Included are rituals, exercises for developing psychic talents, and information on all major "sects" of the Craft, sections on tools, beliefs, dreams, meditations, divination, herbal lore, healing, ritual clothing and much, much more. This book unites theory and practice into a comprehensive course designed to help you develop into a practicing Witch, one of the "Wise Ones." It is written by Dr. Ray Buckland, a very famous and respected authority on witchcraft who first came public with "the Old Religion" in the United States. Large format with workbook-type exercises, profusely illustrated and full of music and chants. Takes you from A to Z in the study of Witchcraft.

Never before has so much information on "the Craft of the Wise" been collected in one place. Traditionally, there are three degrees of advancement in most Wiccan traditions. When you complete studying this book you will be the equivalent of a "Third Degree Witch." Even those who have practiced Wicca for years find useful information in this book, and many covens are using this for their textbook. If you want to become a Witch, or if you merely want to find out what Witchcraft is really about, you will find no better book than this.

0-87542-050-8, 272 pgs., 8-1/2 x 11, illustrated $14.95

WITCHCRAFT TODAY: The Modern Craft Movement
Edited by Chas S. Clifton

For those already in the Craft, and for those who stand outside the ritual circle wondering if it is the place for them, *Witchcraft Today* brings together the writings of nine well-known Neopagans who give a cross-section of the beliefs and practices of this diverse and fascinating religion.

The contributors live in cities, small towns and rural areas, from California to Ireland, and they have all claimed a magical birthright—that lies open to any committed person—of healing, divination, counseling and working with the world's cycles.

Written specifically for this volume, articles include:

- "A Quick History of Witchcraft's Revival" by Chas S. Clifton
- "An Insider's Look at Pagan Festivals" by Oz
- "Seasonal Rites/Magical Rites" by Pauline Campanelli
- "Witchcraft and Healing" by Morwyn
- "Sex Magic" by Valerie Voigt
- "Men and Women in Witchcraft" by Janet and Stewart Farrar
- "The Solo Witch" by Heather O'Dell
- "Witchcraft and the Law" by Pete Pathfinder
- "Witchcraft and Shamanism" by Grey Cat
- and more!

Also included are additional resources for Wiccans: publications, mail-order suppliers, Pagan organizations, computer bulletin boards and special-interest resources. The Principles of Wiccan Belief are also restated here.

0-87542-377-9, 208 pgs., 5-1/4 x 8 $9.95

CRAFTING THE ART OF MAGIC: The History of Modern Witchcraft, 1939-64
by Aidan A. Kelly, Ph.D.

This is a history of the development of modern Witchcraft as a religion during the later lifetime of Gerald Gardner, the religion's most important founding figure, from 1939 to his death in 1964.

Modern Witchcraft is a vital religion in the process of being created by its members. Since the publication of Gerald Gardner's *Witchcraft Today* in 1954, Gardnerian Witchcraft has blossomed, carried by Gardnerian initiates and admirers throughout the Western world.

No other book before now has relied solely on the historical evidence to reconstruct the history of modern Witchcraft. *Crafting the Art of Magic* doesn't rely on unverifiable (and often simply false) statements from any individuals, but on the application of standard scholarly techniques to the available documentary evidence, which consists largely of drafts of materials for the Gardnerian Book of Shadows written by Gardner and/or Doreen Valiente.

0-87542-370-1, 224 pgs., 6 x 9 $10.95

Prices subject to change without notice.